Also by Terry Pluto

The Curse of Rocky Colavito
Tall Tales: The Glory Years of the NBA
Loose Balls: The Short, Wild Life of the American Basketball Association
Bull Session (with Johnny Kerr)
Tark (with Jerry Tarkanian)
Forty-Eight Minutes: A Night in the Life of the N.B.A. (with Bob Ryan)
Sixty-One: The Season, the Record, the Men (with Tony Kubek)
You Could Argue but You'd Be Wrong (with Pete Franklin)
A Baseball Winter (with Jeff Neuman)
Weaver on Strategy (with Earl Weaver)
The Earl of Baltimore
Super Joe (with Joe Charboneau and Burt Graeff)
The Greatest Summer

FALLING FROM GRACE

Can Pro Basketball Be Saved?

Terry Pluto

SIMON & SCHUSTER

New York   London   Toronto   Sydney   Tokyo   Singapore

SIMON & SCHUSTER
Rockefeller Center
1230 Avenue of the Americas
New York, NY 10020

SIMON & SCHUSTER and colophon are registered trademarks
of Simon & Schuster Inc.

Designed by Irving Perkins Associates

Manufactured in the United States of America

10 9 8 7 6 5 4 3 2 1

Library of Congress Cataloging-in-Publication Data

Pluto, Terry
     Falling from grace: can pro basketball be saved?/Terry Pluto.
        p.   cm.
     Includes index.
        1. National Basketball Association.   2. Basketball—Social
aspects—United States.   3. Basketball players—United States.
I. Title.
GV885.515.N37P675   1995
796.323'0973—dc20   95–33430
                                                          CIP

ISBN: 978-1-4767-4863-4

To my teachers: Father Dominic Mondzelewski, Dr. Susan Gorsky, James Muth, Phil Hodanbosi, Don Robertson, Augie Bossu, Hal Lebovitz, and Jeff Neuman.

And to those who hired me when it wasn't easy: Bill Tanton and Irwin Smallwood.

Contents

Panel of Experts   11
Introduction   15

Part I   **PLAYERS**   **25**

   1. Modern Players   27
   2. Capping the Draft   57
   3. Why Johnny Can't Shoot   76
   4. Violence and the Culture of Disrespect   99
   5. When the Players Run the Show   126

Part II: **COACHES**   **139**

   6. The Voices of Coaches   141
   7. Stranglers on the Sidelines   157
   8. Coaching Lines   174
   9. The Worst Job in the NBA   202

Part III: **THE LEAGUE**   **213**

   10. Bad Boy$ 215
   11. The Official Rules   234
   12. Selling the Game   261
   13. The Toughest Basketball League
       in the World   277
   14. Improving the Game   293

   Afterword   303
   Index   309

Panel of Experts

1. RICHIE ADUBATO: An assistant coach with the Orlando Magic, who broke into the NBA as Dick Vitale's assistant in Detroit.
2. CHARLES BARKLEY: The NBA star and a critic of today's young players.
3. RICK BARRY: Hall of Fame forward who has the second-best free throw percentage in NBA history. He can't understand why Shaquille O'Neal won't shoot free throws underhanded.
4. HUBIE BROWN: Longtime NBA coach, respected TV analyst, and spiritual father of the Five-Star Group of NBA coaches.
5. LARRY BROWN: The veteran NBA coach who worries that the NBA marketing departments are "turning the league into a burlesque show."
6. JERRY COLANGELO: Veteran basketball executive, owner of the Phoenix Suns, and a man worried that NBA basketball is losing its entertainment value.
7. DOUG COLLINS: Former Bulls coach and TV analyst, now head coach of the Detroit Pistons.
8. BOB COSTAS: NBC broadcaster, former play-by-play man of the ABA's Spirits of St. Louis.
9. BOB COUSY: Hall of Fame point guard who believes the NBA has too many coaches, too many plays, and not enough freedom for the players.
10. CHUCK DALY: Hall of Famer and father of the Bad Boys in Detroit who saw nothing wrong with their style of play.
11. MATT DOBEK: The public relations man for the Detroit Pistons and the co-author of *Bad Boys* with Isiah Thomas.
12. WAYNE EMBRY: General Manager of the Cleveland Cavaliers

who is an outspoken critic of the violence and the attitude of many of the game's young players.

13. BILL FITCH: Veteran coach now sentenced to the L.A. Clippers.

14. COTTON FITZSIMMONS: Vice president of the Phoenix Suns, and a former coach who advocates a return to the running game.

15. GARY FITZSIMMONS: Player personnel director of the Cleveland Cavaliers, and son of Cotton Fitzsimmons.

16. MIKE FRATELLO: Coach of the Cleveland Cavaliers and a Hubie Brown disciple.

17. JOHN HAVLICEK: Hall of Famer with the Boston Celtics.

18. MARK HEFFERNAN: A former member of the Cleveland Cavaliers marketing department who thinks that the hyping of the game with blaring music has gone too far.

19. TOM HEINSOHN: Former Celtics great and coach, now a Boston broadcaster with Bob Cousy.

20. JUWAN HOWARD: Washington Bullets forward and a member of Michigan's Fab Five.

21. PHIL JACKSON: Coach of the three-time champion Chicago Bulls who is offended by how the New York Knicks nearly won the 1994 title.

22. STAN KASTEN: President of the Atlanta Hawks.

23. JERRY KRAUSE: General manager of the Chicago Bulls.

24. FRANK LAYDEN: Former coach of the Utah Jazz.

25. GENE LITTLES: Assistant coach with the Denver Nuggets who replaced a burned-out Dan Issel on an interim basis.

26. JACK MADDEN: The veteran NBA official who retired after the 1993–94 season.

27. RED McCOMBS: Former owner of the San Antonio Spurs.

28. AL MENENDEZ: Veteran scout for the Indiana Pacers.

29. DICK MOTTA: The veteran NBA coach.

30. ERIC MUSSELMAN: Coach and general manager of the CBA's Rapid City Thrillers and the Continental Basketball Association's most successful executive.

31. JOHN NASH: Washington Bullets general manager.

32. PETE NEWELL: Hall of Fame coach, now a scout for the Cleveland Cavaliers.

33. KEVIN O'KEEFE: Veteran basketball writer and columnist in San Antonio who had a close look at the brief NBA coaching career of Jerry Tarkanian.

34. MARK PRICE: An all-pro point guard with the Cleveland Cavaliers and a member of Dream Team II.
35. WILLIS REED: Hall of Fame center now serving as general manager and trying to make some sense out of the New Jersey Nets.
36. WALLY ROONEY: Veteran NBA official who retired after the 1992–93 season, and whose career began in the ABA.
37. CHARLES ROSEN: Longtime CBA coach who has found salvation coaching a Division III women's team.
38. BOB RYAN: Legendary Boston basketball writer and author of books with Larry Bird and Bob Cousy.
39. BILLY SAAR: The veteran NBA official who retired after the 1993–94 season.
40. DOLPH SCHAYES: Hall of Fame forward.
41. DAVID STERN: NBA commissioner.
42. EARL STROM: The late Hall of Fame official.
43. JOE TAIT: Veteran Cavaliers broadcaster.
44. JERRY TARKANIAN: The winningest (percentage) college coach of all time, who took over the San Antonio Spurs for twenty games. Now coaching at Fresno State.
45. MARK TERMINI: Attorney for such players as Rod Strickland and Ron Harper.
46. ISIAH THOMAS: Former star guard with the Pistons, now general manager of the new Toronto franchise.
47. ROD THORN: Director of NBA Operations and the man in charge of levying fines for fighting.
48. JOHN VANAK: Former official in both the NBA and ABA.
49. CHRIS WEBBER: Washington Bullets forward and a member of Michigan's Fab Five.
50. HARRY WELTMAN: Former general manager of the New Jersey Nets, Cleveland Cavaliers, and Spirits of St. Louis.
51. LENNY WILKENS: Hall of Fame guard, and the coach who has won more NBA games than anyone else. Now coach of the Atlanta Hawks and the 1996 Olympic team.
52. PAT WILLIAMS: Vice president of the Orlando Magic.

# Introduction

A lot of people who love pro basketball dearly are worried. They know that the game has always belonged to the players; they are proud that the National Basketball Association has been a players' league, because the players have usually handled themselves so well.

It wasn't just the fans who loved the NBA—the players did, too. They treated the league as if it were family. They nurtured it, disciplined themselves, and made sure that business on the court was usually conducted according to their own code of honor. Even in their squabbles, they remembered that playing in the NBA is a great gig and they had better not mess it up. Perhaps it was because pro basketball was the third sport—maybe even the fourth sport after baseball, football, and boxing—on the national sports agenda in the 1950s and 1960s.

In the 1970s, the game began to lose itself to greed, drugs, and the duel between the NBA and the American Basketball Association. Then came Larry Bird and Magic Johnson. Then came Commissioner David Stern and Players Association President Larry Fleisher. Then came a drug policy, a salary cap and a commitment on the part of the entire league—from the boardrooms to the locker rooms—to clean up the game and make it fan-friendly.

The result was the 1980s and early 1990s—the glory times of the NBA.

Then suddenly the league and its players began to act fat and sassy. We went through a period of taunting, brawling, and championship teams that couldn't shoot straight. More importantly, we have too many players running amock, consumed by their own wants and needs, oblivious to what has made the game great.

"These guys just don't respect the NBA," said Cleveland Cavaliers general manager Wayne Embry.

Is this the National Basketball Association as we head into the next century? It could be, unless the league and the people who care about the sport do something, do it now, and make it dramatic.

Yes, the 1995 playoffs were a throwback to the early 1990s. Orlando and Houston put on a good show. They ran. They didn't fight. In fact, Houston can serve as an object lesson for the entire league.

QUESTION: Why did the Rockets win back-to-back titles?

ANSWER: Because they had guts enough to tell Vernon Maxwell to take a hike.

Mad Max didn't like it when the Rockets traded for Clyde Drexler. He whined and complained because Drexler took his starting job. He even screamed at Coach Rudy Tomjanovich in front of several players. But the Rockets told Maxwell, "If you don't like it, go home."

He did—right before the playoffs—and Houston was a better team despite losing one of its most talented players.

But most franchises don't have the guts of Tomjanovich and the Houston Rockets. Look at what Dennis Rodman did to San Antonio when the Spurs needed him the most. Look at teams such as New Jersey, Minnesota, and others where the players run wild.

Now is the time for the NBA and the basketball men—this includes front office people, coaches, and veteran players—to take their league back from those who would destroy it.

No less than Michael Jordan thinks so.

"Part of the reason I came back is that I see players who don't have enough respect for the game," he said. "We are making a pretty nice living from this game and we ought to take care of our responsibilities to it."

Jordan said that there is nothing wrong with making money or having endorsements—and Jordan admits to being the king of endorsements—but the essence of the game is winning. "But some guys need to remember that," he said.

Or, as Philadelphia coach John Lucas said, "We've got a lot of guys coming into the NBA who love what the game brings them, but they don't love the game."

There are players such as Derrick Coleman, who says that practice has nothing to do with game performance—so sometimes he goes to practice, and sometimes he doesn't. Then he attacks one of the NBA's model citizens, Karl Malone, by calling Malone "an Uncle Tom, a fake."

Malone is a future Hall of Famer, a self-made star who came into the league with half the ability of Coleman but has accomplished twice as much. Remarkably, the NBA brass said little in defense of Malone, and that made Malone very mad—and for good reason.

"There is a problem with some of the young players," he said. "I can't believe how many of them are complaining out there. You want to tap them on the shoulder and say, 'Hey, have you forgotten that we're being paid to do this? This is our job. How many jobs are going to pay you $3 million a year?' "

That's a good idea, but many young players already have other agendas and priorities.

"Guys have chips on their shoulders," said veteran NBA center Sam Bowie. "If the coach says to go to the right on this play, they go to the left. The way they are paid today, you'd think they'd want to please the coach."

Instead, they have come to believe they are more important than the coaches. "If a guy has a bad game, his usual response is to say that they didn't run enough plays for him," said former Celtic Kevin McHale.

This is not to say that the 1980s were the good old days when everyone got along and coaches were kings. But you can't dismiss what is happening today as simply "more media coverage that blows things out of proportion," as Stern did.

Heck, some of these players don't even understand that there was basketball before them. The Lakers' Nick Van Exel has said he has no concept of the Laker-Celtic rivalry of the 1980s. "I never watched basketball, too boring," he said. "But I heard that Larry Bird and Magic Johnson had a pretty good thing going."

Chew on that for a while, and then you'll understand why so many good guys—big names in the sport such as Jordan, Malone, and Charles Barkley—are worried about the state of the NBA as we head into the next century. They believe the NBA's never-ending quest to create new stars from its young players has turned out a group of Frankensteins.

"You've got a group of guys in this league like David Robinson, Hakeem Olajuwon, John Stockton, and myself who have spent their careers trying to do the right things on and off the court," said Malone. "But we're not cute enough for the league, so they promote all the craziness, all the yelling and taunting. Now they have gotten what they deserved, and they better get out and change it. What happens when we retire? Who is coming behind us to take care of the integrity of the league?"

This isn't meant to trash all the young players. Yes, Shawn Kemp sounded foolish when he said that Malone's "time has passed. Now it is my time," even though Malone remains the top power forward in the game. But, in contrast, third-year pro Jimmy Jackson graciously accepted being left off the 1995 All-Star team in favor of veteran Mitch Richmond, even though Jackson was having a better season.

"Mitch deserves it," said Jackson. "He has been there a while. I know that my time will come."

The trouble is that there seem to be too many Derrick Colemans, J. R. Riders, and Christian Laettners, and not enough Jimmy Jacksons.

While the NBA doesn't have to worry about losing its hold on the winter sports fan to hockey—as *Sports Illustrated* warned in the sping of 1994—it is very true that the league can be "butt ugly," as *USA Today* claimed in the summer of 1994. That came during the 1994 playoffs, which fortunately were televised mostly at night since they were not fit to be seen by children. Among the notorious incidents was a fight between the New York Knicks' Derek Harper and Chicago's Jo-Jo English that ended up in the stands only ten rows below where David Stern sat and watched. "I was embarrassed for the players and for the league," he said.

He should be, but not just because of the trash talk and cheap shots.

The game itself has gotten bogged down in hand-to-hand combat that is passed off as great defense, combining with control-freak, unimaginative coaches who have strangled the offense and turned fast break into a dirty word.

The league was concerned about the severe drop in scoring and how playoff records were set in 1994 for fewest points scored in a single game and in a seven-game series. We had 8-point quarters and six-minute stretches where no one could score a field goal. Was this the NBA of the 1990s, or was it the Tri-Cities Blackhawks vs. the Fort Wayne Pistons?

The league came up with some new rules, but the Band-Aids didn't stop all the bleeding. Despite tighter handchecking rules and moving in the three-point line for the 1994–95 season, the scoring in the league continued to drop—down from 101.5 in 1993–94 to 101.4 in 1994–95.

In fact, what the new rules really produced were 11,982 three-point-shot attempts and 855 more illegal-defense calls. In the words of Indiana coach Larry Brown, the average game has become boring. All of this should scare the NBA. It should warn them that they are in danger of becoming a fat, unimaginative business, more concerned with halftime shows and other marketing gimmicks than the product on the court. No matter how David Stern spins it, basketball is no longer riding the tidal wave of the Jordan-Magic-Bird era of the 1980s and early 1990s.

During the 1994–95 regular season, scoring was out, and defense was in—or what was supposed to be defense, but often was nothing more than conservative coaches making their teams sit on the ball. From 1986 to 1995, scoring in the average game dropped by 18 points, and the NBA's response of moving in the three-point line to twenty-two feet may have slowed the decline but is not the answer. It is time for those who love the game—players, coaches, executives—to face the problems and find some solutions. With that in mind, what follows is a basketball think tank, featuring some of the game's sharpest minds all called together for the purpose of saving the game.

COTTON FITZSIMMONS: It's time for us to take our league back. We can't have all this taunting. We can't have players running wild off the court, then starting fights on the court. What I am talking about is discipline. Some teams let players do anything they want, and the coaches feel helpless.

BOB RYAN: Anyone who claims that the NBA is purely a players' league is missing the point. The coaches may not have control of the players away from the court, but it's another story during the game. I'm here to tell you that coaches are strangling basketball. They are trying to take the game away from the players. They have slowed the game down to a crawl. Some teams don't play defense, it's hand-to-hand combat.

WILLIS REED: Maybe I'm getting soft in my old age, but I sit there and watch the games today and think to myself that they didn't allow this much contact back when I played. Under the basket, it's like a wrestling match when a guy tries to get position. When I went against Wilt Chamberlain, we pushed and shoved, but it was nothing like this. I can't believe some of the stuff I'm watching.

PHIL JACKSON: When I played, I wasn't exactly known as a finesse player. But what has happened in basketball today is that we have beefed up our players to the point where many of the big men are weight-lifters and musclemen. They are bumping, holding, and body-checking each other to the point where some teams are lucky to score 85 points, which is about 12 under what Detroit averaged in the late 1980s—and we thought the Pistons were bad. Pat Riley's defense with the Knicks was unprecedented in the history of basketball. What the officials and the league allowed the Knicks to get away with is the crescendo to what has been building up in the league since the Pistons of the late 1980s. Now it has reached the point to where it's a real intrusion to the game. You cannot fault the players. You cannot fault the coaches. They are doing what they think is best to win.

CHARLIE ROSEN: Phil is a good friend of mine. I was an assistant coach with him in the CBA. We agree on the 1994 Knicks. They weren't basketball players, they were stormtroopers. I know that Phil would never allow his teams to play that way.

PHIL JACKSON: I would think that I'd never have a team play like the Knicks, but I bet Pat Riley felt the same way when he was in L.A. He used to complain about the Pistons and other teams being overly physical. Now, he's had to eat his words. I just hope I don't end up in that position.

AL MENENDEZ: Well, I think you can blame the coaches to an extent. I keep hearing, "You have to do anything to win." What does that mean? Kidnapping? Maiming? Where will it end? Do we have no self-control? Do we want this to be like Rollerball? Do we want our players just to go out there and kill each other? Are we going to be like Tonya Harding with Nancy Kerrigan, trying to take the opponent out before the competition? Maybe we have become such a big business that things such as sportsmanship and the beauty of the game don't matter anymore. If that's the case, then we should just junk the NBA and go back to having rival gangs meet in the schoolyard and deciding the issue with guns, knives, and chains.

WAYNE EMBRY: Maybe I am an idealist, but the NBA has done a lot of good for men of all races. It shows how blacks and whites can work together for a common goal. A good, unselfish basketball team exhibits so many of the right kind of values. But I look around now and say that if we become a league that promotes violence, trash talking, and utter disrespect for the opponent— and we simply say that society is like that, so what can we do to control our players?—then we are missing a chance to be a model that promotes the right kind of values, the values we saw in many of our teams and players in the 1980s.

CHUCK DALY: I am a defensive coach, and I am not as alarmed as some people about the state of the NBA. But I am concerned about the game. A lot of people believe that with all the contact that is being allowed now, this is not basketball. To me, a big problem is that the court was set up a million years ago for a bunch of guys who were 5-foot-7. The size of the people has changed, but the court hasn't. Unless we do something to help the game, you won't be able to score much because some teams will be coached so well that they just won't let you score. Each year, more teams keep getting better and better defensively, and I just don't see it changing. In fact, I expect the scoring to continue to go down right into the next century.

JERRY COLANGELO: It better not, or we are completely forgetting what made the NBA what it is today. We are in the entertain-

ment business. What fans love is the poetry in motion, the un-
predictability of the NBA—and that comes from a running,
open-court game. We need to develop new stars to replace
Michael, Magic, and Bird. You can't do that in a bump-and-
grind half-court game. You need to give the young players room
to run, or they'll never show their stuff.

BOB RYAN: I know this in my heart, that the problem with the
NBA isn't just the lack of stars. It's not just that Magic and Bird
retired and Michael went away. It's the way they are playing the
damn game. All this half-court crap is boring. In the middle of
the 1994 Finals, I got Pat Riley by the side and asked him, "Do
you honestly think that the game would have been as popular as
it was in the 1980s and early 1990s if these 80-point games were
the kind on display?" Pat looked at me and said, "I won't argue
with that premise." Yet here was one of the guys inflicting those
awful games on us.

WAYNE EMBRY: Look at the 1995 Finals—Houston and Orlando
showed you can run and win. That was great basketball, like the
NBA of a few years ago. If you have the atheletes, let them run.

ROD THORN: We need to change the mind-set, especially in the
media. We have coaches who would rather lose 85–80 than
110–105 because they try to sell the idea that if they play an
80-point game, well, their team lost but they sure played hard
and played good defense. But if they gave up 110 points and
lost, instead of it being an exciting game, a lot of people would
insist no defense was being played.

CHUCK DALY: That's because most coaches would rather be known
as defensive coaches. It's a macho thing.

COTTON FITZSIMMONS: Macho my ass, what a lot of these guys are
doing is playing boring basketball. They don't want to run because they want to call every play from the sidelines and keep
control. And what kind of offense do you have? Maybe 80 percent of the teams in the league walk the ball up the court. They
throw it to the big man under the basket. The big man holds the

ball until the double-team comes. Then he throws it back out, and that guy takes a three-pointer. They call that good ball movement. It's just plain boring.

DOUG COLLINS: I agree with everything that is being said about the lack of scoring and the running game, but I also have a major concern about the players. When you give rookies gigantic, guaranteed, multiyear contracts where they make more than established NBA players you take away the incentive. You look at great players such as Michael, Magic, and Bird. They always knew the score, the time left on the 24-second clock, and the significance of each possession. They knew their teammates' strengths and weaknesses, and they knew how to attack the man guarding them. Today's athletes are greater than ever before—in terms of size, strength, and raw ability. But where have the fundamentals gone? So many of these guys have been able to get along solely on their God-given talent, then they come to the NBA, sign a $25 million contract, and you expect them to listen to the coach when the coach tells them that they don't understand the game?

HUBIE BROWN: It comes down to this—we have to stop rewarding the morons. You want to know who can stop the taunting and all the other garbage? The league can. The front offices can. The coaches can. But it's hard. It means hiring coaches who are disciplinarians and supporting them. It means telling some of the kids that they are wrong, and punishing them. You see such crap during games today that you'd like to go out there and break some of these guys in half.

CHUCK DALY: It's the MTV generation. Kids want the $150 shoes. They want the commercials. They want the dunks and the flash.

WAYNE EMBRY: A very sad sign of the times is that we have players wanting to skip practices to make shoe commercials—and the teams allow them to do that.

DAVID STERN: I hear a lot of people overreacting. I know there are trouble spots, but these things are cyclical. In the early 1980s, I heard how there was no defense in the league and how we should raise the baskets. I remember when we had a major drug problem with our players. We overcame that and we'll overcome this.

PETE NEWELL: The league can solve a lot of the problems, but the NBA first must be willing to admit there are problems and then be willing to take some chances, try something new. I don't know if we have enough basketball people in the league office who understand what is really going on down on the court.

RED McCOMBS: The only enemy the NBA has is itself. We can't have teams suing the league and each other. We need to remember that what made this league great was how everyone—the players, coaches, and franchises—worked together to put basketball on its feet in the 1980s. But I don't know if we have the same spirit now as we had back then.

WAYNE EMBRY: I have spent a lifetime in basketball and I am here to tell you that something is terribly wrong.

We have lost nearly 20 points a game since the middle 1980s. We have twenty-one-year-old kids making $50 million before they play their first NBA game.

We have players running around with guns and players openly defying their coaches.

We can't find enough good young players with basic shooting skills and other fundamentals, and we can't find or develop enough qualified men to coach all of our teams.

By nature, I am a conservative man. But I have seen enough. What happened to sportsmanship? To people from diverse backgrounds working together for a common goal? What happened to the integrity of competition, to playing hard—but also playing fair? Are we in the NBA strong enough to overcome some of the forces in society? I believe we are, but not if we just go with the flow. If we want to save our game, it is time for us to change it.

PLAYERS

1 Modern Players

When Kevin Willis was traded to the Miami Heat, he needed a big truck to carry his clothes from Atlanta to southern Florida in November of 1994. That's because Willis owned 110 suits; he would have had more, but he gave away forty-five before his move.

Willis also owned a Range Rover and a Mercedes 560SEL.

When Billy Owens came to the Heat in a trade, he owned two Mercedes and was preparing to buy a third for his fiancée. That was at the start of the 1994–95 season, when Owens was twenty-five years old and had been in the NBA for three seasons. That's one Mercedes for each year that he was a pro.

When Kenny Norman was traded by Milwaukee to Atlanta, he came with a Mercedes 600SEC and a Mercedes 500SL. Kenny Norman is a decent player but hardly a great one; he has never played on a team that got past the first round of the playoffs. But he has $200,000 worth of cars.

When Butch Beard became the coach of the New Jersey Nets, he asked all his players to wear sports jackets to games. The fine would be $500 for each time a player failed to wear a jacket. Derrick Coleman sent a blank check to the Nets management, telling them to fill in the amount of the fine for a year—he had no plans to let anyone tell him what to wear to games, and he was willing to pay $40,000 for the privilege. Charles Barkley—who is no one's idea of a choirboy—heard this story and some other tales about Coleman. Someone asked him what he thought of D.C., which is Coleman's nickname. "I think D.C. means 'Disturbed Child,' " said Barkley.

In 1993, Lakers coach Randy Pfund called a team meeting at his hotel suite. In the middle of Pfund's talk, there was a knock on the hotel door. Pfund answered and found a smiling man with a big pizza in his hand. Lakers center Elden Campbell had sent out for room service. He didn't even ask the coach if he could order a pizza, he just did. Hey, he was hungry.

In order to have some peace and quiet in meetings and on the team bus, Philadelphia coach John Lucas banned his players from carrying cellular phones. When Magic Johnson did a brief stint coaching the Lakers in the spring of 1994, a team meeting was interrupted when a player's beeper went off. Johnson grabbed the beeper from the player and threw it against the wall. He began to tell the team that this—the beeper—was exactly what was wrong with the team. Why would any basketball player need a beeper?

Remember, this was Magic Johnson, not Hank Iba, Bobby Knight, or Adolph Rupp. Magic is a man of the 1980s and 1990s—or at least he thought he was until he coached the new breed of players with the Lakers.

Johnson was stunned that his players didn't push themselves hard in practice, and they didn't seem obsessed with winning. He called them selfish, spoiled, and lazy. He tried to teach his team a lesson: Frustrated with the players' yawning through practice, Magic challenged the Laker starters to a game. He put together a team with assistant coach Larry Drew, Continental Basketball Association callup Reggie Jordan, and old-timers Danny Schayes and Kurt Rambis, who were sitting on the end of the bench. That fivesome—led by Magic—beat the Laker starters in three consecutive games.

It was Magic who learned the lesson: that coaching today's players was not for him. The Lakers were 5-11 under Magic when he resigned.

"Magic has tremendous leadership qualities," said Chuck Daly. "He knew that being a great player is more than talent, it's an intellectual level. It's a competitive level and a leadership level. He had a hard time understanding why the players couldn't make the same demands of themselves as he did—and the players today just aren't willing to push themselves as hard as the players of Magic's era."

When Daly says "Magic's era," it sounds as if he's talking about the age of the set shot—but what he really means is the 1980s.

"I take the losses too hard," Johnson said on the day he announced his resignation. "I hurt. I take them home with me. It's tough for me to sit there and watch when I don't get the effort [from the players] that I think I should. With this team, we don't have the mental side of the game, they don't understand it."

"When Magic quit as coach, a lot of us career coaches said, 'Now he knows how tough it really is,' " said Richie Adubato. "He found out that the same guys who didn't hustle for Randy Pfund stopped hustling for him after a few weeks."

"Players always talk about wanting to be respected," said Doug Collins. "But they don't respect the game. They are being paid so much money, and they equate money with power. The long, guaranteed contracts for $50 million or whatever make some of these guys think that they can do anything they want—and if you, the coach, do or tell them something they don't like . . . well, they think you don't respect them."

As Bill Fitch says, "Individualism has taken over."

Given the fact that they were in the movie *Blue Chips* before their twenty-second birthdays, Anfernee Hardaway and Shaquille O'Neal have been solid citizens in Orlando. Still, both are in their early twenties. They each are worth at least $50 million. They have starred next to Nick Nolte. O'Neal has made two rap tapes, and the first (the immortal "Shaq Diesel") sold over 1 million copies. Now we have "Shaq Fu: Da Return" at your favorite record store—and it may be a million seller, too.

During the 1994–95 season, Hardaway and O'Neal were young players with old NBA blood running through their veins. Yes, O'Neal had what became a public clash with coach Brian Hill over how the pick-and-roll play is to be defended, but that was just a flareup. Early in his career, Jordan stormed out of practice one day because he believed that coach Doug Collins wasn't keeping a fair score during a scrimmage. These things happen when star players and coaches are together every day for eight straight months. But Hardaway and O'Neal were there when Hill needed them. They followed the team rules off the court and led the Magic to the NBA Finals on the court. In fact, it wasn't their fault Orlando was swept by Houston in the Finals; rather, the secondary players such as Dennis Scott, Nick Anderson, and Donald Royal played miserably.

But what if Hardaway or O'Neal didn't like the coach or his strategy? What would the coach do?

Just ask Bill Blair.

On December 12, 1994, the Minnesota Timberwolves lost to Phoenix. No big deal; the Wolves always seem to lose, and that defeat dropped their record to 3-15. Minnesota's J. R. Rider had a terrible game, scoring only 3 points and being lit up for 25 points by Suns rookie Wesley Person. Rider is a wonderful talent who has been maddeningly inconsistent and immature during a pro career that began in 1993 when he was the team's first-round draft pick.

"J. R. needs to grow up and step up his game," Minnesota coach Blair told reporters after that loss to Phoenix. Rider learned of Blair's comment, and then the forward went into the press room. He told the writers, "Right now, I'm a C-minus player. I know that. . . . But why is it all on me? . . . How can you expect my attitude to be good when we're 3 and 15?"

Then Rider shocked the writers by saying, "I'll have a press conference tomorrow after practice."

Teammate Stacey King asked, "What's he going to do? Retire?"

Rider went ahead with his news conference, and said that he thought Blair was showing him no respect by saying that he needed to grow up. Then Rider said, "What does growing up have to do with basketball?"

Yes, he actually said that. He also said, "Growing up and basketball are two different things."

The amazing thing is that Rider believes this. Just because you're paid $2 million a year to play basketball . . . well, that doesn't mean you have to act like an adult, does it?

Or how about this:

After he forced a trade to the Washington Bullets because he didn't like Golden State coach Don Nelson, Chris Webber promised to be a model citizen. For a month, he was fine in the dressing room, then he suffered a separated shoulder. He was on the injured list for a month when the subject of the Bullets' travel was raised by some players, who complained to reporters that the team should have its own plane instead of flying charters. Remember, the objection was to a *charter* flight, not a commercial flight. Webber and the other players didn't like the food on the charter flights.

"I can't keep living like this," Webber told Washington reporters. "You can't keep eating Taco Bell after games. When you look at it, if I'm a race car driver, I've got to have the best car. I've got to have the best body I can have, and it's hard to maintain your body with this kind of food."

When Webber raised this beef, he hadn't even traveled with the Bullets for a month because of his injury. He had been with the team only seven weeks. Then a few months later the Bullets had a food fight on their chartered flight and did $15,000 worth of damage.

"It's just scary," said Cavaliers general manager Wayne Embry. "We have players missing practices and meetings to tape commercials. We have guys challenging coaches every day. That bothers me. Too many guys want to just go their own way."

But New Jersey's Derrick Coleman insists, "There's a new breed of players and it's a new day and age. We speak our minds and we have opinions and a lot of people can't deal with that. They can't deal with our names and our status."

Coleman, Webber, and the rest do represent a new breed. In the past, players judged themselves and their status on the basis of their accomplishments in the league—particularly championships. For the players of today, it's all the peripheral things—the contracts, the endorsements, the commercials—that determines who you are and where you stand. They want the right to complain and dictate how they should be treated, but they don't want to be held accountable for their own play or that of their teams. For the record, Coleman's team has never made it past the first round of the playoffs. The same is true for Webber. For Larry Bird or Magic Johnson or Michael Jordan, the bottom line that mattered was measured in rings. For the new breed, it's solely in their paychecks.

Consider J.R. Rider again. A month into his rookie season, Rider was averaging fewer than 10 points a game for Minnesota. Still, Rider was summoned to make a commercial for Converse. If you happened to see the commercial, you'd never know it was Rider; all you saw were his feet in a pair of Converse cross-training shoes. The Converse people had Rider working out for fifteen hours, more or less, and all they did was film his ankles and shoes. No dialogue, either, just loud music. The next day, Rider said he felt like he had "tired legs" at practice. Wonder why? The Wolves also could have asked exactly what was more important to Rider, basketball or endorsements. This isn't to pick on Rider; several players have been late or skipped practice to film commercials.

"You fine a guy for that and it doesn't faze him," said Embry. "Hey, that commercial could mean $50,000, $100,000, or a lot more to the player. Whatever you fine him, it still will be worth it to the player. That is the kind of world we in the NBA now live in."

Later in the season, Rider taped another commercial, and this time he had his own shoe named after him, and he was allowed to speak and everything.

That's wonderful, but who was J.R. Rider during the 1993–94 season?

He averaged 16 points. He grabbed about 4 rebounds a game and shot about 47 percent—very respectable—but he wasn't Rookie of the Year. It's hard to imagine that anyone other than his relatives and old friends from University of Nevada-Las Vegas actually bought tickets to see Rider play. As for his team, it won 20 games and lost 62. In fact, in their first five years of existence, the Wolves had a 105-305 record, so you couldn't say that Rider was somehow going to be the next generation of a grand tradition.

But he already had a shoe contract worth at least six figures . . . even before he averaged those 16 points.

"It creates big trouble," said longtime NBA assistant Gene Littles. "When a kid comes into the league making $2 million and already has a shoe contract, he also better have the work ethic. You are not going to be able to give it to him. There is nothing you can threaten him with. You jump on his case, and he tells the coach, 'Hey, I got my five-year contract. I got $15 million coming in. I'll get to practice when I get to practice. If you want to fine me, go ahead. I'll write you the check.' His attitude is that he's probably going to be there longer than the coach."

Littles's point is that kids come into NBA—and most of them really are nothing but kids—with the attitude that they are already stars in the league. Rider was suspended three times during the 1994–95 season for various indiscretions. But it obviously didn't turn him into a model citizen.

"That's because they are given the trappings immediately," said

Chuck Daly. "They didn't have to earn the big money or the endorsements, it's handed to them."

In 1993–94, the Seattle Supersonics were 63-19, the league's best regular season record, but the Sonics were upset by Denver in the first round of the playoffs. They were up 2–0, then dropped the next three games.

At halftime of Game 2, Sonic players Gary Payton and Ricky Pierce had a screaming match. Pierce wanted to see the ball more, and Payton said Pierce was selfish. Then it got personal.

After losing to Denver in Game 3, Payton screamed at several of his teammates in the dressing room until he was restrained by veteran Sam Perkins. Then Payton and Pierce got into it again after Game 5.

"That was disgusting," Seattle coach George Karl told reporters after the playoffs. "My biggest problem in the series wasn't Xs and Os, but management of character. Today's players don't even have loyalty to each other. . . . I let the winning affect my instincts. You're winning games. Shawn [Kemp] comes late here and there for practice and the bus . . . Gary [Payton] doesn't practice hard. What do you do? Blow up a bomb when you're on an 11-game winning streak? . . . There is no player who wants to take responsibility for losing. . . . I conceded to the blackmail of minutes. If I started to take minutes away from Shawn [Kemp], Michael Cage or Vincent [Askew] to play Ervin Johnson, then I don't think those three guys would have played as hard. . . . He'll soft-shoe and say all the right things, but the truth of our game is that the individual very seldom concedes to the team."

The 1995 playoffs were more of the same for Karl and the Sonics. They had a regular season record of 57-25, but were upset in the first round by the young L.A. Lakers. Again, players complained about their lack of minutes. There were no fights in the dressing room, but Karl had too many egos to juggle. Instead of pulling together to avoid another first round disaster, the only thing upon which the Seattle players would agree is that it was all Karl's fault. Yes, Seattle did play relatively hard in the first round, but the Sonics didn't play together.

Karl's characterization of his team rings true, because the players of today are being raised by a basketball world that is far different from the one that gave us Michael Jordan, Larry Bird, and Magic Johnson.

Pat Riley is supposed to be the epitome of the modern coach, but even he has asked, "Why is it necessary to sit down every single time and explain why you are doing something? Why has it gotten so that players say, 'He didn't talk to me'? These guys are pros, making millions of dollars. Their job is to come to play, to accept a role."

That may be what coaches think, but players have another opinion. To understand this, you have to look at where some of today's future stars have come from.

The current generation of young NBA players say that most of us can't understand them.

They're right.

That doesn't just go for the fans, but also for older NBA players, and certainly NBA coaches and executives.

How do we know what it's like to be thirteen years old and already be interviewed on television?

That happened to Chris Webber after he scored 64 points and had 15 dunks in a junior high school game. Pretend you are Webber for a moment. You are in the eighth grade. You are already 6-foot-5 and wearing a size 16 tennis shoe. You have already been to Los Angeles, Las Vegas, and Seattle—all because you can play basketball, and you were a member of a traveling summer AAU team out of Detroit that included a kid named Jalen Rose.

You are thirteen years old, and one day you receive an invitation from Michigan State coach Jud Heathcote. He wants you and your family to stop by his office in East Lansing and maybe go out for dinner. That sounds like fun, so your dad drives you up there—remember, you are only thirteen, so you can't drive yet.

Not long after the Michigan State visit, Michigan coach Bill Frieder drops by your house to say hello and meet your parents.

You are Chris Webber. You aren't even in high school, but major universities are recruiting you.

No wonder Don Nelson couldn't understand Chris Webber.

Nelson thought Webber was a rookie at the age of twenty-one. Webber hadn't felt like a basketball rookie since he was thirteen.

Webber's college teammate at Michigan was Juwan Howard.

They are different, but they also are the same.

To fully understand how Webber, Howard, and Michigan's Fab Five were assembled, pick up Mitch Albom's terrific book, *The Fab Five,* which is the source of some of the background material used here about Howard and Webber.

Webber comes from a middle-class family. His father was an autoworker, his mother a teacher. They forced him to attend Detroit Country Day School in suburban Birmingham, Michigan. It's a place known more for its National Merit Scholars than its McDonald's All-Americans. Webber sometimes likes to act like a city kid. He tries to let you know that he can handle himself on the streets. Maybe he can, but he's certainly not a street kid.

Howard comes from Chicago. His mother was seventeen when he was born, a junior in high school. She was no more ready to take care of a baby than the infant Howard was capable of stepping into the NBA. Howard was raised by his grandmother, Jannie Mae Howard. The family was so poor that he spent the first week of his life sleeping in a drawer lined with blankets because they couldn't afford a crib.

By the time he was a sophomore in high school, Howard was 6-foot-8 and was considered the best high school big man in the city of Chicago. There was a twenty-eight-day period in 1990 when college coaches were allowed to watch players work out, but NCAA rules would not permit the coaches to speak to them. The coaches couldn't even wave or wink. Okay, maybe a little eye contact, but that was it.

Michigan assistant Brian Dutcher was there *every day* watching Howard work out. Imagine being sixteen years old and from one of the poorest projects in Chicago, yet knowing that a grown man from a major college basketball program was there, watching you for a solid month—even though he couldn't say a word to you.

Why wouldn't that make you believe that you might be the most important person ever to step on this earth?

Fortunately for Howard, his grandmother was a strong woman

with little time for fools. She made him study and made him listen. She could deflate his ego when it got a little too big. Howard had decent grades, and while he could handle himself on the streets if he had to, he stayed out of trouble. He was a good kid.

He was the first member of the Fab Five to commit to Michigan.

Howard and Webber had known each other from the summer AAU games. They were rivals—the best high school big man in Chicago and the best from Detroit. But when Howard signed with Michigan, he began calling Webber, saying that he should come to Michigan, too.

"Actually, we didn't like each other much when we were in high school," Howard said. "But I told Chris that if we both went to Michigan along with some of the other guys they signed, we could win an NCAA title in our freshman year, and we almost did."

The Fab Five spent their lives being recruited—by summer league coaches, by high school coaches, by college coaches, and by agents. So when Howard and Webber became first-round draft picks in the NBA, they didn't consider themselves rookies—just as they never considered themselves freshmen when they were at Michigan.

The Fab Five was together for only two years at Michigan. The spiritual leader was Jalen Rose, a kid who did grow up on the mean streets of Detroit. Rose and Webber were best friends from the seventh grade, which was when they began playing together. Rose taunted Webber about being soft and going to a wimpy suburban school, telling him that he needed playground grit.

At Michigan, the Fab Five took on Rose's personality. They talked trash. They were the first notable team to wear long, baggy shorts.

"If I had known that the shorts would get to be such an issue, I'd have not gone along with it," said Michigan coach Steve Fisher.

Well, Steve, if some of your players hadn't worn the shorts seemingly halfway down their butts . . . and if Howard hadn't grabbed his crotch as he taunted the Michigan State crowd . . . if Webber hadn't taunted Michigan State coach Jud Heathcote . . . if the Fab Five had just conducted themselves with a little more class . . .

"I blame myself for some of that," said Fisher. "First, we weren't nearly as bad as people said. But I also could have done a better job of preparing the kids to deal with interviews. Instead, I gave them free rein and they came off like cocky eighteen-year-olds. We had a group of kids who were eighteen years old, but never had the luxury of being eighteen. Because of the spotlight on our program, we had to learn on the fly. And when we made a mistake, the entire nation saw it. Now, I'd tell them to be careful what they said. I really winced at some of the things they said because I knew it would come out wrong."

In other words, Fisher now would be like Crash Davis in the movie *Bull Durham*, when he tells the phenom pitcher, "Today, we are going to learn a lesson in clichés. The first one is, 'I'm working hard and just trying to improve.' Now write that down."

Veteran NBA scout Al Menendez insists that the Fab Five was a direct product of the Detroit Pistons' Bad Boys, the team that won championships in 1989 and 1990. The college kids simply copied the pros, and put their own individual stamp on it.

"At Michigan, we were the guys in the black hats, but I liked it," said Webber right after he was traded to Washington. "We were criticized a lot. Some of the things they said about us on TV would make my mother cry. But it didn't bother us because we were in it together."

The team identified with the tough guys on the street. They revelled in the image because they believed it gave them respect.

"It did bother me that they made us out to be gangsters," Howard said recently.

Maybe that's because Howard really knew gangsters, given where he grew up in Chicago. He even said that when he first walked the Ann Arbor campus, he had to resist the temptation to dive for cover when he heard a car backfire. In his neighborhood, you took no chances because odds were it was a gunshot.

"I look back on it now and we were just a bunch of college freshmen having fun," Howard said. "I don't think the critics were fair to us."

Fair or not, the Fab Five came to symbolize the coddled, spoiled big-time college basketball player. It appeared that they weren't coached in high school, and then Fisher let his players do what they wanted. His players even called him "Fish." His critics insist that Fisher signed kids who had never been disciplined or coached, and he was not about to take a chance on alienating them—and having them transfer—by laying down the law of the gym. Fisher sort of went with the flow. Fisher would say that there was no other way to go.

"I've always told my players that I'll treat them fairly, but I won't treat them the same," he said. "It's like that in a family. No father treats all his children the same."

But handling spoiled brats isn't easy, and the basketball system had already spoiled the Fab Five by the time they reached Michigan. Of course, schools such as Michigan recruiting thirteen-year-old kids such as Webber is a big part of why today's modern player is a prima donna before his first professional game.

Webber was the number one pick in the 1993 draft. Golden State traded three future first-round draft picks plus the rights to number three pick Anfernee Hardaway for the rights to Webber.

The man behind the deal was Don Nelson, the Warriors coach and general manager. He has been a true force in the NBA, a three-time Coach of the Year and a strategic innovator. With the Warriors, Nelson has been a man in search of a center, and during the draft day press conference he said he finally had one in Webber—even if Webber would be a bit undersized at 6-foot-10.

Webber heard that and wasn't thrilled. Howard was the center at Michigan; he was a power forward. He was lukewarm at best about being an NBA center and he didn't hide that opinion from the press.

Nelson fits the classic old-line coach profile. He was an undertalented, overachieving player. He was a low draft pick out of Iowa. He was traded and then cut before hooking on with Boston and becoming an excellent role player on five championship teams. His career average was 4.9 points. It's safe to say that no one ever kissed Don Nelson's butt, either when he was thirteen or thirty-three years old.

Wayne Embry gave Nelson his first coaching job with Milwaukee in 1976. Both men believe in players of strong character, players who work hard and listen to the coach. They believe in the Celtic way, where the team really did come first and a rookie was at the bottom of the food chain. They still talk about how Bill Russell wouldn't even learn a rookie's name until midseason; he just called them "rook," or by their number. To Russell, a free agent was "F.A."

Even though Nelson had been a pro coach for sixteen years and had obviously changed with the times, nothing prepared him for the new wave of players symbolized by Chris Webber.

Nelson can be sarcastic. He will criticize a player in front of others. He is not the kind of coach to put his arm around a young guy and say, "Tell me, what's on your mind?"

Most of his players know that and accept it. That's because Don Nelson is a damn good coach. His team wins, and players like to win because it's fun. Winning also means more money—or at least it used to. But Webber signed a fifteen-year, $74 million contract that gave him the right to become a restricted free agent at the end of his rookie season. It was hard to tell Webber about how winning and sacrificing for the team would lead to more money, because he already had more money that anyone else on the team.

Webber and Nelson alternated between an uneasy truce and a verbal form of guerrilla warfare.

"There was a game where he took me out and screamed that he never should have drafted me," said Webber. "He said it right by the bench in front of a bunch of kids. That's not right."

Webber believed his own press clippings. He was a franchise player. He was worth $74 million. He had a multimillion-dollar shoe contract. He didn't understand why a coach would scream at him for something like failing to help out on defense.

Nelson looked at Webber and saw a twenty-year-old. In his mind, twenty-year-olds need coaching. Sometimes, twenty-year-olds need a verbal kick in the ass.

When Nelson told Webber that drafting him was a mistake, he didn't mean that; he was trying to motivate the kid. He was doing what Red Auerbach had done, when he'd tell a player that no one's job was safe, that everyone in the NBA wanted to play for the old Celtics. He wanted Webber to try to prove to him that he was wrong.

Webber didn't hear it that way. He didn't think he had to prove anything to anybody.

"I don't care if you're a dog, a five-year-old, or a grown man with ten kids, it's the way you respect people and treat people that counts," said Webber. "Nor does it matter how much money you make. What matters is giving a person respect."

Nelson surely thought that Webber had done nothing in the NBA to deserve the same respect as a veteran such as Chris Mullin or Tim Hardaway. Such respect had to be earned, not merely granted because a player is a top draft pick.

"I just don't know what I did to make Chris so angry at me that he didn't want to play for me," said Nelson. "I didn't treat him different than any other rookie. I probably was even softer with Chris."

Webber and his friends were suspicious of Nelson. Webber wondered why the coach played him only thirty-two minutes a game. Stars usually are on the court for thirty-eight to forty minutes a night. They thought Nelson made too much an issue of Webber's weak free throw shooting, which was a mere 53 percent. Webber averaged 17.5 points and 9.1 rebounds and was voted the 1994 Rookie of the Year, but it seemed to him that Orlando did a much better job of promoting Anfernee Hardaway for the award than the Warriors did for him.

Near the end of the 1993–94 season, Webber began to seriously consider using the option in his contract that allowed him to become a restricted free agent after his rookie year.

Why you sign a guy to a $74 million contract and give him an out after a single season is the $74 million question that the Warriors have never answered. Basically, they screwed up. Because of the arcane workings of the salary cap, which we'll see in greater detail in the next chapter, Webber played for "only" $1.7 million in his rookie season, since that was the highest salary slot the Warriors had available. Because that was considered low for the number one pick in the draft, the Warriors agreed to give Webber the right to restricted free agency after one year. It was a great deal for Webber for three reasons:

1. If he were seriously injured in his rookie year, he would have a contract that would pay him $74 million over fifteen years even if he never played again. That's a terrific insurance policy.
2. By allowing Webber to become a restricted free agent, the Warriors could rip up the contract and pay him anything they wanted. Salary cap rules do not apply to re-signing your own free agents. But this also gave Webber the right to ask for $100 million or whatever his heart (and agent) desired.
3. If Webber wanted to sign with another team, the Warriors

would have the right to match that offer sheet and retain Webber. But this restricted free agency also gave Webber the chance to leave Golden State if he wanted to stand firm and simply refuse to sign with the Warriors.

Webber took a stand. He never publicly said that he didn't want to play for Nelson, but Warriors owner Chris Cohan said, "This wasn't about money. It was mostly about Don."

Nelson even offered to resign as coach and just retain his title as general manager if that would bring Webber back. Instead, it infuriated Webber.

"He just lied," said Webber. "Saying that was the last straw. That was phony. The only reason he [offered to resign] was to pressure me to come back to training camp."

Webber may have been right; Nelson has been known to try and shape press coverage to get what he wants. If he wanted to make Webber look bad, he did. As Larry Brown said, "What has the NBA come to when a rookie can force a great coach like Don Nelson to offer to quit?"

Webber became a whipping boy on sports talk shows, often with the sound effects of a whining infant.

But Webber viewed this as another attack on his manhood and a lack of respect. His resolve hardened. He had his millions from his shoe contract and other endorsements. He may have been only twenty-one in the fall of 1994, but he had enough money in the bank to wait out the Warriors and Don Nelson.

His agent informed the Warriors that the best thing to do would be to sign Webber and trade him. That way, at least they'd have something to show for their former number one pick. The bottom line was that Webber was not going back to Golden State.

Meanwhile, Juwan Howard had become the fifth pick in the 1994 draft by the Washington Bullets.

"We offered him $30 million over ten years," said Bullets general manager John Nash. "It was the biggest contract in the history of the franchise. I couldn't believe that I actually was willing to pay a rookie that much, and I was absolutely stunned when his agent quickly turned it down."

David Falk represented Howard, and he reportedly was more

interested in something like a $24 million deal over six years—an average of $4 million annually. That wouldn't fit into the Bullets' salary cap slot. Falk represented two other Bullets—Rex Chapman and Calbert Cheaney. He offered to restructure their contracts to create a higher salary slot for Howard.

That is one of Falk's favorite maneuvers and what has made him an effective agent. Often, he understands the salary cap better than general managers do. He also represents a lot of players, so he can come up with a salary cap plan whereby he'll rework the contracts of his veteran players on the roster—getting them more money and more years later—in exchange for their earning a little less now. That money can be used to sign a rookie, especially one represented by Falk. So Falk gets the rookie what he wants, and he also gets his established players a raise.

More than one team has gone along with Falk's ideas of how to juggle their payroll, but the Bullets were not about to bite.

As Nash said, "I can't feel ashamed about offering a player $30 million."

The obvious question is, how can Juwan Howard, who grew up with his grandmother in the projects of Chicago, pass up $30 million? He should crawl on his hands and knees over broken glass to sign that contract before someone changes their mind. But remember how the system works, how players such as Howard are recruited, coddled, and told that they are the center of the universe. The Fab Five never won a national title, but down deep they believe they were the greatest college team *ever*. And they believe they will be great pros.

So when an agent tells a player in this state of mind that he's worth more than $30 million, guess what? The player believes his agent. So Howard sat out all of training camp.

Meanwhile, the Bullets watched the Webber case with interest, and then decided to make a pitch for him. Howard's draft rights were mentioned as part of a possible deal, but Webber squashed that offer.

"Chris made it very clear that if he came to play in Washington, it would be because Juwan was here and they could play together," said Nash.

Bullets owner Abe Pollin met with Webber and Howard. He was expecting the worst, and instead found both young men to be intelligent and charming. He decided he wanted both of them on his team.

Webber's agent told the Warriors to sign his client to a one-year, $2.1 million contract. Then he said that the Warriors could trade Webber to the Bullets for Tom Gugliotta and three future first-round picks.

"It was not the kind of deal we wanted to make, but it was the best we could do," said Nelson.

So the trade went through. Then Howard signed a twelve-year, $37 million contract with the Bullets.

So here is what Webber did:

1. He pried himself away from Golden State.
2. He helped convince Howard to sign with the Bullets, and he also helped Howard get an even larger contract.
3. He set himself up to become a restricted free agent again in the summer of 1995, and he could put the Bullets through the same thing he did Golden State. Suppose he doesn't like the coach, or the city, or he thinks he didn't play enough, or believes that Howard deserved more minutes.

When Webber joined the Bullets, he said all the right things. He said he hoped to sign a long-term contract with them. He said he "didn't want to be a free agent every year." He said he would hang on coach Jimmy Lynam's every word and that the world would see that he was a good guy.

The Webber situation, however, destroyed Don Nelson mentally. He went into the hospital with "exhaustion," and wound up resigning before the end of the season. So the Warriors lost both Nelson and Webber.

"This was one of those things where it seemed that the inmates were running the asylum," said Phoenix Suns owner Jerry Colangelo. "You have to respect Golden State for standing up for their coach. We need more of that in the NBA. But I also applaud Washington for taking a shot with Webber. They were mired at the bottom and had to try something."

The Bullets had seven consecutive losing seasons before the Webber deal (and the trade would not keep them from making it eight straight). They were one of the NBA's most boring teams and a terrible draw, but within twenty-four hours of the deal they sold 2,000 new season tickets—this for a team that had only 5,000 season ticket holders.

"This is a first for me when a coach like Nelson is challenged by a young player like Webber and, essentially, the player wins," said Indiana general manager Donnie Walsh. "I don't like it. It sets a dangerous precedent. Right now, the monster is out of the cage."

A footnote to this story came when Webber and Howard joined the Bullets in late November of 1994. Both players were horrendously out of shape.

Why?

Because neither had played full-court basketball since the spring of 1994.

Why not?

"Because my agent told me not to play," said Howard. "He didn't want me to take a chance on getting hurt. It was the longest I ever remember where I didn't play competitive basketball."

Webber gave a similar answer.

So that is another aspect to this story: when an agent tells the modern player not to play, he doesn't play.

Eleven years before the Chris Webber situation, there was Magic Johnson and Paul Westhead. Given what Magic said about the character of rookie players after he quit coaching the Lakers in 1994, this story hangs heavy with irony.

It began in 1979, when Johnson left Michigan State as a sophomore, joined the Lakers, and led them to the 1980 title. He was twenty years old. Jack McKinney had coached the first 14 games of that season, before sustaining a serious head injury in a biking accident. He would never coach the Lakers again. Assistant Paul Westhead took over. He stuck with McKinney's fast break offense, and full-force, Magic motored them to the title. The next season, the Lakers were 54-28, but were upset in the first round of the 1981 playoffs by San Antonio.

Westhead viewed the playoff flop as an indictment of the running game—or, at least, he thought that the Lakers needed more structure. He installed a half-court offense with twenty-five new plays. He put the brakes on the team, pulling down the curtain on Showtime. While several Laker players didn't like it, Johnson was the only one who spoke out publicly. Eleven games into the season, the Lakers defeated Utah, 113–110—yes, they scored 113 points, but Johnson considered that to be Slo-Ball. That shows you how times have changed. Anyway, that victory in Utah was their fifth in a row. Johnson had 17 points, but there had been a confrontation during a timeout, apparently because Westhead wanted Johnson to run certain plays, but Magic wanted to just run, period. After the game, Magic told writers that he could no longer play Westhead's style and he wanted to be traded.

The Lakers were 7-4. The next day, they fired the coach, replacing Westhead with a tandem of Jerry West and Pat Riley. Johnson was twenty-two years old and was painted nationally as a symbol of the spoiled modern athlete. Even teammate Jamaal Wilkes told *Sports Illustrated,* "Does this mean if Magic got mad at a player, then the player would be gone the next day?"

When Magic was introduced before the next game, he was booed. Then the Lakers beat the Spurs, 136–116. Magic had 20 points, 16 assists, and 10 rebounds. Fans cheered him. Riley grew into the coaching job and became this generation's Red Auerbach. The Lakers went on to win the 1982 title, and everyone decided that Magic must have been right about Westhead after all. Johnson also never had another major clash with a coach. Is that because Westhead was so wrong, or was it because Magic learned from the Westhead controversy to bring his gripes to the coach behind closed doors? No one is sure, but it is obvious that someone learned something.

Westhead may have learned something a little too well. When he next coached in the NBA, with the Chicago Bulls from 1982 to 1983, they averaged 111 points per game to rank ninth in the league. And when he returned to coach Denver in 1990–91, his hypermodern, hyperactive style of play disdained set plays or defense; his team averaged 120 points per game, but gave up an NBA record 130.8, including 107 in a *half* against Phoenix. He may have been the laughingstock of the league, but no one said the Nuggets' style was boring.

Webber's and Howard's situations are not unique. If anything, today's and tomorrow's young players will receive even more coddling than the Fab Five.

You may not know it, but the next Shaquille O'Neal is already supposed to be among us. Hard-core hoop fans already know his name, and the first newspaper stories began appearing about him in the fall of 1994. He is Terry Wallace from Miami, Florida. He is 6-foot-4 and 220 pounds and the syndicated story telling us about the kid they call "Baby Shaq" mentioned that he's twelve years old.

Yes, twelve years old—and in the seventh grade.

When Wallace enrolled at Rubén Darío Middle School in Miami, one of his teachers told him, "I'd love to be your agent. I'd love to have 10 percent." It was meant as a joke, but it also was true. Between the eighth grade and whenever Wallace becomes eligible for the pro draft, there will be a lot of people who will want to be this kid's agent. But isn't it a bit of a stretch to assume that a seventh-grader not only is headed to the NBA, but that he's the next Shaquille O'Neal? Aren't we assuming the kid will continue physically to grow into an NBA body, that he will mentally mature, do enough in school to stay eligible and not fall with the wrong crowd and end up in jail? Aren't we assuming a lot about his development as a basketball player and as a person?

Of course we are, but it is done all the time in the business of basketball.

As a sixth-grader, Wallace averaged 18 points, 8 blocks, and had a couple of 30-rebound games—games that were played on eight-foot baskets, by the way. Already, the basketball meatgrinder wants a piece of him—*and all he's played on are eight-foot baskets!* High school coaches attend his games, and you know that college coaches can't be far behind. Didn't Bob Knight watch Damon Bailey play when he was in the eighth grade? And didn't Knight tell author John Feinstein that Bailey "already is better than any of our guards"?

It turned out that Bailey became a great high school player, a good college player, and an afterthought as a pro. In fact, Knight told some people that he failed to maximize Bailey's talent. The Indiana Pacers picked Bailey in the second round of the 1994 draft—more as a courtesy to a local hero than anything else. After leaving college, Bailey had two knee operations. Maybe he'll come back and play a bit, but his pro career looks as promising as Steve Alford's.

This is not meant to trash Bailey, but to remind everyone that a lot of strange things can happen to a kid on the road to the NBA. Consider our Baby Shaq. Remember, he is only twelve years old and he already weighs 220 pounds. He supposedly carries the tonnage well, but if his body composition changes as he matures, Baby Shaq could end up looking like Baby Huey. Who knows?

More importantly, why not just leave the kid alone for a few more years and let him at least reach the age of sixteen in peace?

A few years ago, Dick Vitale was broadcasting a college game with Keith Jackson on ABC. Vitale launched into one of his stream-of-consciousness monologues about a couple of kids who were supposed to be great high school players, but who were just starting their sophomore seasons.

"But Dick, why talk about these kids?" asked Jackson.

"Because they are real diaper dandies," said Vitale. "All the big-time colleges want them now."

"But Dick, they are only fifteen years old," said Jackson. "Why can't we just let them be fifteen?"

For once, Vitale was silent because he knew Jackson was correct.

When it comes to these youngsters, what we should be talking about is the cottage industry that hypes kids like Terry Wallace, a system where the top twelve-year-olds in a city play in summer tournaments all over the country.

"These AAU teams travel to places like Las Vegas, Los Angeles, Boston, you name it," said veteran basketball scout Al Menendez. "Obviously, these things go on because someone somewhere is making money off them. That's one story. But a bigger issue to me is the kids. What do you do with a kid who has already been to Vegas and New York before he's in high school?"

In high school, basketball remains a wonderful road show. During the 1992–93 season, St. Raymond's from the Bronx played in tournaments in Hawaii, San Diego, and Alaska. Yes, these are high school kids, and St. Raymond's isn't even one of the premier high school programs in the country.

Al Menendez just shakes his head when he hears stories like that. He scouts for the Indiana Pacers. For years, he was player personnel director of the New Jersey Nets and he's a New York native. He also was an assistant coach at Hawaii with Rick Pitino and an assistant under Jerry Tarkanian at UNLV. He says there are disturbing trends in amateur basketball that will eventually have an impact on the colleges and pros.

"How do you coach a kid who has had summer coaches fawning all over him, giving him shoes and shirts and God knows what else to play for their teams?" he asked. "Doesn't anyone realize that we are taking our best young basketball players and creating a generation who will go through life with their hands out? How are you supposed to discipline kids in college or the pros, when the kid has had his ass kissed ever since he was in the seventh grade? He has been taught that if he doesn't like one coach, don't worry, another coach will be glad to take him. These summer coaches get into bidding wars over kids. Some of these summer teams in New York are backed by drug dealers. It's a cesspool. The high school coach used to be the most important person in a player's life, at least after his parents. Or he sometimes was like a parent when there was no father in the home. That wasn't always a great situation, but a high school coach was usually a better influence than most of these summer league coaches. At least a high school coach is supposed to be a teacher. Today the most important coach often is not really a coach at all. He's coaching the summer league team, but he could be a used-car salesman, a drug dealer, an older wealthy guy who likes basketball and thinks he knows more about it than Dean Smith. Sometimes, the summer coach is a legitimate guy who has the best interests of the kid at heart. But too many of these guys have their own agendas. A summer league coach can be anybody, and that bothers me."

Menendez and other basketball men said that a player used to establish his credentials by playing for his high school team. Now, the summer means just as much or more.

The classic example is Lloyd Daniels, who was a complete creation of the summer leagues. Daniels played only one full year of high school basketball—even though he attended four different high schools—and never received a diploma from any of them. He later earned his high school equivalency certificate while attending Mt. San Antonio Junior College in California. That came with the help of Mark Warkentein, an assistant at UNLV. Warkentein became Daniels's legal guardian and helped the player with his studies and in other areas, the idea being to get Daniels's books in shape so he could play for the Rebels. Jerry Tarkanian loved the guy; he was convinced that Daniels was the "next Magic Johnson."

It turned out that he wasn't even the next Avery Johnson.

Daniels played a grand total of two games for Mt. San Antonio Junior College. He transferred to UNLV and was busted in a sting at a Las Vegas crack house, where Daniels was in line with several other junkies waiting to buy cocaine. He never played a game for UNLV, but was around the program long enough to earn the school two years of probation.

"But after he left us, I got calls from schools such as Kansas and St. John's, and they were interested in signing Lloyd," said Tarkanian.

What does that tell you?

Here is a guy who had played one year of high school ball and two junior college games. He was a convicted drug user. He was a terrible student. Yes, he was a "playground legend," but he also was known for jumping from one summer league team to the next, always looking for the best deal.

Yet major colleges wanted Daniels after his drug arrest.

The summer leagues—where Daniels caught the eyes of college scouts—are tied in to the summer camps. That industry began with Howard Garfinkel's Five-Star Camps—because Garfinkel was known for rating the nation's top high school players from one to five stars, with five stars meaning the kid was a future all-pro. Soon Nike entered the summer camp business. The Nike camp is considered the best in the country because Nike pays all the expenses of the top 120 high school players—twenty-four at each position—to take part in their week-long camp. Nike tries to say that its camp is about more than basketball, because players take morning courses in math and English—but the messages are so mixed. They tell the kids that basketball should not be the most important thing in their lives, then they pay all the kids' expenses, put them up in nice hotels, and shower them with Nike shirts, shorts, socks, shoes, and bags—all because the kids can play basketball. The kids know this. In fact, Nike seems to be recruiting these kids just in case they grow into pro stars—they'll know whose shoes they should wear.

It seems that every college coach and major shoe company has its own camp, and they often compete with one another to convince the best players to attend. The more talented players they attract, the more prominent college coaches will show up to watch—and everyone's ego is stroked.

A kid in this situation has to feel like the best-looking girl at an old high school sock hop. She is in the middle of the dance floor, knowing that all those shy boys standing against the wall want her to see them, to pick them. But we aren't talking about teenagers here, but fifty-year-old coaches who have contracts worth over $1 million. The kids know that, too. This can't help but turn most sixteen-year-olds into egomaniacs.

Lost in all this hyperventilating over teenagers whose bodies usually are far ahead of their brain is this fact: most of these kids won't make it.

Let's take a look at *The Sporting News*'s top seventy-five high school players for 1986. Here are the first ten in order: J. R. Reid, Terry Mills, Rex Chapman, Michael Christian, Rumeal Robinson, Steve Thompson, Anthony Pendleton, Chris Munk, Chris Brooks, and Scott Williams.

No great players here. Only Reid, Mills, Chapman, and Williams have had NBA careers of at least four years. Christian, Pendleton, and Brooks never even made it to the NBA.

If you examine the entire list of seventy-five, you find only one real star—Derrick Coleman. On the list of seventy-five, only ten have had NBA careers of at least four years.

The Sporting News also listed the top thirty junior college players for 1986, and only three even lasted a full season in the NBA—Mitch Richmond, Gerald Paddio, and Ledell Eackles.

Those should be sobering numbers, and they are more the norm than the exception.

In 1988, *The Sporting News* rated the top fifty high school players—and this was a much stronger class. Eleven of the top twelve have had significant NBA careers. The names are Alonzo Mourning, Billy Owens, Stanley Roberts, Kenny Williams, Shawn Kemp, Chris Mills, Chris Jackson, Todd Day, Lee Mayberry, Don MacLean, Laphonso Ellis, and Christian Laettner. The only miss was a fellow by the name of Cesar Portillo.

But after that twelve, only seven of the remaining thirty-eight players had an NBA career of at least three seasons.

The 1988 JUCO list is even more revealing, as only two of the top thirty made it in the NBA—Chris Morris and Cedric Ceballos.

Let's take a look at one more list. This one came from the *St. Petersburg Times* by Bill Cronauer, who was considered one of the top evaluators of high school talent in the 1970s and early 1980s. Cronauer listed his top thirty-three players for 1981. Only seven had pro careers of at least five years—Greg Dreiling, Patrick Ewing, Eddie Pinckney, Sam Vincent, Ennis Whatley, Chris Mullin, and a fellow by the name of Michael Jordan.

But there were other can't-miss types who did. Remember Keith Lee? Stuart Gray? Bobby Lee Hurt? Nigel Miguel? John Flowers? Anthony Jones?

He had ten names on his "All-Sleeper" team. Only one played in the NBA—Lorenzo Charles, whose career lasted 36 games with the Atlanta Hawks. Charles is best known for the dunk that gave N.C. State's Jim Valvano his only national title.

"You can talk until you're blue in the face about how the odds are stacked against the kids, but they don't believe you," said Wayne Embry. "That's because there are so many people in these kids' lives telling them how great they are, how the NBA is just waiting for them. Between the street agents, the shoe companies, the summer leagues, and even some of the high school and college coaches, no one is going to tell these kids the truth. There are guys in the NBA who can't even balance their own checkbooks."

But at least they can pay someone to do that for them.

"I know," said Embry. "But what about the kids who don't make it? They can't read, they can't add, and then they find out that they can't play ball anymore. Then what?"

The NBA has made a series of commercials telling kids to Stay In School, but many of the players used in the spots left college early for the NBA. Charles Barkley is one. Jordan is another. Isn't that a mixed message? An NBA spokesman said that what the league really meant is for kids to stay in high school, and all of these players did that. But that creates another dilemma. Are they saying, "Stay in school so you can get to the NBA like me?"

To make matters worse, high school star Kevin Garnett entered the 1995 draft and was selected fifth. What message is that? Not exactly "Stay In School."

One of the best ways of dealing with this issue is the approach taken by Brad Daugherty. The Cavaliers center is from Black Mountain, in western North Carolina. When he talks to schoolkids in his area, he brings along an old high school teammate. This guy is now a noted attorney. Daugherty talks about how he was smart enough in grade school to skip a year, how he graduated from high school at sixteen and earned a degree from North Carolina by the time he was twenty. He says he's lucky that he's tall and could play basketball. Not everyone can do that. But a lot of people can become a lawyer; just listen to my friend tell you how it is done.

The clearest demonstration of the result of all of this long-term warping of priorities was on display at the basketball World Championships in Toronto in 1994—the occasion for the so-called Dream Team II.

The first team truly was a dream. It was Magic, Michael, Larry, Karl Malone, John Stockton, Charles Barkley, Patrick Ewing, Scottie Pippen, David Robinson, Chris Mullin, Clyde Drexler, and Christian Laettner, who was the token college player. That group owned eleven NBA championship rings. It was coached by Chuck Daly, winner of two titles in Detroit, and he was assisted by Lenny Wilkens, the all-time-winningest coach in NBA history. The college assistants were Seton Hall's P. J. Carlesimo and Duke's Mike Krzyzewski.

Daly talked about how the players were treated like rock stars as they rolled to the 1992 Olympic gold medal in Barcelona. There was a lot of hype around the Dream Team, but most of it was deserved; any team with Jordan, Bird, and Magic Johnson on the roster—even if those players were aging—must be discussed when talking about the greatest teams ever assembled. The only ugly incident in the 1992 Olympics came when Barkley elbowed a poor Angolan fellow under the basket. Barkley was chastized for it, and for his subsequent explanation, "How did I know he wasn't carrying a spear?"—a dumb comment, as he later admitted.

Then came Dream Team II in 1994, which the NBA used to showcase its next generation of stars.

How many championship rings did these guys have? Two, and they belonged to Detroit's Joe Dumars. Yes, Isiah Thomas (who also had two rings) was on the roster, but he couldn't play due to a ruptured Achilles tendon.

Dream Team II came with an inferiority complex. By dubbing

them a Dream Team, the NBA set them up to be compared to the first group. The Blessed Trinity of the original dreamers was Magic-Michael-Larry. But who was it on Dream Team II? Shawn Kemp, Shaquille O'Neal, and Reggie Miller? Derrick Coleman, Larry Johnson, and Alonzo Mourning?

My Lord, Steve Smith was on Dream Team II, and what did he ever do?

"I don't think those guys had as much fun as we did because they spent too much time worrying about how they stacked up next to us," said Barkley. "They were too preoccupied with us. There will never be another team like us and as the years pass, you'll see that more and more."

So what did Dream Team II do? They talked about how great they were.

"I was really surprised at how some of the guys ran their mouths," said Mark Price, a member of Dream Team II. "Joe Dumars and I would hear some of that stuff, and we'd look at each other and roll our eyes. So this was the next generation."

As Dream Team II was crushing Australia, 130–74, at the 1994 World Championships in Toronto, players such as Coleman, Miller, and Kemp insulted the beleaguered Aussies.

"There were a lot of 'bleeps' out there, but I guess that's part and parcel of the NBA today," said Andrew Gaze, Australia's leading scorer. Gaze played college basketball at Seton Hall, so he doesn't exactly have virgin ears.

As the U.S. hammered Russia, 137–91, there was a play where Kemp fell to the court. Russia's Mikhail Mikhailov offered Kemp a hand to help him up. Kemp scowled at the Russian center, and got up on his own.

Nice guy, Shawn Kemp. In the next life, you won't have to worry about him coming back as the next Henry Kissinger. Kemp spent most of the World Games dunking, then screaming right into the camera.

After one game, Rick Fox—playing for Canada—said Kemp "was the heir apparent to Michael Jordan."

Fox plays for pay with the Boston Celtics. All we can do is hope he was kidding. Kemp can no more be like Mike than Fox will become the next Sam Jones.

During the Dreamers' 134–83 trashing of Puerto Rico, several players got into a trash-talking, finger-pointing exchange with Puerto Rico's Orlando Vega. Actually, Vega played some high school and college ball in the U.S. When he scored, he began yelling at O'Neal. To his credit, O'Neal smiled, shook his head and walked away—knowing that this gnat was not even worth a playful swat. But Larry Johnson stepped in—as if O'Neal needs a bodyguard—and the 6-foot-9 Johnson began waiving his finger in the face of the 6-foot-2 Vega.

There was no fight, but the whole thing was just ridiculous, and it's hard to imagine anything like that happening with the original Dream Team.

According to Price and others, O'Neal conducted himself with class and dignity during these games. But others whined about their playing time to such an extent that Joe Dumars offered to sit out the game against Puerto Rico so coach Don Nelson could have his minutes to give to the other players. But did the younger players get the message—that this is a team game and you should be willing to sacrifice?

Dumars wasn't sure, as he told *Sports Illustrated:* "It's like a tree falling in the forest. It's hard to know if anyone hears it."

"Coach Nelson tried to get the guys to cut down on the trash talk," said Price. "When you are beating a team by 50, 60 points, there is no reason to put them down. It was sort of like pouring salt in the wound, but I guess it's just part of these guys' personalities."

Even NBA director of operations Rod Thorn admitted, "We had too much taunting. It didn't portray us in a positive light to be taunting teams when you are beating them handily. . . . The league didn't like some of the things that went on."

Not all the second Dream Teamers were an embarrassment. Kevin Johnson, Dan Majerle, Dumars, and Price represented the league well. Perhaps the most impressive show was by O'Neal, who was only twenty-two but acted like a mature thirty-two with the grace worthy of a member of any Dream Team. Yes, he refused to drink out of a Coke cup—the official sponsor of the World Games—because he had an endorsement deal with Pepsi. But don't forget that in 1992 Jordan refused to appear in some of the Dream Team pictures because of his deal with Nike.

One of the sponsors of the 1994 World Games was Converse.

"Larry Johnson wears Converse shoes, and there was an eighty-foot statue of Larry as Grandmama on top of the building," one of the assistant coaches, Pete Gillen, told the *Cincinnati Enquirer.* "I was wondering, how do you coach a guy who has an eighty-foot statue of himself on the building?"

Gillen laughed as he asked the question, but his point was valid.

How do you coach any of these guys who are marketed into legendary status—at least in their own minds—before they accomplish anything that approaches greatness on the court? Where do these players learn how to act?

"Over the years, I've done some things that I regret," said Barkley. "But no one can ever question how I played the game. I played hard. I never would do something like refuse to go into a game. When I was a young player, I talked a lot to Moses Malone. He showed me the value of hard work."

Barkley is worried that the rookie mega-contracts and the instant stardom from the NBA marketing machine has convinced young players that they have arrived in the NBA when they are still unpacking their bags.

"These guys can be colorful," he said. "I'm not talking so much about what they do away from the court. They can have their own personalities. But on the court, they just can't take a short step."

Barkley said it was ridiculous that players such as himself, Karl Malone, Joe Dumars, and other veteran stars are not the highest paid players in the NBA.

"When they make that kind of money right away, why should they [young players] listen to anyone?" he asked.

Barkley is now famous for his line about how kids shouldn't use NBA stars for role models. Instead, we should ask: With the retirement of Magic, Michael, and Larry, who is going to be the role model for the players?

Barkley actually can help in that area. He has made more than his share of mistakes. There have been the bar brawls, the fights on the court, the criticism of his teammates in the newspapers, and the infamous spitting incident.

"The thing about Charles is that he can be eccentric," said Suns coach Paul Westphal. "Charles is part competitor, part clown. He loves an audience and he loves to entertain. He'll say outrageous things just to get your attention. But I never thought he meant things to be malicious. I'm not sure that's true of some of the other younger players."

Westphal believes that Barkley has things to tell today's players.

"But I don't think these guys will hear me," Barkley said. "I've tried to talk to a few of them. They are so volatile. They get defensive. I realize that they come from families that you see on the TV news [families with drug and gang problems]. They cop an attitude, and there really isn't much you can say to them."

And when they won't listen to a Charles Barkley, what chance does a coach have?

2 Capping the Draft

When we have reached the point where a rookie signs a $68 million fully guaranteed contract, something is wrong.

When veterans such as Charles Barkley and Karl Malone say that there needs to be a rookie salary cap, something is wrong.

When teams allow themselves to be held hostage by rookies, something is wrong.

But there is even more to worry about when it comes to the NBA and the college draft. Listen to Doug Collins.

"I worked the draft for TNT, and as I was walking through the hotel lobby on the morning of the draft, Glenn Robinson was there," said Collins, the former NBA star and now the Detroit Pistons coach. "He was going to be the first pick in the [1994] draft that night. There was a crowd of people around him. His agent had his arm about Glenn. He had TV cameras following every step he took and a couple of microphones waiting for him to say something. I mean, they were hanging on this twenty-one-year-old kid as if what he said would tell us if there would be world peace. When he spoke, he talked about how whatever money he got from the draft wasn't going to change him. Okay, Glenn is a good kid and I am sure he was sincere, but you give any kid $70 million—I'm sorry, he is going to change. Any of us would."

Ninety minutes before the draft, Robinson was doing a live TV shot for the Home Shopping Network. He was shilling for his autographed rookie card—limited edition, of course. The price was a mere $69. He also was selling autographed basketballs for $119. He had a shoe contract in his back pocket worth over $1 million.

Remember, all of this was before he'd even played his first game, before he'd signed his contract—*before* he was even drafted. How much would those Glenn Robinson rookie cards have been worth if Milwaukee had pulled a last-second deal and traded his rights somewhere? In this crazy world where there is a market for cards of serial killers and porn stars, a bogus Glenn Robinson Bucks card probably would have doubled in price.

Bob Cousy's top salary was $30,000. He has made a decent living since, first as a pro and college coach and later as a broadcaster for the Celtics. But the odds are that Cousy will not earn $2.9 million in his lifetime—which is what Robinson made his first year with the Bucks.

"I've always been happy that I made enough money at a kid's game so I didn't have to go out and do card shows, charging some kid ten bucks for an autograph," said Cousy. "I could have made a lot of money doing that, but to me it's unconscionable."

No, that is basketball as it heads into the next century.

"That bothers me," said Collins. "I was the first pick in the 1973 draft. I was sitting at home. I knew I'd be drafted, but I didn't know where. The phone rang and I was told that I was the first pick in the draft, taken by Philadelphia. I thanked the man and that was about it. This was in 1973, which wasn't that long ago."

But Doug, weren't you among the 20,000 people at the Hoosier Dome for the 1994 Draft Show on TNT?

"That's very true," said Collins. "I'm one of the guys doing the draft on television. We are promoting these guys to be larger than life. These guys are going into a situation where they will be paid millions of dollars. They are literally on this gigantic stage in front of a national television audience—and most of them are not even going to start for their teams! What kind of message is that?"

What kind of message is it when a rookie is making more than the guy starting in front of him? Or even the best player on the team?

"It makes you mad, is what it does," said Charles Barkley. "Michael Jordan, Magic Johnson, and I should always have been the highest paid players on our teams—by far. But that wasn't always the case."

The Robinson contract talks became very obstinate. He held out through all of training camp. Word was that he wanted to be the first $100 million player in pro sports. His agent sort of denied it. The Bucks offered $60 million and were quickly rejected by Robinson's representatives. You would have thought the Bucks were trying to buy a Mercedes with a check for $25. Anyway, the two sides occasionally talked, then spent a lot of time talking trash about each other to reporters. Bucks owner Herb Kohl said that he had a deal for Robinson: "You take my franchise, I'll take your contract." (The Milwaukee franchise is only supposed to be worth $75 million.) In the final week of training camp, the Bucks went public with their offer of a little over $60 million. They said that Robinson was fixated on $100 million. Robinson's agent, Dr. Charles Tucker, responded by saying the Bucks were trying to portray his client "as a greedy little black kid."

Suddenly, the element of race reared its ugly and divisive head— the last thing the Bucks or Robinson needed. The Bucks had put Robinson on the cover of their media guide. They were using him as a tool to sell tickets, a ray of hope for a depressed franchise that was 48-116 in the previous two seasons. Indications were that Robinson was a nice enough person, one who had no trouble playing for Purdue's Gene Keady, a disciplinarian who has never suffered egomaniacs very well. He has a neat nickname, Big Dog, and the Milwaukee fans called talk shows to say they could rename the Bradley Center the Dog House if Robinson indeed turned out to be the Real Thing.

"He has the marquee potential to be a true national star," said Milwaukee Bucks vice president John Steinmiller. "That means you're on national TV more, merchandise sells well, and tickets are more in demand. If it happens according to the script, it's a good thing."

Of course, that's a big IF. The last time the Bucks had the number one pick, they drafted Kent Benson in 1977. He was more like the next Neal Walk than Kareem Abdul-Jabbar, who was Milwaukee's other number one pick in the draft.

Robinson finally signed for $68 million over ten years right before opening day. It was a contract not far off from the original offer from the Bucks. It should have been a reason to rejoice. But after all the nasty exchanges, the best that could be said was that Robinson and the team that needed him so badly had called an uneasy truce.

*   *   *

Robinson may very well turn out to be a star for the Bucks. He is 6-foot-8, and he averaged 30 points and 10 rebounds for Purdue, a team that is not one to run-and-gun. He could score inside or out, and clearly was the best player in the 1994 draft; he played well as a rookie, averaging 22 points despite his long holdout.

But making marketing assumptions can be very dangerous. When the Cleveland Cavaliers traded for the draft rights to Danny Ferry, they not only gave the former Duke star and NCAA Player of the Year a ten-year, $32 million contract, they also presented Ferry with a $3 million bonus for which they received a percentage of the dollars he received for commercials and certain endorsements. But Ferry flopped, and the Cavs didn't get back a dime on that $3 million. As one Philadelphia writer suggested, "The Cavs thought they had the next Larry Bird, and they ended up with Big Bird."

"There are more misses than hits in the draft lottery," said Cavs general manager Wayne Embry. "I admit, we missed on Danny. What happened to him is the most puzzling thing I've ever seen in all my years of talent evaluation."

It also turned out to be one of the most expensive, as Ferry often couldn't break into the group of substitutes that came off the Cleveland bench. Meanwhile, he was the highest paid player on the team for most of his time in Cleveland. While they never went public with it, this could not have been a happy situation for Mark Price, Brad Daugherty, and Larry Nance. Price is the best player in the history of the Cavs franchise, Daugherty the best center, and Nance the premier forward. Ferry earned more than all of them in his first three seasons. While Daugherty eventually signed an extension worth $38 million after making five All-Star teams, Nance and Price never received long-term deals that would rival Ferry's.

"The least they could have done was give all that money to a white guy who could play," Charles Barkley said of Ferry in his autobiography.

More to the point, the money should have gone to a player who had proven himself in the NBA. But it doesn't work that way.

The number two pick in the 1994 draft was Jason Kidd, who signed a nine-year, $54 million deal with Dallas. Here is what that package looks like in round figures: $275,000 signing bonus; $2.7 million as a rookie; $3.5 million in 1995; $4.3 million in 1996; $5.1 million in 1997; $5.9 million in 1998; $6.7 million in 1999; $6.8 million in 2000; $8.4 million in 2001; $9.2 million in 2002. The first eight years are guaranteed, and Kidd is promised $3 million of the last $9.2 million in 2002. If he thinks his contract has fallen below the market value, he has the right to become a free agent after six years. This was despite the fact that Kidd was hit with three lawsuits before he played his first pro game, with allegations ranging from assault on a girlfriend to a paternity suit from another girl to a hit-and-run traffic incident. By the way, while Kidd is strong, quick, and can dribble, he is not much of an outside shooter.

The number three pick was Duke's Grant Hill, who took $45 million for eight years from Detroit. Hill is a class act, who immediately donated $500,000 to some inner-city Detroit charities.

The number four pick was Donyell Marshall, who pocketed $42.6 million for nine years from Minnesota, but was an early disappointment and was traded at midseason to Golden State.

Or how about this? The L.A. Clippers made Lamond Murray the number seven pick in the 1994 draft. They signed him for $20 million. A forward from the University of California, Murray was interviewed on TV about why he had the reputation as occasionally loafing.

"I had a hard time getting up for teams like Oregon and Oregon State," Murray said. For the record, Oregon and Oregon State were league games for Murray and California in the Pac-10. If he couldn't get excited about them, how was he going to feel when the Clippers and Wolves met in Minnesota in the middle of a February blizzard—when both teams were already dead in the playoff race?

Why all this money for rookies? Who are these teams negotiating against? And why do rookies have to get the biggest slices of the NBA's financial pie when they had nothing to do with baking it?

For a little perspective, we can go back to the days when Lenny Wilkens had to fight to get $7,000 out of the St. Louis Hawks in 1960—after he was their first-round selection. Wilkens nearly decided to forgo pro basketball and take a graduate assistantship in economics at Boston College while working toward his Ph.D. He thought he would make more money teaching business than in the business of pro basketball, but then he decided to try the pro game for a year.

Can you imagine that today? A first-round pick trying to decide if he should attend graduate school or turn pro?

Okay, you can say that was the stone age, but how about this: in 1986, Wilkens coached a Cleveland team with Daugherty and Ron Harper. Daugherty was the top lottery pick, signing for $6 million over six years. Harper was the last lottery selection, number eight overall, and he held out for two weeks before signing a four-year, $2.2 million deal.

In 1990, Derrick Coleman was the number one pick in the draft, and he signed for $10.8 million over four years with New Jersey.

How did the NBA go from those numbers to a player bummed out because he didn't get $100 million?

The players will say that the gross revenue of the NBA was about $25 million in 1986, when Daugherty signed that six-year, $6 million deal; by 1994, it was over $100 million.

Okay, so let's be really generous and say that revenues have increased five times over. If you multiply Daugherty's contract by five, you get a six-year deal worth $30 million.

But that doesn't tell the story, either.

The problem is the salary cap. Teams can't pay rookies anything they would like—which is not true of veterans. In effect, your own veterans are exempt from your salary cap. If you already have them under contract and want to extend—or if they become a free agent and you want to re-sign them—you can pay them anything you want, as long as the increase is no more than 30 percent per season. So say you have a guy making $500,000 in the last year of his contract. If he becomes a free agent, and you think he's a future star, you can give him a five-year, $10 million deal—or whatever you like. In NBA terms, you can "go through the cap" to retain your own players.

But draft picks are different. Draft picks do count against the cap. To sign them, you need a salary slot.

After a draft day deal, the Orlando Magic made Anfernee Hardaway the number three pick in 1993. Their highest salary slot was

$1.6 million. That would be Hardaway's starting salary. They could only increase it by 30 percent per year—standard salary cap rules. The result was a $48 million deal over thirteen years that also included a loan and other incentives. The Magic even talked about how Hardaway made a "sacrifice" to play for $1.6 million as a rookie. They talked about how other players in his area of the draft played for $2 million to $3 million in their first seasons, so they allowed Hardaway to become a restricted free agent after his rookie season—permitting Orlando to re-sign him without salary cap restraints since he was the Magic's own player. The new deal was $70 million for nine years. Ah, what a country!

Complicated? Of course. The NBA's salary cap is the only thing that would make the IRS code read like Jack and Jill Went Up the Hill to Fetch a Pail of Water.

But why don't teams just say no?

Why do teams have to give a player 10 percent more than the guy who was drafted in the same spot last year? Or even 30 percent more?

"All drafts are not created equal," said Cavs player personnel director Gary Fitzsimmons. "But we pay them as if each year the quality of a player coming into the league is better than it was the year before."

But why?

"We've created our own monster," said Fitzsimmons. "We hype these kids and the draft to death. It is part of the league's publicity machine. Listen to what is said on draft night. The kids are compared to all these stars already in the league. The kid and his family and his agent hear that junk, and they want to believe it. Why not? They want to believe the kid is going to be the next Michael Jordan."

Doug Christie was the seventeenth pick in the 1992 draft, chosen by Seattle. He didn't like the salary slot the Sonics had open, and Seattle was not about to cut a veteran to create a higher slot in which to sign Christie, so he held out all of training camp and most of the regular season. On February 22, 1993, he was traded to the L.A. Lakers with Benoit Benjamin for Sam Perkins. For the Sonics, it was a great move. They dumped two problems on L.A.

First was Christie, whom the Sonics didn't know if they even needed because they had several veterans his size (6-foot-7) who were playing well. They also weren't sold on his ability, and he had a history of knee troubles.

The second problem was Benjamin, a coach-killer ever since he was the number three pick in the 1985 draft. He was an under-motivated kid who was handed a million bucks primarily because he was seven feet tall. After five frustrating years with the L.A. Clippers, he was shipped to Seattle. The Sonics thought they would be able to get this guy to play; besides, he was still seven feet and they needed a seven-footer. But as the trade was occurring, Benjamin was approaching his free agent year. So what did Sonics do? They gave him a six-year, $18 million contract! After five years in the NBA, Benjamin was still being rewarded for his potential instead of his production. Naturally, he was no better with the Sonics than he had been with the Clippers.

But the Lakers were in the market to make changes. They really liked Christie, and if they had to take Benjamin—fine, they'd do it. They figured they'd find another sucker to take Benjamin later—which they did, sending him on to New Jersey—the Nets and Benjamin being a perfect marriage.

The Sonics were thrilled to add Perkins, a good guy and a solid pro who fit into their team and helped them become one of the powers in the Western Conference. Perkins was a guy who had shown that he was worth his $2 million paycheck.

Meanwhile, Christie ended his six-month holdout and signed with the Lakers. At his press conference, Christie began talking about not being able to replace Magic Johnson. No one had asked him about stepping into Magic's shoes. No one even wrote about it or suggested it. The reporters knew he was the seventeenth pick in the 1992 draft, he had yet to play an NBA game, and he was nothing more than a young player with promise. But someone had put Magic Johnson into Christie's head, or maybe he had such an ego that he thought he could be the next Magic—or he thought others believed he would be—so he brought it up on his own.

It said a lot not just about Christie's state of mind, but what the hype does to these young players.

NBA people know this, so why do teams do it?

"Sometimes, they want to make their own picks look good to their media and fans," said Fitzsimmons. "It has always been a temptation to compare college kids to someone in the pros."

But it is only recently that they began to pay the rookies like they were All-Stars.

"When you draft a kid, you know that if you decide to take a tough stand on his contract, the kid could end up sitting out part or all of the season," said Harry Weltman, a former NBA general manager. "The other possibility is Europe, but after Danny Ferry went over there and after what has happened to his career since, I don't think that is a big threat. But kids do sit out. They miss training camp. They miss part of the regular season. Then when you do sign the kid, he's behind. He's not in shape and usually doesn't play well. It's almost as if you wasted his first year—and all the money you paid him for that first year."

Richie Adubato can tell you about wasted years.

He was the coach in Dallas when the Mavericks made Doug Smith their first pick in the 1991 draft. Dallas was 24-58 the season before and in a rebuilding mode, but the Mavericks couldn't sign Smith until opening night. When he showed up, he was so out of shape that he couldn't do twenty minutes on the Stairmaster.

"His whole game was getting out on the fast break and running, and he was twenty pounds overweight," said Adubato. "He couldn't shoot a lick from the outside. Because of his conditioning, he couldn't run. But I had to play him anyway because he was our first-round pick. He didn't deserve the minutes or the money he was getting. As the coach, you knew that. The other players knew that. But you had to play him anyway."

Then you lose, and make a bad situation even worse.

That season, Smith averaged 8.8 points and shot a miserable 42 percent. Dallas had a 22-60 record. That entitled them to the number four pick in 1992, and they selected Jimmy Jackson.

"We were either going to get Christian Laettner or Jackson," said Adubato. "I met with both kids and came away believing that we'd be better off with Jackson. I knew that all Laettner ever did at Duke was win. He didn't understand losing. Put his personality into a losing situation, and after 11 games when your record was 1-10, Laettner was going to be pointing fingers at every guy in the locker room and at the coach for the losing. He'd think everyone was terrible. And why not? Coach K. and the players at Duke won all the time, so it couldn't be him. But Jackson had been through a rebuilding situation at Ohio State. He had a real grasp of what we were going through in Dallas. Laettner went to Minnesota and did exactly what I thought [being disruptive and distraught by losing]. I couldn't wait to get to Jimmy Jackson."

It turned out that Adubato couldn't wait long enough.

Jackson and the Mavericks engaged in a long, bitter contract dispute. Jackson's attorney, Mark Termini, determined that his client was worth a six-year, $19 million deal—slightly less than what Laettner received as the player drafted in front of Jackson. Termini also had draft day newspaper stories in which Dallas general manager Rick Sund compared Jackson to Oscar Robertson. If the team thinks the kid is going to be the next Big O, if it has the room under the cap (as Dallas did), and if you weren't asking *more* money than the player picked ahead of you, why should you take less?

So Jackson sat. The Mavericks lost. After twenty-nine games and a 2-27 record, Adubato was fired. Smith was still a bust. Jackson was holding out. "I learned just how vulnerable a coach can be to what happens on draft day and with the contract talks," said Adubato.

Making it worse for Adubato, Jackson finally signed with twenty-eight games left in the season. You guessed it, he received the same six-year, $19 million deal he wanted in the first place. Furthermore, the Mavericks were 7-21 with Jackson after being 4-50 without him. Adubato can't help but wonder if he would still be coaching in Dallas today if Jackson had signed before training camp, because he is one of the players who turned out to be one of those rare lottery picks—nearly as good as advertised.

Negotiations with players—especially rookies—are often very weird.

"A general manager heads into the contract talks feeling pressure from his owner, his coach, and the team's fans to get the kid signed," said Weltman. "The coach and the fans really don't care what you pay the kid. They may say that they don't want the kid to get too much money, but what they really want is the kid in camp and ready to play. Now, your owner wants you to 'hold the line,' wherever that line happens to be. Of course, the line on salaries keeps moving, but you keep doing your best. So that is what is on a general manager's mind as he begins the talks.

"Then the agent comes in and says that what the kid really is looking for is security—whatever that means. You mention a figure, say $12 million. The agent looks at you as if you just offered him 12 cents. You mention that there was a time when $12 million could bring a young man a certain degree of security. The agent says that the $12 million isn't the kind of security he has in mind. You say, 'Tell me, what will it really take for the kid to feel secure. What kind of number is going to trigger his peace of mind? I mean, we're talking $12 million here, and if he has twelve members of his family, well, that's a million for each of them.' Then you find out that what will really buy security is more like $30 million. Or $50 million. It changes all the time."

Wayne Embry has been in two memorable negotiations.

The first was when he was with Indiana and the Pacers were trying to sign Wayman Tisdale, the number two pick in the 1985 draft. Tisdale had seven different "representatives," including his father, the Reverend Tisdale. Before contract talks began, the Reverend Tisdale asked everyone in the room to stand, bow their heads and pray for guidance.

"When we hit a snag in the talks, the Reverend again asked us to bow our heads and pray for divine guidance," said Embry. "The Reverend asked the Lord to 'let wise men prevail.' I thought, 'Boy are we in trouble now, because Wayman is being represented by a guy who has a direct line to the Supreme Being.' "

Embry also entered into a unique negotiation with Uncle Johnny Keys and his friend, a guy named Jim who was a jeweler by trade. They represented Randolph Keys, the Cavs' number one pick in the 1988 draft. Sometimes, Uncle Johnny called to talk contract. Sometimes, it was Jim the Jeweler, who was a Friend of the Family and was a big supporter of basketball at Southern Mississippi, where Keys played forward. To Embry, part of his job was making sure that each of Keys' agents knew what the other one had agreed to, because there were some communication breakdowns. In the end, everyone met in the same room and a deal was cut. Embry had no complaints.

But Atlanta president Stan Kasten has an even better story.

When Kevin Willis was a rookie, Kasten thought he had to talk contract with Willis' brothers—Robert and Keith Willis. Sometimes, he thought he was talking to Robert Willis. On other occasions, he believed it was Keith Willis. All negotiations were done on the phone. It was only two years after Willis signed his first contract that Kasten learned an astounding truth: Keith Willis and Robert Willis were the same guy—Robert Keith Willis!

Kasten also said that after Jon Koncak received his $12 million contract from the Hawks, Mrs. Moses Malone knocked on Kasten's door demanding to know what he planned to do for *her* husband now that Koncak was making more money—and playing behind *her* husband!

It may sound like anyone can be an agent. Well, almost anyone can. All a person has to do is attend a couple of seminars a year run by the NBA Players Association, and suddenly they become a certified agent. In fact, since 1990, there reportedly have been more certified NBA agents than there were NBA players.

At the final NBA predraft camps, there are more agents than prospective pros. Some agents hustle players who won't even be drafted—they don't know the difference or they don't care. They just want a client. That leads to illegal payoffs and other horror stories. A couple of executives insist that a few years ago at the Orlando Classic—a predraft camp—one wannabe agent hired a limo and a couple of hookers, and then he and a young player would "go for a ride." Word of this technique got out among the players. A number of guys indeed "went for a ride," but most were already signed with other agents.

This time, it was the agent who was taken for a ride.

"Because not all of the people in this business are wonderful human beings, when you are negotiating contracts, you can't take it personally," said Weltman. "Sometimes, you can't even think about it logically or you would realize the insanity. I ended up telling myself, 'Look, you are not going to break the order of the game. The framework is already there and you had better just adjust to the fact that you are going to have to pay these kids a lot of money if you want them to play for you. That is how business is done.' You're not even dealing with the value of the player to your team. You're dealing with precedent, what the number eight player in the draft last year made—and your kid who is now number eight expects to get more. That is how the system has been working for years. It doesn't matter if you expect the kid to start, or if you think he'll be lucky to play fifteen minutes a night . . . you are going to pay him more than the guy drafted in his spot received last year."

There are other considerations.

"Sometimes, an agent will insist that their kid should get more than the going rate for a player drafted in his spot simply because he is bigger," said Weltman, "They tell you that big guys have always gotten more money—unless they happen to be representing a little guy. I love the argument that, 'I know my guy was drafted tenth, but he's seven feet and you know how rare seven-footers are, so we should be paid more than the guy drafted ninth, because that guy is only 6-foot-5.' When you get into one of those discussions, you really feel like you're banging your head against the wall."

But the general manager must be careful not to pay the draft picks too much, or he will have wives and agents all pounding on his door the next day.

"You have to keep in mind that these guys [the players and agents] network constantly," said Weltman. "For some of these guys, they seem to spend all their time doing that. If most of these guys spent just half the time reading a book that they do talking on the phone about Who Is Making How Much, then they'd all have their Ph.D.'s by now."

Another aspect of the draft that adds drama—and economic pressure—is the lottery.

The lottery was inspired by the 1982–83 season, although it wouldn't come into being until 1985. Before then, the teams with the worst record in the Eastern Conference and the Western Conference would flip a coin to determine who'd get the first pick.

In 1969, the Phoenix Suns called tails and lost. They ended up with Neal Walk. The Milwaukee Bucks won. They picked Lew Alcindor, who will be known in the Hall of Fame as Kareem Abdul-Jabbar.

Fast-forward to 1982–83. Everyone knew that the best player in the draft was 7-foot-4 Ralph Sampson. Many scouts thought he was the next Abdul-Jabbar. Certainly, he was better than Jammin' James Bailey, who was holding down the middle along with a very old Elvin Hayes for the Houston Rockets. In fact, coach Del Harris benched Hayes in favor of Bailey at midseason.

"From the start of the season, we were hoping to get Ralph Sampson or a player of his caliber to mend the ship," Harris told *Sports Illustrated* in 1983. "There was never any time when we said, 'Let's lose games.' On the other hand, there were times when we could have acquired talent to help us this year. But it would have been at the expense of the future."

The Rockets lost by 33 points in the opener and began the season with 10 straight defeats. Then Harris uttered this wonderful line: "All of our players belong in the NBA. I'm just not sure that they all belong on the same team."

As the losses piled up, the *Houston Post* ran the standings as the "Sampson Sweepstakes," with the teams in the Eastern and Western Conferences with the *worst* record on top. When the season was over, the Rockets were 14-68. The next worst team in the West was the San Diego Clippers at 25-57, so Houston buried them.

In the East, Indiana had the worst record at 20-62, followed by the Cleveland Cavaliers at 23-59. Houston became very big Cavs fans that season, because the Rockets also owned Cleveland's number one pick.

Anyway, the coin was flipped, and Houston won. The Rockets picked Sampson first and Rodney McCray with the number three selection. Indiana's pick was center Steve Stipanovich, whose career was cut short because of various injuries.

Then Harris was fired, and replaced by Bill Fitch.

The NBA really didn't like how the Sampson Sweepstakes developed in 1983–84. They liked it even less the next season when the Rockets again had the worst record and won the coin toss—even though Sampson was the 1984 Rookie of the Year. No matter, Houston's 29-53 record was one game better (or worse) than San Diego's 30-52. In the East, Indiana again was last at 26-56. The coin flipped right for Houston, which picked Hakeem Olajuwon. (Had they lost, they might have had to settle for Michael Jordan, but that's another story.)

NBA commissioner David Stern didn't like the stench of this run for the worst. He never accused anyone of dumping games, but he realized that the reward for losing could be too high, so the lottery system was created.

In the first year, the commissioner pulled envelopes out of a hopper with the names of the eight bottom teams sealed inside. The New York Knicks drew the top pick (and the rights to Patrick Ewing)—and there were unsubstantiated rumors that a corner of the envelope was wrinkled and the whole thing was a fix because the NBA office supposedly wanted the Knicks to have a good team since it made for excellent TV ratings. A nice theory, though one contradicted by the ratings for the 1994 Finals.

That led to the current Ping-Pong ball system. And that has worked. You don't hear nearly as many rumors about teams losing games as you did in the prelottery days—although it certainly seemed like Dallas was in the business of collecting as many Ping-Pong balls as possible in the early 1990s. Furthermore, the NBA turned the lottery itself into a TV show, with the owners and general managers having their fifteen minutes of fame as they dragged their lucky charms into the studio in the hope of securing a high pick thanks to a ball pinging at just the right time for them. In this age of state lotteries, the NBA once again was ahead of the public relations curve. For better or worse, no other league gets nearly the publicity of the NBA—not when you consider a lottery of popping Ping-Pong balls actually being carried on national TV.

The league had tried different weightings in the system. The current method gives teams more Ping-Pong balls for having a worse record; only the top three picks are chosen by lot, with the others going in ranking order from worst to least worst. But this system also leaves something to be desired.

So far, the best thing Allan Bristow ever did for Charlotte was to be good on lottery day. In 1991, the Hornets had the fourth worst record in the NBA (tied with New Jersey at 26-56), but their ball pinged at the right time. Their number one choice became Larry Johnson.

In 1992, the Hornets were 31-51—the seventh worst record in the NBA. But this time, the Hornets drew the number two pick, and Alonzo Mourning packed his bags for Charlotte.

In 1992, Orlando (21-51, the second worst record), ended up with the top choice—Shaquille O'Neal. But in 1993, Orlando was 41-41, the best record among the eleven lottery teams, and still the Magic ended up with the first pick again! A deal brought them Anfernee Hardaway and three future first-rounders in exchange for the rights to Chris Webber.

The odds against a .500 team winning despite having only one ball out of sixty-six—yes, a one in sixty-six chance—were supposed to be worse than that of Chris Dudley shooting 90 percent from the foul line in a season. It brought back rumors of a fix, that the NBA wanted Orlando to have a good team and have O'Neal surrounded by excellent players for marketing purposes. No charges were made, much less proven, but it happened, and those two top picks made Orlando the team to watch as we head into the next century.

Meanwhile, teams such as Dallas and Minnesota had to understand that they were not only lousy, but unlucky, too.

While the NBA keeps tinkering with the lottery system—trying to determine how many games equals how many Ping-Pong balls in the hopper—the concept remains the same: let every nonplayoff team have some sort of chance at the number one pick so that teams don't lose on purpose.

That is a valid idea, and one worth keeping.

How did the NBA get into this draft mess?

Until the dawning of the American Basketball Association in 1967, rookies could either play basketball in the NBA or get a real job.

But the ABA entered the basketball world determined to knock the NBA on its side and force a merger. The ABA signed college players before their senior seasons concluded—a mortal sin until then. Even though Wilt Chamberlain actually dropped out of Kansas before his senior season, he had to play with the Globetrotters for a year before entering the NBA—despite an inside deal that gave the old Philadelphia Warriors Chamberlain's draft rights after his senior year at Philadelphia's Overbrook High.

The NBA and NCAA had a cozy setup. The colleges served as a farm system for the pros, and the NBA kept their hands off the kids until their college eligibility was up. It was supposed to be good for everyone.

"Everyone but the player," said Steve Arnold, one of the first agents who helped bring underclassmen such as Spencer Haywood to the pros. "Suppose a kid was a genius at MIT and IBM wanted to hire him after his junior year. That kid could quit school and take the money on the table. But the same didn't hold true in pro basketball. We thought it was absolute hypocrisy."

But grabbing the moral high ground in the free market was not what the ABA had in mind—it just wanted to beat the NBA to the young talent. So players such as George McGinnis, Julius Erving, and Johnny Neumann left school early. Lew Alcindor, Pete Maravich, and Artis Gilmore triggered vicious bidding wars between the two leagues, making agents key players and the new power brokers in this game.

But even after the two leagues merged in 1976, high salaries for rookies remained. Yes, competition between the two leagues for players was over, but now the players had agents—and those pesky men in suits and with briefcases were not about to go away, not as long as there were big contracts to be negotiated and percentages to be pocketed. Today, agents are limited to a 4 percent take by the Players Association. But in the 1970s and early 1980s, agents could charge anything—and many of them did, 10 percent or more. Some would take their fee up front. For example, an agent would negotiate a five-year, $1 million deal. He'd say, "Well, I know you get $200,000 in your first year—but half of that is mine. You see, the contract is worth $1 million. Ten percent of $1 million is $100,000."

Since an agent received a player's check before the player did, he could take out his outrageous fee before the player even saw the money.

Now, besides capping agent fees at 4 percent, the NBA Players Association says that you can only take your cut out of what the player receives each year. In other words, the agent's fee is paid a little at a time.

But in the Anything Goes days of the ABA-NBA wars, agents flooded the market. Some got rich and stayed there. Others saw the dollars flowing and wanted a piece of the action.

So even after the merger, the agents were stronger (at least in numbers) than ever before. To many young law students, having your name on the sports page was a lot more fun than doing Aunt Glenda's will or being another faceless gnome in a huge corporate law firm.

To the distress of the NBA, some of the agents were smarter than some of the owners and general managers—and the big money kept coming even though the NBA no longer was negoti- ating under a threat from another basketball league.

Something else that inflated rookie salaries was expansion.

"A first-round pick just isn't what it used to be," said Colan- gelo. "The league had eight teams in it at one time. After the next expansion, we will have twenty-nine. So you take the number twenty-nine pick—still a first-rounder. Back when there were eight teams, that guy would have been drafted in the fourth round and had a lot less bargaining power."

There used to be a mystique about a first-round pick. That's because he was among the top ten college players in the nation—at least until the coming of the ABA in 1967.

"Now, some teams don't even want their low first-round picks," said Embry. "They'll see a kid who is going to be drafted twenty- something. They know that it will probably cost them at least a million a year over four or five years to sign him—and they don't even know if the kid would make the team if he were just a free agent. Look, the right first-round pick can help your team, but the wrong one does nothing more than clog your roster and pile up needless dollars on your cap. And in the bottom half of the draft, most of the players aren't going to help you. There just isn't that much talent around, but you end up drafting them anyway."

The bottom line on draft picks and big money is this: once the kids started getting the bucks, there was no one around to make the teams stop it. Since most NBA teams have as much self- discipline as a six-year-old at Dairy Queen, the dollars just grew and grew. A strange financial snowball began rolling down the mountain, picking up momentum and size at every turn. Now, rookie salaries could smother the game unless something changes.

When the owners and players association sat down to negotiate a new labor contract, both sides agreed on a rookie cap. Under it, a complicated formula was used, but the results were simple: Rookie salaries would be brought under control.

For example, top pick Joe Smith of Maryland would have been in line for a three-year deal from Golden State worth slightly less than $9 million. No rookie contract would be longer than three years or worth more than $9 million.

But when the union took the deal back to the players, there was a rebellion, and one of the controversies was the rookie cap. Egged on by their agents, stars such as Michael Jordan, Patrick Ewing, and Scottie Pippen moved to decertify the union and negate the deal (and the rookie cap) that the union made with the owners. Many agents did not want to lose the commissions they make from the huge rookie contracts, and the agents convinced many players that a rookie cap was a bad deal for everyone.

Again, greed was over-riding common sense as the NBA was thrown into a summer of labor turmoil.

3 Why Johnny Can't Shoot

There is nothing more discouraging about today's game than the decline of fundamentals, especially that most essential skill of putting the ball into the basket. If you want to find the reason for the atrocious shooting, look no further than your nearest playground.

There you'll find a game called 33 or Scuttle. One guy has the ball, and two or more are supposedly on defense. If there aren't enough players for a full-court game, kids now play 33. Some form of this game has been around forever, but it is only recently that it has become the playground game of choice. In the past, if there weren't enough guys to play full court, most would play two-on-two, three-on-three—some variation of a *team* game. You had a kid on your side. You passed him the ball, he passed you the ball.

"The basic pick-and-roll play came from the playground," said Lenny Wilkens, who learned his basketball on the asphalt of Brooklyn. "If you were playing two-on-two, the only play you really could run was a pick-and-roll. Then when the game was five-on-five, the emphasis was still on team play, passing to the open man and getting good shots. On the New York playgrounds, we had spectacular players like Connie Hawkins. But they were never selfish. Even on the playgrounds, they could play sound, fundamental basketball when it was needed. That is the big difference between playground ball back then and today. Many of these kids—even the best ones—don't have the fundamentals. They can't even run a basic pick-and-roll, and I'm talking about kids coming out of the top colleges. They rely almost completely on their great athleticism."

33 is a game that rewards that athleticism and neglects basic fundamentals such as shooting and passing. One kid has the ball, and the others stand under the basket waiting for him to miss.

There is no passing, because there is no one to catch the pass.

There is little outside shooting; if you take a jumper and miss, you have virtually no chance of getting the rebound because there are so many kids standing by the hoop.

There is a lot of driving. The best way to score in a chaotic game like this is often to miss your own shot, follow it, and put in the rebound.

"You get the guy with the ball saying, 'I'm gonna take you, I'm gonna take you to the basket,' " said Doug Collins. "They tell you what they are going to do to you before they do it. It's the 'I'm gonna dunk on you' mentality."

In games of 33, you see six, sometimes even eight guys just hanging around rather than playing together. One guy takes a shot, then eight guys crash the boards. It's nothing but crazy shots, then guys jumping over each other's backs for the rebound.

Why would anyone want to play basketball that way?

"The only thing I can think of is that we promote basketball as an individual game," said Collins. "It was Bird vs. Magic, Jordan vs. Isiah, Ewing vs. Olajuwon. Of course, these guys are great team players, too, but we don't talk about that on the little thirty-second spots on TV."

That may be partly true, but there is more to it.

"We have a dunk generation," said Isiah Thomas. "Kids today are more concerned with learning how to dunk than learning how to play."

Remember that Thomas isn't some guy from rural Indiana who grew up on the two-handed set shot. He is from Chicago, and he could play the city game as well as anyone—ever. In All-Star Games, he loved to throw lob passes that bounced first. He could go behind his back, through his legs, off his nose—you name it. But he also could run a basic pick-and-roll play, swish an eighteen-footer, and play the kind of game that would have made Gene Hackman stand up and cheer in the movie *Hoosiers*.

"If you watch the highlight films to promote the NBA draft, what do you see?" asked Doug Collins. "There are fifteen straight guys dunking the ball—as if that wasn't just the best play in basketball, but the only play. The dunk isn't even among the five most important plays in basketball. My son Chris and I did a clinic for kids in Chicago. Chris is a good shooter and he starts for Duke. As I was talking about the fundamentals of shooting, Chris was going around the three-point arch, nailing one shot after another. At one point, he made 15 in a row and 19-of-25. It was an incredible display, like Mark Price or Craig Hodges in the Three-Point Shoot-outs. I said, 'Okay, let's give Chris time to catch his breath. Anyone have any questions?' The first kid raises his hand and says, 'Can Chris dunk?' I was stunned, but it tells you the mentality out there. Somehow, we have to figure out how to get shooting back into basketball, because that's the heart of the game.''

Consider this quote from Hank Luisetti: "It's a shooter's game. Now when I hold clinics, all kids are interested in is shooting."

Luisetti told this to *Sports Illustrated* reporter Ron Fimrite. The year was 1975.

If anyone helped make it a shooter's game, it was Luisetti. He is the father of the jump shot, even though he never played in the NBA.

Until the middle 1930s, every player pretty much shot the same way:

Hands together.

Feet together.

Two hands on the opposite sides of the ball and push it out from your chest.

That was it, the two-handed set shot. Players such as Bobby McDermott and Dolph Schayes could throw in the set shot from remarkable distances, thirty feet or more. This was before the three-point shot. The reason they shot from so far out was that they could make it—or at least that is what they would tell you. But there was something else.

It took a long time to get off a set shot.

Hands together.

Feet together.

Push from the chest.

That does not lend itself to a game on the run. It took a lot of passes, a lot of movement and picks to free a player enough to catch a pass, set his feet, put his hands on the opposite sides of the ball, and then—push!

That was why some players kept practicing from longer distances than anyone would attempt today.

When the game began in the late nineteenth century, the ball was bigger and softer than it is today. It had raised seams, or actual stitches. Imagine trying to throw a bloated whale bladder into a peach basket. That was early basketball. By 1930, the rulemakers shrank the ball from thirty-two inches in circumference to thirty inches. The raised stitches disappeared, and the ball was made of a slightly tougher leather.

It was at this point that Luisetti arrived on the scene.

He grew up in San Francisco and began playing basketball on a crumbling concrete tennis court where there also was a hoop on a pole. Luisetti was just a little kid and the ball was very big. Even with two hands, he couldn't get it up to the rim. So he learned to throw it up like a discus, one-handed from the side while flinging his entire body at the basket. When other older kids showed up with their two-handed set shots, Luisetti stuck with his one-hander, only now it had somehow evolved into a one-handed set shot. Then he began to jump when he shot. This was revolutionary. No one had done it before. No one showed him how to do it. He just did it, like the first guy ever to decide to throw a baseball with a flip of the wrist to make it curve.

Luisetti attended Stanford, where he regularly scored over 20 points. That is like averaging 50 today, because most games were in the 40-point range and there was a center jump after every made basket.

On December 30, 1936, Luisetti and his Stanford University team faced Long Island University at Madison Square Garden. There were 17,623 fans on hand—a mob for 1936. Long Island had a 43-game winning streak, but East Coast basketball fans wanted to see this Luisetti kid who shot the ball unlike anyone before him. Furthermore, the Stanford team had the audacity to actually play defense full court. And when Stanford snared a rebound, the players didn't walk the ball up the floor—they ran and tried for layups.

At halftime, Stanford had a 22-14 lead and Luisetti's team received a standing ovation from the New York crowd as they left the court. These guys were fun to watch. Luisetti finished with 15 points, but seldom shot in the second half as his team rolled to an easy 45-31 victory.

"It seemed Luisetti could do no wrong," wrote the *New York Times* the next day. "Some of his shots would have been deemed foolhardy if they had been attempted by anyone else, but with Luisetti shooting, these were accepted by the enchanted crowd."

Luisetti was a 6-foot-2 forward. As a child, his bow legs had been strapped into metal braces so he could learn to walk normally. No one ever imagined he'd become the Michael Jordan of his day. Not only did he shoot differently than everyone else, he seemed to run faster and jump higher. This led many coaches to discount his jumper.

"I'll quit coaching if I have to teach one-handed shots to win," said Nat Holman, the legendary coach at City College of New York. "They will have to show me plenty to convince me that a shot predicated on a prayer is smart basketball. There is only one way to shoot and it's the way we do it in the East. That's with two hands."

That was the attitude of most Eastern coaches. You have to remember that this was long before the age of television. New York was the media center of the universe. A guy playing basketball at Stanford may as well have been in Guam. Luisetti brought the jumper to New York, but then he was gone like Halley's Comet. Add to this the fact that Luisetti went into the navy, contracted spinal meningitis and never played pro basketball. There were some guys on the West Coast who experimented with the jumper, but to the Eastern players who dominated the NBA into the 1950s, the jump shot was a fad that had passed, while the two-handed set shot endured.

Dolph Schayes entered the NBA in 1948. He was twenty years old, but he already had graduated from New York University, having started college at sixteen. He was 6-foot-8, 220 pounds, and the typical New York City player. He had an accurate two-hand set shot—as did most pros in the 1950s.

"Bob Cousy and Bill Sharman had one-handers, but they were one-handed set shots from a stand-still position," said Schayes.

"Even Jumpin' Joe Fulks, who was supposed to be one of the first jump shooters in the pros, well, he only went an inch or two off the ground when he shot."

But the players were aware of Luisetti and the other jump-shooting pioneers. They were intrigued by the shot.

"We didn't believe that jumping would make you a better shooter," said Schayes, "but we thought it would make it much harder to defend your shot. You could get it off quicker. As a defender, you weren't really sure when the guy was going to let go of the ball. Paul Arizin [1950–62] was one of the first pros with a real jumper, but it defied the conventional technique. He jumped, but he kicked his legs back behind him, much like Dick Barnett did later with the New York Knicks. Arizin's shot was sort of a flat line drive."

But Schayes wanted a jump shot of his own, and in the middle of his Hall of Fame NBA career he decided to teach himself a jumper.

"I spent hours and hours working on it," he said. "But the best I could do was maybe get an inch off the ground. It just felt so awkward. A big part of developing a good jumper is shooting within a rhythm, but I never could get that rhythm. I remember talking to Bob Cousy about it, and Cousy told me that he tried to learn a jumper, but he couldn't do it, either."

Bob Pettit, who grew to be 6-foot-9 in the 1940s in Baton Rouge, Louisiana, had a one-handed jumper, but it was purely by happenstance.

"I had no coaching as a kid," said Pettit. "My high school coach was a good man and a dear friend of mine, but he was a football man. I learned basketball on my own. Most kids shot two-handed. I tried it, but the ball wouldn't go in. Then I kept experimenting and I found a one-handed shot where I put the ball over my head."

One of the reasons it worked for Pettit was that he was a bigger man than most who played the game before World War II. Bigger men usually have larger hands, and the larger the hands, the easier it is to shoot and control a basketball with one hand.

More than half of the pros took jump shots.

By 1960–61, the average team scored 116 points per game and most players were taking jump shots. "In high school and college, there was no shot clock, so it was easier for some guys with set shots to survive," said John Havlicek. "But in the pros, you almost had to have a jumper."

Shooting was the name of the game in the 1960s and 1970s.

Think of the names: Oscar Robertson, Jerry West, Rick Barry, George Gervin, Nate Archibald, Earl Monroe, Dave Bing, John Havlicek. In the colleges, Pete Maravich, Rick Mount, and a guy by the name of Freeman Williams all put up huge numbers.

"The thing to remember was that this was all happening before the three-point play," said Rick Barry.

Barry averaged 37.4 points and shot 52 percent to lead the nation in scoring as a senior at the University of Miami in 1965. Then he scored 25 a game as an NBA rookie, following it up by leading the NBA in scoring with nearly 36 points per game in 1967.

Maravich averaged 44 points and shot 44 percent in three years playing for his father, Press Maravich, at LSU. He played in the NBA for the entire 1970s and was a 24-point scorer. Rick Mount was a flop as a pro, but nearly a 40-point scorer at Purdue. Those two college stars created a generation of players who longed to be shooters. So did 5-foot-9 Calvin Murphy, a 33-point scorer at Niagara in the late 1960s.

In the NBA, Jerry West and Oscar Robertson often averaged 30 points in a season. Havlicek averaged in the high 20s with Boston in the early 1970s.

"The game was more wide open, and we shot a lot more," said Havlicek. "That is why our shooting percentages were lower (usually in the 44 to 48 percent range for most high scorers). We just didn't worry about taking a bad shot or two."

Defenders of today's game point to the numbers. They say, "If Bob Cousy was such a great player, then how come he shot only 38 percent?"

Well, Bob Cousy, what about it?

"I thought of myself as a good shooter, and I seldom shot over 40 percent," said Cousy. "Some people have said that the balls were a little bigger [because they were overinflated with air]. Some of the arena conditions weren't like today. We played in a lot of very dark, smoky places where it was hard to see. But I'll be honest, I watch today's games and I know that many of our guys were better shooters than the players we see now—yet the numbers don't show it."

Dolph Schayes was considered a great shooter in the 1950s, but like Cousy, he seldom hit over 40 percent from the field.

"I think the lower percentages back then were due to the fact that we didn't have that much inside play," said Schayes. "Common sense tells you that the closer you are to the basket, the more likely your shot is to go in. Wilt Chamberlain was the first NBA player to shoot 50 percent in a season, and no one would accuse him of being a great shooter. But he was so big and so powerful that he was unstoppable inside."

Late in his career, Chamberlain had shooting percentages of .649, .683, and .727 from the field.

In 1994–95, Shaquille O'Neal led the NBA at .583 from the field, followed by Horace Grant (.567), Otis Thorpe (.565), Dale Davis (.563), and Dikembe Mutombo (.560). All are big men; none of them have even decent jump shots from fifteen feet. The only guard in the top fifteen was John Stockton at .542, which put him eleventh.

But you don't see good players shooting 38 percent, or even 44 percent; John Havlicek retired in 1978 as a 44 percent career shooter. Most of the top scorers today are very close to 50 percent. Michael Jordan has shot nearly 52 percent for his career.

Havlicek and others explain it in terms of sheer volume. There are between 20 to 25 fewer shots attempted in an NBA game today than in the 1960s and 1970s.

"If a team doesn't have a clear layup on a fast break, they often pull the ball back outside and then set up their offense," said Havlicek. "We were never afraid to take a fifteen-footer off the break."

Who was the last coach who went into the game preaching that one of his team's main goals was to take 20 more shots than the opposition?

Remember Doug Moe? He is now considered a dinosaur because of his faith in the running game, the jump shot, and the machine-gun approach. In 1988–89, Moe's Denver Nuggets averaged 118 points and attempted 8,140 shots. In 1994–95, the Golden State Warriors were the NBA's high-power team at 111 per game and 7,233 attempts. The Nuggets averaged seven more points and 18 more shots per game than the Warriors—a huge drop in only six years. In fact, during the 1994–95 season no team other than Golden State averaged more than 106 points. Shooting percentages are higher, yet most basketball men insist the shooting is worse. The real explanation for that is two words: the Dunk.

When was the last time you saw a commercial for a jump shooter? That tells you all you need to know about the state of shooting and the psyche of most basketball fans as we head into the next century.

In the 1960s and 1970s, the heroes were the shooters. Of course, the NBA was definitely number three on the sports scene. West, Robertson, and Havlicek didn't have their own national commercials, their own line of shoes and clothing. Thankfully, they didn't have their own rap songs like a Shaquille O'Neal. The game sold the game, but today commercials sell the game and the players in thirty-second and one-minute snapshots.

Those commercials say a lot of different things about the players and the game. O'Neal discusses some of his dunks as if he had just found the cure for cancer. Watch the CNN highlights from nightly NBA games and you might see a dozen different dunkers, whether or not those plays had any significance in determining the game's outcome. True, there recently was one shooting commercial. It featured Larry Bird and Jordan in a game of HORSE, with the two stars bouncing the ball off the court, than banking it off the Hancock Building—with their eyes closed.

That's not shooting. It's a sideshow.

Analysts such as Doug Collins and Hubie Brown deliver a different message when they discuss the game and the importance of shooting during their broadcasts. But the TV networks sell the sport with dunk after dunk. And the truth about dunking is that it is becoming boring. Not all dunks and not all the time, but the average dunk is a guy wide open on a fast break, with nothing between him and the rim but an empty floor. He dribbles . . . he jumps . . . he dunks.

Two points.

Big deal.

"It got to the point where I didn't like to be out in front on a fast break," said Michael Jordan. "All the fans were on the edge of their seats expecting something spectacular, but I had nothing new to show them. There are only so many dunks. So I'd try something, maybe a reverse dunk, but I still had the feeling that some fans were disappointed."

Of course, there are dunks and there are dunks. It can be a great play, when it is a dunk in traffic . . . a dunk really in your face . . . a dunk when no other shot could do it better.

"I hated having to think before I dunked," said Julius Erving. "My best dunks just happened, in the middle of a game. I would be going to the basket and one guy was in my way, then another, and I had to somehow get the ball around them and through the hole. Sometimes, I didn't even know what I did on a dunk until I saw the replay on TV."

The first NBA star to use the dunk as his main weapon was Bill Russell, who joined the Celtics in 1956.

"That was his shot," said Cousy. "We did it on a lob pass because Bill couldn't hit a bull in the ass with his jump shot. But he could jump over everyone else, so we threw him lobs, he jumped above the rim and dropped it in. Yes, it was a soft dunk, not a slam like we see today."

Russell almost dunked as if he were embarrassed. It was more a layup, like someone gently knocking on the door instead of kicking it down.

"We just didn't consider the dunk to be a skilled shot," said Slater Martin, a star point guard in the 1950s. "All it showed was that you could jump, not that you could play basketball."

Some would argue, "What do you expect Martin to say? He was only 5-foot-10 and couldn't dunk a doughnut."

But Oscar Robertson felt exactly the same way, and he was a 6-foot-5 guard who averaged over 10 rebounds in his first three pro seasons.

"I could dunk even when I was in high school," said Robertson. "I did it once in a game and my coach took me out. He thought I was trying to show up the other team, and I could understand how he felt. He told me never to do it again, and I didn't. If you ask me, the dunk is the most overrated play in basketball."

It was Julius Erving and the old American Basketball Association who really introduced the public to the dunk. When the Virginia

Squires signed Erving out of the University of Massachusetts in 1971, they had no idea he would be a player who'd revolutionize the game. He was a "hardship" case, turning pro after his junior year because he had nothing more to prove in the little Yankee Conference and needed money to help support his family.

"In our first practice, there was a rebound and it seemed everyone on the floor went up for it," recalled Johnny Kerr, the Squires general manager. "I mean, there must have been ten hands going for the ball. But all of a sudden, you saw this one pair of hands and these two elbows above everyone else's. That was Julius, and that was when we knew we had something special."

Erving and the ABA were made for each other. He held that red, white, and blue ball in his huge right hand, and it looked like a grapefruit. The league had few great shot-blocking centers; it was a league that got out and ran, a league designed for a young thoroughbred to strut and stuff.

There were other flashy dunkers, but not all became Doctors of Dunk like Erving.

The most infamous in the ABA was a fellow named Helicopter Hentz, a 6-foot-3 forward from tiny University of Arkansas at Pine Bluff.

"He was with the old Pittsburgh Condors," recalled retired official John Vanak. "They were playing a game in Charlotte against the Carolina Cougars. In the first half, Helicopter went up for a slam—he had this powerful, one-handed tomahawk—and the rim just came down with the ball. It held up the game for an hour. That was the *first* dunk. In the fourth quarter, he unleashed that tomahawk again—and down went another rim. Carl Scheer was the general manager of the Cougars and he found out that there were no more backboards and rims in the old building in Charlotte. He had to go to some high school, and came back with a wooden backboard. I swear, that game didn't end until about three in the morning."

A few years later, Darryl Dawkins would make a reputation breaking backboards, and then write poems to himself and his dunks. Who can forget the Man from Lovetron's best dunk, the one he called the "Chocolate Thunder Flyin', Robinzine Cryin', Teeth-Shakin', Glass-Breakin', Rump-Roastin', Bun-Toastin', Wham-Bam Glass-Breaker I Am Jam"? It wasn't Robert Frost, but it was funny for a while until it began happening too often and people got tired of waiting for a new basket to be installed.

Dunks are a part of basketball lore. You heard a lot of stories about guys named Helicopter, guys who could go up for a dunk and be called for three seconds because they stayed in the air too long above the key. But most weren't even as successful as Hentz, who played one season in the ABA and averaged six points. Even Dawkins was more a good-natured, foul-prone underachiever than anything else in his fourteen-year NBA career.

The ABA was born in 1967 and lasted until 1976. It embraced the dunk. Of course, it loved anything that it thought might put a few extra fannies in the seats, including cow-milking contests at halftime of Indiana Pacers games. In 1976, the ABA held the first Slam Dunk Contest, where Erving did his famed flying dunk, taking off from the foul line and dunking—from fifteen feet away. He actually stepped on the line, but the ABA was never one to let the facts get in the way of a good story.

Shots such as those made Erving a legend, but were not what made him a great player. Erving also became bored with dunks. When he lost the 1984 Slam Dunk Contest to Larry Nance, Erving said that was it—no more contests. So did Nance.

"I didn't want people to think that I was just a dunker," said Nance. "I was a young player and I was developing my whole game. I wanted to be known as a good all-around player."

Nance was a Slam Dunk Champion before he became an All-Star. He could have lived off his legs, but instead he developed an accurate medium-range jumper—much as Erving did—and that is what made Nance the best forward in the history of the Cleveland Cavaliers—that and Nance's defense. When he retired because of knee problems in the summer of 1994, he left the game as the forward with the most blocked shots in NBA history.

Magic Johnson entered the NBA as a 6-foot-9 guard who could do everything, even play center in the NBA Finals. Everything but shoot, that is. So he taught himself to shoot, learning the hook from Kareem Abdul-Jabbar and developing a long-range shot on his own—and it was a one-handed set shot right out of the late 1950s. No matter, it went in.

"The misconception is that players can't make a change in their basic game once they get into the NBA," said longtime assistant

Richie Adubato. "Sometimes, players are too stubborn to listen to their coaches or too lazy to work on things themselves. Other times, coaches just don't go to the trouble to push the guys to learn something new. But the great ones add new shots all the time. Even Michael Jordan taught himself to shoot."

If anyone set the MTV generation of basketball in motion, it was Jordan. No athlete was ever marketed more intensely, made more commercials, or was seen dunking the basketball more often than Jordan.

"When I came into the league, I just wasn't a good outside shooter," Jordon said. "In high school and college, I didn't need to shoot from the outside to score."

He jumped over people, and he even did that in his rookie season. But in his second year, he broke a bone in his foot and missed 64 games. As his foot was healing, he often went to the gym alone to shoot around. There was nothing else he could do because he wasn't allowed to practice. Soon, he became very serious about his jump shot. When he came back and played teams such as Detroit, with players such as Rick Mahorn throwing him to the court whenever he drove to the basket, Jordan realized that he had to develop a jump shot for his own self-preservation.

"In the playoffs, you have to be able to shoot the ball, because they just won't give you anything going to the basket," said Jordan.

Then there was Larry Bird, who lived to shoot and loved to practice his shot. He would arrive at Boston Garden on game night before anyone else, take a ball boy or equipment manager on the court with him, and shoot hundreds of jumpers. The ball boy would rebound, pass to Bird, and he'd shoot and shoot some more—shots that he would take in a game. His goal was the perfect jumper, one with enough arc and backspin that the ball would gently touch only the net, hit the floor, and then bounce back to where Bird took the shot.

That would have made a wonderful commercial, one with a lesson for all young players: no matter how well you dunk, the NBA is still a shooter's league—or should be.

*   *   *

With all the summer camps and summer leagues, you'd think that today's young basketball players would be more skilled and polished than ever. They play basketball virtually all year. In the past, a good athlete was encouraged to play two or three sports in high school. Now, coaches want a kid to specialize, and that's especially true in basketball. Send him to camps and clinics in the summer instead of letting him play baseball. Certainly you don't want him to play football. In the fall, he should be playing basketball in pickup games with other members of the team after school so he'll be sharp once practice starts in November.

"Athletically, the kids today are so advanced from the players of my generation," said John Havlicek. "They are bigger and stronger. They run faster, jump higher, and are more physically mature. They get on weight programs, whereas we were told that weights would mess up your shot. A basketball player didn't want to have too many muscles because it would slow him down. At least, that was the thinking."

So why are shooting statistics in college dropping?

"That's easy," said Cavs player personnel director Gary Fitzsimmons. "Kids today can't shoot. They can dunk. They can finish on the fast break. But leave them open from eighteen feet and it's a different story. Ask them to take a couple of dribbles and then take a medium-range jumper—forget it."

Gary Fitzsimmons's lament can be heard from nearly every scout who discusses the subject of young players.

"They are terrible fundamentally," said Jerry Colangelo of the Phoenix Suns. "I believe that it's because they are so physically gifted, they believe they don't need to take the time to learn the basics."

But with all the camps and the coaching these kids receive at an early age, why wouldn't their fundamentals be solid? They do nothing but play basketball. They have more coaching than any other generation of players, and the coaches appear to work hard and are prepared.

So what gives?

"Some players are beyond fundamentals," said Isiah Thomas.

Say what?

"It's a different kind of athlete from ten years ago," insisted Thomas. "You have 6-foot-11 guys who can run and dribble like guards. But they don't have post-up moves. The athletes have gotten so good that they are better than the fundamentals."

Isiah, if Bobby Knight ever heard you talk like that, you'd be running up and down the bleachers for the next hundred years.

"Fundamentals can hamper athletes," Thomas continued. "Take a guy like Shawn Kemp. A great athlete like that, you give him fundamentals and you can ruin him. What you need to do is just let him play, let his talent flow."

George Karl has a different outlook. He has said that Kemp's game has "too much French pastry." But what does Karl know? All he has to do is try to coach Kemp—and he has to live with Kemp when he triple-pumps before taking a finger-roll layup that kicks off the back of the rim.

At times, Thomas will moan about the modern players' unwillingness to work and their MTV mind-set, but he claims, "These kids do things today on the court that we could never do ten years ago—and they do them without fundamentals."

Thomas's point is that the athletes are changing the game. Some little guys are better off driving to the basket and scoring inside like big men, while some big men are more effective shooting from the outside like guards. It is up to the coach to adjust to the talent.

But it is really hard to accept Thomas' theory about the players being "ruined by fundamentals." All Isiah has to do is look in the mirror.

When pushed, he will admit that he could play any type of basketball, from the basic pick-and-roll to his All-Star hotdog antics.

"It's true, great players can play any sort of game," he said.

The difference is that many of today's young players just want to ignore the basics. That's not being "beyond fundamentals." That's just being lazy.

"The shooting and passing skills are getting worse every year," said Al Menendez. "I remember the 1994 Goodwill Games where the U.S. played China. About every member of the Chinese team could make an outside shot from twenty feet. With only a couple of exceptions, very few of our kids could do the same. We beat the Chinese because we were far superior to them athletically. But a few days later, we lost to the Russians because we shot 13-for-28 from the foul line. Foul shooting in high schools and colleges today is a disgrace."

By the end of the decade, free throw shooting at the major college level will be under 60 percent if the current trend continues.

"Here's the deal," said Menendez. "Kids go from camp to camp because they are getting a free this and a free that. They go to camp and play against the other top kids. They are evaluated by the college coaches. They play a lot of games, but I don't know how many of them are spending two hours a day alone in the gym working on their shooting like a Chris Mullin or an Oscar Robertson did. Kids just seem to live off their natural ability now."

Which brings us to foul shooting.

If you saw the movie *Blue Chips,* you may recall a scene where Bob Cousy is standing at the foul line. While talking to Nick Nolte, Cousy swishes one free throw after another. It was the kind of free throw you don't see anymore—a one-handed push shot.

"I was the athletic director in the movie and Nolte was the coach," said Cousy. "I had on my street clothes and the idea was just for a little action—me shooting the ball—as I talked to Nolte. I didn't even have a warm-up. The first shot I took went in and I kept shooting."

As they filmed the scene, Cousy made about 12 in a row.

The director yelled, "Cut."

The crew told the Cooz to shoot until he missed.

Cousy ran the streak to 17, 18, 19 . . .

"Try one left-handed," a member of the crew yelled.

Cousy put the ball in his left hand . . . swish . . . 20 . . . 21.

Then he missed.

"The guys gave me a standing ovation," said Cousy.

And not just because a sixty-five-year-old made 21 straight free throws while wearing a shirt and tie.

"They told me that the night before while they were filming a game scene for the movie, Shaquille O'Neal missed 14-of-15 at the foul line," said Cousy, who was a career 80 percent free throw shooter.

Nobody shoots free throws with the same one-handed motion that Cousy used. Nor do they shoot the ball underhanded as Rick Barry did. Barry just happens to be the second-best free throw shooter in NBA history.

"I look at some of these guys and I wonder why they don't try it underhanded or something," said Mark Price. "I know if I were shooting free throws like they do, I'd try something else."

Price is the best free throw shooter in NBA history at .906, just ahead of Barry at .900.

"I take pretty much the same shot I do from the field," said Price. "It's not a jumper, but I do go up on my toes. Most guys shoot free throws flat-footed, and their whole shot ends up flat. But my technique—the release, the grip—everything is the same as my jumper. My free throws are always the same. I get the ball from the officials, I take three dribbles and shoot it. As I release the ball, I say, 'Heel to toe,' to myself, to remind me to go up on my toes."

Price's father is Denny Price, a former assistant coach under John MacLeod at Oklahoma University and with the Phoenix Suns. Price also is a compulsive practicer, who shot hundreds of free throws a day at the basket on his driveway while growing up in Enid, Oklahoma.

"I always was a pretty good free throw shooter," he said. "I learned the right way from the beginning and I just took to it. Now, I usually only practice about 25 free throws a day. That's all I need to keep sharp."

But most of today's players didn't have a father who was a pro coach. They seldom practice free throws. Think about playground games. Who takes a foul shot? When a foul is called, the ball is thrown in from the side.

"Today's kids would rather dunk than shoot the ball," said Barry. "The last thing they want to do is practice free throws. That's why you see all these great athletes who are terrible free throw shooters. They are a mechanical nightmare at the foul line. They do so many things wrong that you can't even fix them. Watch poor Shaq at the line. He's a mess. With some of these guys, there is only one thing that can help them."

That's the underhanded free throw, insisted Barry.

Understand this about free throw shooting—it's just going to get worse. In 1994–95, the average Division I player shot 62 percent at the foul line. That's the lowest percentage since 1959, and no one expects it to get any better in the near future. Naturally, some of these rock throwers in college end up missing free throws in the NBA.

"The crazy thing is that the foul line is the one place in the basketball game where you can be completely selfish and still help your team," said Barry. "You can go to the line, and not think about anyone or anything else but making the shot—and all the points go next to your name. Why wouldn't everyone want to be a great free throw shooter? Why wouldn't everyone practice all the time? Why wouldn't they be willing to try anything—even an underhanded free throw—if it would help them at the line and help them score more points?

Okay, Rick, why not?

"No personal pride," he said. "We have guys in the NBA shooting 40 percent or even 50 percent at the foul line and they don't seem to care. I tell you, this is ludicrous."

Then Barry discussed Chris Dudley. To watch Dudley at the foul line is to see a man whose psyche is broken glass. It's not just the fact that he's a career 40 percent shooter. It is how he shoots, and the way he misses. He holds the ball over his head stiffly with both hands. He tries to cock his right wrist. Then he shoots the ball—or he doesn't. If Dudley were a quarterback, it would be known as a pump-fake before throwing a pass. He sometimes does this two . . . three . . . four times before finally releasing the ball.

It is as if he has a mental block. As he prepares to shoot, he knows that terrible things will happen. He will miss. Fans will boo or laugh. Officials often call lane violations, because all his pump-fakes force players to move in too quickly for rebounds. Nothing good ever seems to happen to Dudley at the foul line. Even when he makes a shot, the fans cheer wildly and sarcastically as if he had just won an event in the Special Olympics.

That is why Dudley subconsciously doesn't want to release the ball: he knows people will make fun of him.

"If ever a guy should experiment with an underhanded free throw, it's Dudley," said Barry. "What does he have to lose?"

Good question. Well, why doesn't Dudley do it?

"It doesn't feel comfortable," Dudley has said.

Barry doesn't buy that explanation.

"Guys don't like the underhanded shot because they think it looks dumb," said Barry. "They'd rather shoot 45 percent than try something that might bring them up to 60 or 70 percent. One time, I was doing a TV game in Cleveland and I went to a practice. That was back when Dudley was with the Cavs. I talked to him, showed him some of the basic principles of the underhanded free throw. He threw a few up there, and they bounced around and went in. He wasn't even shooting it right, but it still was soft enough to fall into the basket. Now here was a guy who couldn't even hit the rim sometimes, and I showed him a shot that at least gave him a chance. You'd think he'd follow up on it, right? He never even bothered to ask me or anyone else about shooting underhanded. He just kept embarrassing himself the old way. You have to be a moron to be that stubborn."

Well, Dudley attended Yale, which means he's probably not a complete moron. But he also shot 51 percent from the line in the Ivy League. As a rookie, it was 47 percent for the Cavs. Then it dropped to 43 percent . . . 41 percent . . . 40 percent . . . 35 percent in 1992–93.

In other words, every year Dudley just got worse.

At 6-foot-11 and 250 pounds, Dudley can jump, is surprisingly strong, and has a knack for blocking shots and guarding bigger men in the low post. He's a tough guy you'd want on the floor for thirty-five minutes a night—if he didn't have to shoot free throws.

"Thirty-five percent," said Barry. "And the guy won't shoot underhanded. Give me a break."

But there is another reason Dudley could stubbornly stick to his futile ways. He signed a $25 million contract with Portland in the summer of 1994. Even if he never makes another free throw, he's rich. That's today's NBA.

Wilt Chamberlain could score 100 points in a game and average 50 points in a season. He probably blocked more shots than anyone in NBA history, although statistics on blocked shots were not kept when Chamberlain played.

He was a great 7-foot-1, 270-pound center who could do everything in basketball—except make a free throw.

"To this day, I still don't know why," Wilt said. "I shot 80 percent in high school. I can show you some of the box scores. I look at box scores of me going 9-of-11 and 10-of-12 at the line and I see old stories that say, 'Then they fouled Chamberlain, which was a mistake.' I mean, I wonder what happened to those days because I really was a good foul shooter in college, too."

Maybe he was and maybe not. No one knows for sure what Wilt did at the line at Philadelphia's Overbrook High. But at the University of Kansas, records do show he was a 62 percent shooter from the foul line. As an NBA rookie, it was 58 percent. Not great, but not embarrassing. In his third pro season—1961–62, when he averaged 50 points—he shot a career-high 61 percent at the line. In the 100-point game, he was 28-of-32 at the foul line. Those 28 free throws made are an NBA record for the most in a game.

So Chamberlain could make free throws—he just didn't.

By 1967–68, he was down to 38 percent. He shot 46 percent from the line in the playoffs, and his career mark was .511.

The average NBA player makes 72 percent.

"I'd make 75 to 80 percent in practice," said Chamberlain. "I really would. Just ask my teammates and coaches."

We did.

"I'd say 75 percent is right when we'd work alone in the gym," said Dolph Schayes, who coached Chamberlain in Philadelphia. "But when he'd get in the game, it would be a completely different story. I don't care if he shot them overhanded, underhanded, or what. When I had him, he was always tinkering. I encouraged him to shoot underhanded and he'd make close to 80 percent that way—in practice. It looked good. But in the games, nothing Wilt shot from the line looked very good."

Why is free throw shooting so hard for some people?

"Because it's completely different from any other shot you take in a game," said Bill Fitch. "A jump shot or a driving layup is spontaneous. You do it in a rhythm. You have no 'think time.' You react only to the defense and you have to make a decision to shoot in a split second. But a free throw is static. The whole game stops, they hand you the ball and everyone watches you shoot."

And they love it when a big guy misses. It is a chance for the 5-foot-8, beer-bellied fan to say, "Even I can make a free throw, and look at those guys throwing rocks up there." The average fan can't dunk, he can't make a three-pointer, and he knows that he can't rebound or dribble in traffic. But a foul shot—hey, anyone can make a foul shot.

Those who make free throws can't understand why others don't. And those who don't make free throws can't explain it—they just miss.

"I really think a pro should shoot 75 to 80 percent at the foul line," said Schayes, a Hall of Famer and a career 84 percent free throw shooter. "All you have to do is work at it."

But Schayes did it differently.

"The rim is eighteen inches in diameter," he said. "The ball is ten inches, which means there are four inches on each side of the ball in terms of room to spare. I bought a fourteen-inch rim and I put it inside a regular rim—and I practiced free throws on that smaller rim."

Schayes claimed it helped him improve from a 75 percent shooter early in his career to a 90 percent shooter toward the end. If it worked for him, you would think that other players would try it.

"A few guys took some shots at it, but when they missed, the ball banged out about twenty feet," said Schayes. "Guys would just say, 'Heck with this.' But to me, it was great because after shooting at the little rim, the regulation rim seemed huge. When I coached, I brought the rim to practice a few times, but none of my players seemed interested in it."

One of Schayes's players in Philadelphia, Hal Greer, didn't bother to develop a special free throw. He took his natural jumper from the foul line and shot 80 percent for his career.

"I don't understand why more guys don't do that," said Schayes.

Actually, no guys in the NBA do that. Greer's jumper from the foul line came and went with Greer, who retired in 1973.

When you talk about great players, you usually find excellent numbers at the foul line: Magic Johnson (85 percent), Michael Jordan (85 percent), Larry Bird (89 percent), Oscar Robertson (84 percent), Jerry West (81 percent), and even center Kareem Abdul-Jabbar was a 72-percent free throw shooter.

One player who did get the message of the value of the free throw is Karl Malone. In his rookie season, he shot .481 at the line. But he practiced and practiced. The next year, it was .598. Malone practiced some more, his goal being 70 percent. By his third season, he was at exactly 70 percent. There are points and dollars to be made at the foul line and Malone has cashed in, becoming a career 72 percent free throw shooter and one of the highest paid players in the NBA. Because he is so muscular and so relentless under the basket, and because he has a wonderful point guard in John Stockton feeding him the ball, Malone gets lot of shots. To stop him, teams must foul him. From 1988 to 1993, he led the NBA in free throws attempted and made. He picks up 8 points per game at the foul line. If he had remained a 48 percent shooter, Karl Malone would be on no one's dream team today. Malone did it by shooting free throws with a standard motion. He simply taught himself how to do it.

As we head into the next century, the player destined to draw more fouls than anyone—including Malone—is Shaquille O'Neal.

In two years at LSU, he shot 58 percent from the foul line. In the NBA, he has shot 58 percent. In the last six weeks of the 1994–95 season, he was slightly over 40 percent.

"Shaq would be the perfect candidate for the underhanded free throw," said Barry. "He would be so much more relaxed. The shot is very natural. Your arms hang down and you flip it out toward the rim. The great thing about the underhand shot is that it guarantees that you put the ball up there soft. There is very little motion, no great wrist action. It is a soft shot, and a soft shot has a lot of room for error. It doesn't have to be perfect to go in."

O'Neal reportedly isn't interested, and he once referred to Barry as "that underhanded guy."

A coach who was intrigued by the underhanded free throw is John Wooden, but he never forced the shot on his great players at UCLA.

"[When I coached] in high school, virtually all of my players shot underhanded," Wooden has said in clinics. "We typically shot 75 percent as a team that way. Only two or three of my teams at UCLA shot as well as my high school teams. But it just seemed to me that by college, it is just too late to change a player to an underhanded free throw."

Why? Why can't coaches demand that lousy foul shooters try shooting underhanded—or at least try Hal Greer's jump shot? Have the players taken that much authority away from the coach? Or do the coaches believe that free throws just aren't a crucial enough battleground to risk alienating a player? And if a coach doesn't think free throws are important, is he on the same planet as the rest of us? Coaches demand that players defend and rebound; why can't they require a player to make a full-faith effort to improve at the foul line?

Most of the 1994–95 Orlando Magic could have used remedial free throw lessons. Orlando was the worst free throw shooting team in the regular season at 67 percent. The only other team under 70 percent was Portland at .697. The Magic lost Game 1—and momentum for the entire Finals—when Nick Anderson missed four free throws in the final seconds. O'Neal had a playoff game against Indiana where he was 0-for-8. During their 21-game playoff run, the Magic shot only 67 percent from the foul line—compared to 77 percent for their opponents. O'Neal was a 57 percent shooter at the line in the post-season.

"No NBA team has ever asked me to work with their shooters," said Barry. "Let me work with Shaq and pay me so much for each percentage point that he improves from the line from the previous season. Shaq would get better, his team would win more games, and I'd make a lot of money. He can make 70 percent underhanded if I worked with him and he stayed with the shot."

But it doesn't seem likely to happen, because Shaq and the other brick throwers from the foul line probably don't know that "the underhanded guy" also happens to be in the Hall of Fame. The underhanded shot is ideal for Dudley, O'Neal, or anyone else who can't make 2-of-3. The fact that "No one does it" is a silly rationalization. What made the NBA great was attempting new shots, finding out what works best for you. If it has become cool to miss free throws and coaches can't do anything about it, then the game is in bigger trouble than any of us ever thought.

4 Violence and the Culture of Disrespect

Wayne Embry has been a general manager since 1972. He is in the basketball talent business, and that means he spends much of his time looking beyond a young player's physical ability.

"People get tired of hearing me say it, but character still counts for a lot in this game," said Embry. "If I didn't think so, I'd get out."

Embry said it's now more important to search through a player's background than ever before.

"It used to be that you'd hear some player was a bad kid," said Embry. "But ten or twenty years ago, a bad guy drank beer, smoked, and maybe stole hubcaps. Basically, he was a small-time hood. But today, some of these kids don't come from families, they come from battle zones. You listen to stories of how they grew up, and it scares the hell out of you. Right now in the NBA, you can see most of society's problems."

One of Embry's best friends in the NBA is Phoenix Suns owner Jerry Colangelo. They often talk about the league, and where the young players are taking it.

"Did you see the commercial with Dennis Rodman and Santa Claus?" asked Embry. "What is that? You have Rodman asking Santa for all these things. Santa is telling Rodman how he didn't go to practice, how he was late for games, how he led the league in personal fouls and ejections. Then Rodman said, 'But I led the league in rebounds.' And Santa agrees to give Rodman the shoes he wants for Christmas. I was offended by that commercial. What are we telling our kids? That's it's okay to act like a jerk? To be irresponsible? That nothing matters if you get enough rebounds? That is what it looked like to me. You've got the Worm there in all his tattoos and nose rings and he's a hero? Why would Nike make a commercial like that? I wrote the president of the company to ask him just that."

Colangelo knows exactly what Embry is talking about.

"Emotionally, so many of the players we are getting are nothing but basket cases," he said. "Some of them are morally bankrupt. We get kids from the broken families, kids who don't respect authority, don't understand discipline, and really have no value system—or a completely different value system. It's a microcosm of society."

Consider Dennis Rodman. His life was a mess. He was from a broken home. He lived with a white family in Dallas for a while. He was a janitor at the Dallas–Fort Worth airport after high school, and sometimes he just slept in the airport because he had nowhere else to go. He once spent a night in jail for stealing a watch.

He enrolled at Cooke County Junior College in Texas. He grew from 6-foot-1 to 6-foot-8 in less than a year. He became a basketball player, good enough to receive a scholarship from Southeastern Oklahoma State. He averaged 25 points in three years and was picked by Detroit in the second round of the 1986 draft. He was twenty-five years old when he began his pro career.

Rodman adopted Pistons coach Chuck Daly as the father he never had. He took to Pistons veterans Isiah Thomas, Bill Laimbeer, and Rick Mahorn as the family he never had. He became a tremendous rebounder and defensive forward.

As long as the Pistons were winning and Daly was there, Rodman showed up on time and "was the most unselfish player in the history of the NBA," according to Daly. "He can win 6 to 10 games by himself with his defense and rebounding."

But after the two championship years of 1989 and 1990, the Pistons aged. Veterans were traded or retired. Daly became the head coach of the New Jersey Nets in the fall of 1992. In Detroit, Rodman felt abandoned. He wouldn't listen to new coach Ron Rothstein. He started being late for practice—or skipping workouts entirely. When he came out of games, he occasionally sat on the floor at the end of the bench and took his shoes off in protest. He was in the middle of a messy and public divorce.

Rodman still led the league in rebounding in 1992, and again in 1993. But the Pistons had to trade him because his behavior became even more erratic. One morning, police found him in the parking lot of the Pistons' arena, the Palace of Auburn Hills. He had a loaded rifle in his lap and he was sleeping. It was 5 A.M. In October of 1993, he was traded to San Antonio, where Spurs coach John Lucas allowed Rodman to do pretty much what he wished, with the stipulation that Rodman show up on time for games and grab rebounds as if they were his last meal. Rodman grew more bizarre. He began covering his body with tattoos. He dyed his hair blond, then green and red. He dated Madonna. He added earrings, a nose ring, and even a navel ring. His navel is at the center of a spiderweb tattoo, and the ring has been compared to a door knocker. It was as if he wanted to punish his own body for sins that neither he nor anyone else could explain.

He kept telling anyone who would ask, "Don't let them control you. They always try to control you."

He periodically received psychological help, but he seemed to be working at being outrageous and rebellious. He was fined, suspended, and threatened with trades. None of it mattered. He also was coddled and treated like a misunderstood child who deserved patience and a wide berth—but that didn't work, either.

In the fall of 1994, Rodman was suspended by new Spurs coach Bob Hill and general manager Greg Popovich. In an exhibition game—one of the few where Rodman actually showed up—he threw an ice bag at Hill after the coach took him out of the game. A meeting with Popovich followed, and Rodman told San Antonio writers, "Popovich told me to grow up. I guess I have to go back to kindergarten and learn my ABC's. But that doesn't prove who is the child and who is the man."

Rodman was still on the suspended list when the 1994–95 season began and when the Dennis Talks to Santa Nike commercial was televised.

"Rodman has made a mockery of the NBA, and we publicize him," said Embry. "That just galls me."

Rodman did decide to show up for practice and be somewhat responsible in early December. Once again, he led the league in rebounding.

"When Dennis got to know Madonna, he discovered how being outrageous will get you attention," said Daly. "A lot of the things he does like the tattoos are to get attention. He does it on purpose. That's just him. He also hasn't been happy because he thought the Spurs should have reworked his [$2.6 million] contract."

Rodman is a time bomb for any team. At his best, he is a unique force, a player who does the dirty jobs on the court and is genuinely uninterested in scoring—a key piece of a championship-caliber team. At his worst, he is capable of going off at the worst possible moment, as in the 1994 playoffs when his one-game suspension led to the Spurs' first-round loss to the Utah Jazz. He also spent a lot of his time in Salt Lake City with Madonna.

Then Rodman sunk the Spurs again in the 1995 playoffs. In the Western Conference Finals—when the Spurs needed him the most—Rodman showed up late for practices. He was supposed to be at the arena 90 minutes before games—he usually showed up about 45 minutes before tipoff. During timeouts, he sat on the floor with his shoes off instead of taking part in the huddle. When he did manage to wander to the huddle, he stood just outside of it, letting everyone know that whatever was being said by the coach wasn't worthy of his attention. Coach Bob Hill benched Rodman for one game in the second round against the Lakers. In one game of the Houston series, Hill didn't start him. Rodman seemed to love the attention and the controversy. He claims he is an unselfish player because he doesn't want to shoot—his artistry is rebounding and defense. But he is the most selfish player in the league because he turned the playoffs into his own personal sideshow. And the Spurs deserved to lose because they allowed him to do just that; they let him take the games away from good guys such as David Robinson, Avery Johnson, and Sean Elliott. This is Rodman, and any general manager who acquires him knows that this is the chance he's taking.

When NBA general managers checked out Gary Trent, the 6-foot-8, 240-pound All-American forward from Ohio University, they didn't have to look very far to find out that these were not the 1950s anymore—or even the 1980s.

Trent's father spent six years in jail for conspiracy to distribute drugs, specifically cocaine.

One of his grandmothers was convicted of killing her son.

Five of his uncles served jail time, one of them on a murder charge.

His mother was jailed for three months on a drug-trafficking charge.

Trent talked about all this in *USA Today*.

"Jail was just a part of my life," Trent told the newspaper. "It's like my whole family was mobsters and gangsters. But I love every one of them."

Trent told *USA Today* that he never used drugs, but he had sold cocaine. He once had $12,000 on him—when he was thirteen!

Trent said he stopped his involvement in the drug trade during his sophomore year in high school. He had no brushes with the law, or at Ohio University.

But the value system he reflects is different from the world of most general managers.

"What I did [selling drugs] was wrong, but what I did with the money was right," Trent's father, Dexter Trent, told the *New York Times*. "I dealt drugs. I was damned good at it. But the money I made was for my kids so they wouldn't grow up for nothing like me."

Dexter Trent went to jail. His son sold drugs when he was only thirteen. It is amazing that Gary didn't follow his father's footsteps right through the jailhouse door—because that is what happens so many times in families such as these. That he didn't may suggest the strength of character a team wants to see in its prospects today. There hasn't been a hint of problems with Gary Trent at Ohio U. But with millions of dollars at stake, how would you as a GM evaluate this volatile, delicate issue of character and chemistry for your team?

In 1994, the Philadelphia 76ers' first-round pick was Sharone Wright.

Wright's father was separated from the family. When Wright was a seventeen-year-old senior at Southwest Macon High School, he signed a letter of intent to play college basketball at Clemson on the morning of November 14, 1990. That afternoon, his father was shot after a standoff with police.

"My father was a recovering addict," Wright told Phil Jasner of the *Philadelphia Daily News.* "He had problems with cocaine and heroin and he started drinking again. He got drunk and called the detox center to come get him. Then he called back to say he didn't want them to come."

The detox people showed up—as did twenty-eight policemen. Wright's mother tried to convince her husband to come out of the house, but the phone hookup failed. Wright's father had a gun inside the house. For three and a half hours, no one moved. Then Wright's father came out of the house. Wright said he was going to surrender. A Macon newspaper report said that his father was firing a gun. The police shot and killed his father. It was ruled justifiable, and no charges were ever filed against the police.

What professional basketball players of the past had to overcome obstacles like this one?

In 1991, the Phoenix Suns knew about a player named Richard Dumas. They knew he had the long arms and the huge hands of a young Julius Erving. They knew that he had some moves that made you swear that you'd just seen another Doctor J.

But they also knew that Dumas had been asked to leave Oklahoma State because of drug problems.

"It was no secret," said Colangelo. "That was why when it came our turn to make a second-round pick (No. 46), Dumas was still there. If he had been drug-free, he was a lottery pick."

The Suns had experience with drug problems in the middle 1980s when several players received treatment. Rumors concerning other players led to trades and a public relations nightmare.

According to Colangelo, the meeting between himself and his coaches about Dumas went like this:

COLANGELO: "I don't want to draft Dumas."

COACHES: "Why?"

COLANGELO: "Because we are not in the rehab business."

COACHES: "We've checked the kid out. He may be able to straighten his life out."

COLANGELO: "Guys like this don't change. I've been there."

COACHES: "So you are worrying about wasting a pick?"

COLANGELO: "No, my worry is that he'll make our team."

COACHES: "Why?"

COLANGELO: "Because then we'll have a bag of troubles like we had here before, and I hate the thought of that."

But Colangelo allowed some of his coaches to convince him to take a gamble on Dumas. They signed him for $150,000, and he flunked a drug test during the 1991 training camp. He sat out the 1991–92 season to receive treatment.

Dumas returned in the fall of 1992, saying all the right things. He confessed to coach Paul Westphal that he had never played a game since the age of thirteen when he wasn't high on drugs or alcohol. He said that he loved the idea of playing basketball sober.

Two months into the 1992–93 season, the NBA reinstated Dumas. He worked his way quickly into the lineup, averaging 16 points and shooting 52 percent for a team that advanced to the NBA finals. But during those 1993 Finals, Dumas was spotted in some Chicago bars. The media was still writing stories about how he had turned around his life, when he really was slipping back into the world of drugs and booze.

Dumas flunked another drug test before the 1993–94 season and was suspended until March of 1995, when the Players Association said that Dumas had successfully completed the league's drug program—and the union urged Colangelo to give Dumas yet another try. Colangelo reluctantly brought him back one more time.

"We've had him for three years and he was straight for only half a season," said Colangelo. "He just came with too much baggage. I knew that, and I'm still upset with myself for allowing him to be drafted by us. I knew better."

At the end of the 1994–95 season, Colangelo announced that he had released Dumas—he wasn't worth the trouble.

*   *   *

There are many other examples of players whose lives bear witness to society's problems.

Lloyd Daniels' mother died when he was three years old. His father had a drinking problem. Daniels told *Sports Illustrated* that he smoked marijuana when he was ten, and was selling drugs regularly by the time he was fifteen. He had no home, often moving between relatives and friends. His youth was chaos. He grew up on the street and learned how to take advantage of situations. Because he was a great basketball talent, he transferred from one high school to another—four high schools in all. But he played only one full season.

He played a grand total of two college games—and it was at Mt. San Antonio Junior College in California. He averaged 17.5 points.

Then Daniels enrolled at UNLV. Before he could play a game for the Rebels, he was arrested outside a crack house during a Las Vegas police department drug raid. He was tossed out of school. In 1989, he was twenty-one years old, back in New York, where he was shot over an $8 drug debt. He lost six pints of blood, but survived. Then he went into John Lucas's rehabilitation center.

Daniels played in the CBA, and Jerry Tarkanian brought him to the NBA in 1993–94. He played in the league for two unspectacular seasons with San Antonio.

Then there is Scott Williams. When he was at the University of North Carolina, a senseless tragedy struck his family in Los Angeles. His father murdered his mother, then killed himself. How can any of us know what something like that does to a son? How can any of us understand what kind of family life there was for someone who grew up in a home that ended in gunshots?

There are many more examples, but the point is that the problems faced by some of the new breed of NBA players really are unlike anything the league has ever seen before.

"Athletes have always come from the lower classes," said Embry. "But now, those lower classes are more violent and have sunk to depths the likes of which many people can't understand."

Or as Charles Barkley said, "Today's players are like what you see on TV. It's gangs, kids killing kids. If they didn't play basketball, some of these guys would be in gangs that killed somebody."

Some people thought Barkley was a bad kid back in Leeds, Alabama, because when he was twelve years old he and some friends would stake out a supermarket and wait for the bakery truck to come. They'd steal cakes off the loading dock. That is nothing compared to what he sees today.

"There have always been fights in basketball," said Barkley, "but it was just talking, posturing, and stuff like that. But some of these guys are really fighting, like they want to kill each other. They are violent."

General managers, coaches, and veteran players are trying to understand the new generation of NBA athletes. Over and over again, you hear them use the words "violent . . . hostile . . . selfish . . . undisciplined."

"A lot of these kids grew up on the streets and the playgrounds," said Cotton Fitzsimmons. "In those places, you are told that you can't back down. It's drilled into your head. Well, what if two guys square off on an NBA court, two guys who have been told all their lives that they can't back down? Well, what happens? A real fight, that's what."

"It is the whole welfare society," said Embry. "It's kids without male role models. It's how they fall into gangs for an identity, and they bring that gang attitude to basketball."

Every NBA general manager, coach, and scout should be required to read an article by Elijah Anderson in the May 1994 issue of *The Atlantic Monthly.* Anderson is a professor of social sciences at the University of Pennsylvania. The article is entitled "The Code of the Streets." Basketball is never mentioned, nor is the NBA, but the article says more about what's going on in pro basketball today than a hundred pieces about the sport itself.

The first sentence sets the tone: "Of all the problems besetting the poor inner-city black community, none is more pressing than that of interpersonal violence and aggression." Anderson describes two kinds of families: "decent families," who have traditional values often anchored in a church, and "street famlies," whose children are lost, rootless, and angry.

How does this relate to basketball?

"Among young people whose sense of self-esteem is particularly vulnerable, there is an especially heightened concern with being disrespected," wrote Anderson. "Many inner-city young men crave respect to such a degree that they will risk their lives to attain it."

It happens with alarming regularity in the ghetto. Read some of the police reports. James thinks that Charles is a wimp and a punk, so he beats Charles and steals his Chicago Bulls jacket. Then James tells the neighborhood about what he did to Charles, and he presents the jacket as a trophy. Charles has been disrespected. He can either slither around in shame—and be a target for more attacks—or he can fight back. So he gets a gun and blows James away, reclaiming his jacket.

There have even been reports of killings simply because one guy "looked at me wrong."

It comes down to what is perceived as respect. It's why some young men simply walk right out in the middle of traffic, expecting cars to stop. They want respect. No, it's more than that; they are demanding respect by stepping in front of a car, putting their bodies on the line and daring the car to run them over.

"One way of campaigning for status is by taking possession of others," wrote Anderson. "The ability to violate somebody—to get 'in his face' . . . to 'dis' him, and thus enhance one's own self-worth by stealing someone else's."

Players such as Walt Frazier seldom changed expression during a game. They didn't want you to know if they'd won or lost, if the shot went in or banged off the rim. Being cool was keeping cool.

But today, the code of the streets is that scoring on a guy isn't enough, you have to tell him about it. Hence, trash talk. Or, as Anderson characterized it, "This is a zero-sum game . . . the extent to which one person can raise himself up depends upon his ability to put someone else down."

This describes a lot of the recent fights in the NBA. Remember the brawl between Miami's Grant Long and Atlanta's Duane Ferrell in the 1994 playoffs?

Ferrell dunked on Long. He simply overpowered Long, who sort of ducked as the ball was hammered through the rim. That should have been the end of it—two points with an exclamation point.

But Ferrell wanted more. Ferrell waved a finger right in Long's face. He was challenging Long's manhood, insulting him in front of a sellout crowd in his own arena—and a national cable television audience.

Ten years ago, Long might have just bitten his lip and let it go. Coaches told players, "The way to get back at a guy is to beat him on the scoreboard." Most of the time, the players believed it. You picked your spots to fight. Lenny Wilkens—Ferrell's coach in the game—said that when he was with the old St. Louis Hawks in the 1960s, the Hawks players would tell Wilkens not to fight if he was being roughed up.

"Dribble our way and bring the guy with you," they'd say.

Wilkens would dribble to the side of the court, where someone such as Cliff Hagan or Bob Pettit would level the guy with a blind pick or an elbow. It might not happen until the next quarter, but eventually the score would be settled—and the guy who was decked usually knew he had it coming, so he took the punishment.

But now, no one waits. The code of the streets is that you can't back down, not even for a second.

After Ferrell put a finger in Long's face, Long grabbed Ferrell by the throat, trying to shut him up in the most direct way possible.

"Alienation permeates the inner-city community," wrote Anderson. "Its basic requirement is to display a certain predisposition to violence . . . to maintain his honor, a man must show that he is not someone to be 'messed with' or 'dissed.' In general, a person must 'keep himself straight' by managing his position with respect to others [and show] that one is capable of violence and mayhem when the situation requires it."

Violence and mayhem is exactly what happened after Long grabbed Ferrell's neck. Both benches emptied, players threw punches and jumped on each other's backs. The remarkable thing is that only one person was hurt—Miami assistant coach Alvin Gentry, whose arm was broken. He was trying to be a peacemaker by pulling away bodies, but wound up falling under several players, and his arm was smashed against the hardwood floor.

Why did the fight happen?

Because Ferrell wanted to embarrass Long. This was the ultimate "face job." You dunk in a guy's face, then you get in the guy's face to tell him about it.

Long was publicly humiliated. He had to show that he was "capable of violence and mayhem" if that was what the situation required—or what he felt he needed to do to keep his honor and stature in the eyes of his teammates and the public. So he went after Ferrell.

For neither player was the play enough. They just couldn't let it go. Just as today in the city young men are very concerned about what others think of them, so they show off by wearing $100 tennis shoes and $200 team jackets. In almost any high school, kids love to dress up—and thus put themselves above the pack. But in the city, Anderson maintains, having a lot of nice things makes you a target. Someone wants your jacket or shoes for two reasons: 1. So they can have the status symbols they can't afford. 2. Because they raise themselves up and put you down at the same time when they take your prized possessions.

Deadly fights can break out over a jacket, because just giving it up makes you less than a man. There is more honor in the eyes of your friends to die in the attempt to keep your jacket than to live without it.

The disintegration of the family lies behind this behavior and attitude. Many young men come from homes that are "fraught with anger, verbal disputes, physical aggression and even mayhem," according to Anderson. Some kids grow up fighting because it's all they know and because they have learned to like it. There is a perverse satisfaction that comes from beating someone to a pulp, especially if you have decided that the person has done something to deserve it. That is why revenge movies have always been so popular.

But what works well on the big screen often doesn't translate well to reality. It's the difference between reel life and real life, though many kids fail to understand the distinction. And some of these kids grow up to be NBA basketball players.

"There were fights when we played [in the 1960s]," said John Havlicek. "Maybe we even had as many fights as they do today. But what I've never seen before is how much anger these players have today. They seem to step on the floor angry about something. Then it festers and blows up. Some of the fights really don't have much to do with basketball. It's like all this anger just builds up and explodes."

*   *   *

Not all NBA players are from hard-core street settings. Many are the product of "decent families," as Anderson characterizes them. But living in the city means that "even youngsters whose homes reflect mainstream values—and the majority of the homes in the community do—must be able to handle themselves in a street-oriented environment," wrote Anderson.

There is a war between the "decent families" and the "streets" for the hearts and souls of the children. You can see that in the macho setting that is today's NBA. You see it in the games on a play such as a dunk. A guy doesn't just slam, now he hangs on the rim and growls. *Look at me. Fear me. I am a man.* We have dunkers and growlers such as Chris Webber, who came from a two-parent, middle-class family and attended Detroit Country Day High, a prep school. But he hung out on summer teams with Jalen Rose, who was from Detroit's mean streets. And he took on Rose's demeanor.

A similar kind of clash of values plays itself out in the physical—if not brutal—defense played by teams like the bad boy Detroit Pistons or today's New York Knicks. Consider Derek Harper. He played for ten years with the Dallas Mavericks, who in their glory days with Sam Perkins, Rolando Blackman, and Mark Aguirre were known as a highly skilled finesse team. Their critics insisted that the Mavs may have been "too soft." Certainly no one considered Harper to be a thug or a player you'd picture in a playoff brawl that spilled into the stands, only ten rows away from where commissioner David Stern was sitting.

In 1994, Harper was traded to the Knicks, and the 6-foot-4 guard moved into the lineup. The Knicks under Pat Riley had adopted the Bad Boys persona. They scowled, growled, and led the league in flagrant fouls. They were from the nation's biggest city, where life is perceived to be ugly, harsh, and tough. Only the strongest survive.

The message Harper received when he joined the team was never spoken, but was still clear: "You're in New York now. Are you man enough to play for the Knicks?"

In the 1994 Eastern Conference semifinals, Harper was being guarded by Chicago's Jo-Jo English.

"You could see something coming," said Bulls coach Phil Jackson. "It started in the back court, with them bumping, scratching, and pushing each other. You had two guys who didn't want to back down."

Jackson said that Harper put his face in English's face—almost, but not quite, head-butting English. Others—including Harper—insist that English was trash-talking and baiting him. English was the twelfth man on the Bulls, Harper a starter; if both players got into a fight and were ejected, the advantage certainly would go to the Bulls.

Anyway, after the bumping and talking, Harper threw a forearm at English's head. The two sort of body-slammed each other and rolled on the floor and into the courtside seats. Riley and Jackson ran onto the court along with several players. Riley grabbed Harper and screamed at his point guard for losing his cool. Yes, most of the coaches and players tried to be peacemakers, but several fans sitting in the first row still found themselves in the middle of a brawl.

John Starks—a product of the mean streets of Tulsa—supposedly was kicked by a female fan. He was grabbed by a security guard. He cursed the guard, then reportedly looked at the woman and grabbed his crotch.

Sitting near Georgetown coach John Thompson, Stern stared at the fight with the same sense of shock, and feeling the same sick stomach that Robert E. Lee must have felt as he watched Pickett's Charge at Gettysburg.

"I was embarrassed for the players and for the league," said Stern. He added that he knew Harper wasn't a bad guy, and this was out of character for him. Harper had clearly started the incident. He said he was embarrassed. He apologized to everyone. He said he didn't like fighting. He just lost his cool.

"I had Harper for a [television] interview the next day," said NBC's Bob Costas. "I asked him directly if there was something about the atmosphere on the Knicks, something either implied or directly stated by Pat Riley or someone else in the dressing room that made him a different player than he was before. He said, no, there was nothing about the Knicks that led to the incident. He said he had never been in anything ugly like that before, and it just happened."

Maybe Harper was telling the truth. Or maybe he was complying with another code of the streets: you don't snitch on your friends. On the street, guys have been known to take a bad rap and go to jail for a few years rather than admit who really did the deed—and suffer even more dire consequences on the street. A guy who keeps his mouth shut and takes a fall for his friends is considered a hero on the street.

"What bothered me about that incident was the attitude after the fight," said Jackson. "My players heard and read that they shouldn't complain about the physical nature of those games with the Knicks. They should just bite the bullet and understand that this was how the game is played. I was saying, 'Why should the game be played this way?' That kind of attitude just leads to more fights, more explosions."

"Whenever you played the Bad Boys or the Knicks after them, you had a feeling that when they fell behind, they were going to do something to alter your concentration," said Doug Collins. "You knew they were thinking, 'We're getting our asses kicked, so we've got to get them thinking about something else.' Then there would be an incident."

But that attitude is the code of the streets. When the police (or in this case, the officials) cannot establish control, you build your own order any way you can—and any way you can get away with.

"We have to take a stand," said Willis Reed. "I know there are a lot of problems in the world. I know some of our players come to us with problems. But we can control how the game is played. The way the league let Detroit and New York play should not have been allowed to go on. If you want football, go to a football game. If you want wrestling, go to a wrestling match. We know how basketball should be played and we have to demand that they play that way."

"Everyone may be criticizing our style of play," said the Knicks' Anthony Mason. "But if you look around, everyone is copying it."

And a lot of players like it. As Detroit's Bad Boys and Riley's Knicks have proved, if the league allows the bullies to bully, then the style will work because there are plenty of young men in the NBA who are very comfortable in the role of the bully. The one hope is that with the Knicks' second round elmination in 1995, teams and coaches will stay away from those tactics. But a lot of coaches are attracted by it. As Chuck Daly said, coaches like to be known as being "macho."

*   *   *

Talking is nothing new to the NBA. In the 1960s, Sam Jones loved
to torment Wilt Chamberlain. The Boston guard would drive into
the middle of the lane, then loft a ten-foot shot right over Chamberlain's outstretched hands. Sometimes, Wilt would swear he got
a fingernail on the ball, but it would still go in.

To make things worse for Wilt, Jones would say, "Too late,
baby." Then he'd turn and run to the other end of the court.

Wayne Embry remembers Chamberlain catching the ball and
saying, "You can't stop me, Wayne." Then Wilt would dunk on
Embry.

"When I played in the 1950s, I don't remember much trash
talk," said Dolph Schayes. "About the only guy who'd say anything to me was Bill Sharman. We were the top two free throw
shooters in the league. As I'd step to the line, he'd be at the top of
the key and I'd hear him say, 'You're gonna miss.' Other times,
he'd wipe his brow and flip sweat at me just as I was going to
shoot. But that was as provocative as it got."

Larry Bird talked trash.

"Bird would say, 'You better hope I miss, because that's the
only chance you have against me,' " said Charles Barkley. "Larry
talked a lot, but it wasn't personal stuff. It was the 'You can't stop
me' sort of thing."

Former Knicks forward Louis Orr recalled Bird telling him,
"Louie, why are they having you guard me? You have no chance,
Louie."

In the 1991 playoffs, Indiana's Chuck Person and Bird got into
a shoot-out—with both the ball and their mouths.

"That was legendary, trash talking in its purest form," Person
told the St. Paul Tribune: "I was telling him, 'No one on the
planet can guard me, especially a slow guy like you.' Then Larry
would say, 'You can't guard me on the other end.' I'd say, 'I'm not
going to guard you. I'll let someone else guard you. I'm going to
guard McHale.' It was that kind of stuff."

And it was harmless. Why? Because no one was pointing fingers.
No one was screaming in the other's face.

"I talk trash," said Barkley. "Most players do. But in the last few
years, the talk has gotten dirtier. It's real rude, real personal. Now

some of these young guys talk to you after every basket. They make a shot, and they stare at you as they run down the court. Sometimes, they run right over to you and stare."

And that's a problem.

"In the past, guys would talk to each other the whole game but none of the 20,000 fans in the arena or the people watching on TV could tell," said Embry. "It was done in the flow of the game. They would stand near you, be looking away from you—but be talking to you at the same time. Now, they run over to you. They get in your face. Everyone can see that you are being put down."

When an incident like that happens, then the player must react. His manhood is being challenged.

"I recently saw a game where [Houston's] Robert Horry dunked on [New York's] Charles Oakley," said Phil Jackson. "Then he screamed right in Oakley's face. He couldn't have been more than a few inches away from Oakley. What does Oakley do? He gives Horry an elbow in the chest. Luckily, some players stepped between them. But it was clear that Horry was just trying to provoke Oakley into throwing the first punch."

Right now, we need to draw a distinction between trash talk and taunting.

Trash talk is verbal. As Embry mentioned, it's the subtle soundtrack of the game, seldom noticed by the fans. There is no reason to worry about it unless it becomes demeaning, foul, or downright nasty.

What's nasty?

As the late official Earl Strom once said, "I know it when I hear it." A good example would be what Lonnie Shelton said to Paul Pressey in 1985. Shelton was with Cleveland, Pressey with Milwaukee. Shelton thought that Pressey had intentionally tried to trip one of Shelton's teammates. Shelton was a massive guy, 6-foot-6 and 275 pounds. He was out of the old enforcer mode. He once became angry at Buck Williams, and chased Williams from one end of the court to the other—then right up into the stands! Security guards cut Shelton off not far from the popcorn stand. On another occasion, Shelton and his wife were buying ribs on Cleveland's near east side. As they walked out, a mugger pulled a knife on them. Shelton knocked the knife out of the mugger's hand. His wife called the police. When the officers arrived, they saw the 275-pound Shelton sitting on the mugger, quoting the Bible to him.

So Shelton had a reputation and everyone in the NBA—including Pressey—knew it.

When he went up to Pressey and said, "I'll end your career," Pressey took it seriously and stepped back. But some other Milwaukee players heard that and came between Pressey and Shelton. Now Shelton was really angry. He literally threw aside two Milwaukee players and ran after Pressey, who wisely bolted from the court to the dressing room—where once again, Shelton was stopped by the security guards.

We can safely say that things like "I'll end your career" cross the line from trash talk to taunting.

Or we can say that comparing an opponent to a part of the female anatomy is out of line.

Scottie Pippen dunked on Patrick Ewing, then he told Ewing about it. Ewing had fallen down. Pippen looked down at the Knicks center and waved his finger. Later, Pippen defended his actions by saying, "You wait all game for a moment like that."

Only if you are playing a game other than basketball.

It has been suggested that taunting could be for the 1990s what drugs were to the NBA in the 1970s. That was when Bill Russell said, "If ten guys on the court sneezed, eight were losing money."

Drugs are still a concern, but the league's drug program has been reasonably successful. Now, you hear that it's taunting and fighting that could kill the game in the eyes of the public. "That's why we've drawn up rules to stop the taunting," said NBA director of operations Rod Thorn. "Jumping up and down in front of a guy is taunting. Waving a finger in his face is taunting. Making a shot, then running over to a guy and screaming at him is taunting. Anything that an official considers an intent to provoke an altercation is taunting. Look, it has become a sociological thing, how city kids are raised. Trash talking is a part of their lives. They also see it on TV, and that just encourages them. Well, we are going to try and cut down what the kids see from our players by putting a lid on taunting."

Before the 1994–95 season, the NBA said a player who is taunting in the opinion of an official will receive a technical foul and a $250 fine. The second time he does it, he is ejected and subject to further fines.

"The mentality of trash talking is one of the dumber things I've come across," Chamberlain told *Sports Illustrated.* "You're saying, 'Hey, world, I'm the best! Only I can do this right here!' and everybody really knows that it's done by everyone all the time."

Until the late 1980s, throwing a punch didn't necessarily mean a player would be ejected, so taunting wasn't always a good idea, because in the words of Hubie Brown, "If you said something to me that insulted me, in the old days I could just kick your ass."

In the 1960s, the fine for throwing a punch was $25. Often, players would square off and punch each other, the fight would be broken up and a timeout would be called. Everyone would cool off. The game would resume, and the two combatants would be allowed to continue.

"When I coached Cleveland in 1976, we had a highly charged seven-game series with Washington," said Bill Fitch. "But we didn't have any fights. Of course, Washington had big Wes Unseld. When Wes was on the court, no one was interested in fighting."

When the 6-foot-6, 300-pound Unseld later coached the Bullets, there was a game in which Bill Laimbeer went after one of his players. Unseld came on the court, put a bear hug on Laimbeer and threw him down.

End of fight.

"I think fans sometimes like to see fighting," said Chuck Daly.

If nothing else, you have to give Daly credit for being honest. In the 1950s, many NBA teams were owned by men who had hockey backgrounds. They were convinced that a great fight meant good box office, and that was another reason the fines for fighting were so paltry in the early days of the NBA.

But Daly insists that the attraction still holds today—at least for some of the audience.

"There was that big fight between Atlanta and Indiana [involving Ferrell and Long in 1994]," said Daly. "Well, the TV ratings for the game the next night went through the roof—because people wanted to see what would happen, if there would be another fight. I don't think that people in basketball want to see fights. It fits in hockey, but not our sport. I know that the commissioner and the league have come out strongly against it. But when you have combative people who have tempers and when emotions are running high, you're going to have some fights."

Bob Costas said that as far as he knows, there is no research that indicates a consistent pattern of higher TV ratings for teams that are known to fight. But it also is true that the networks "sometimes promote these games as if it was the WWF," said Costas, referring to the World Wrestling Federation.

"What I hate seeing today are coward fights," said Fitch. "A coward fight is when you do something to provoke me, but you do it because you know that I can't hit you back."

In its efforts to crack down on fighting, the league instituted its One Punch and You're Gone rule. This may eventually create more problems than it solves.

"Here is how it works now," said Hubie Brown. "You're a professional. You can kick my ass playing the game every night of the week. I know this. I'm also an asshole. I know that if I can get you to throw a punch at me, you're gone. I may get fined for taunting, but you're history if I can get you to throw a punch. So me, the idiot, gets in your face. I bump your chest and yell at you. You, the professional, can just take it and look like a coward to the other players and fans. You have been emasculated in public, now what are you going to do? If you react, you get thrown out. The professional player should not have his manliness challenged by some moron—and the moron gets rewarded if you knock his head off, as anyone else in the building would do if they were in the professional's position. Players are people, too. Some nights, they just can't take the crap from the idiots. But when the rules protect the idiots, something is wrong."

Okay, Hubie, fix it.

"We have to quit rewarding the morons," said Brown. "Make the first technical $1,000. The second technical [for taunting] is $5,000 and an automatic suspension. The coaches also can do it. They can just tell their players not to act like morons, and punish them if they do. But if the coaches don't do it, then the league must and it should come down hard."

Actually, Brown should go even further with his suggestion. The league should come down hard on the player *and the coach*. If your player is ejected for taunting and/or fighting, so is the coach. The coach also should receive a fine similar to what the player receives.

If players from the same team are continually involved in these incidents, suspend the coach for five games. That will get people's attention.

There are going to be some fights. The players are too big, the stakes too high, and often the court feels too small. The remarkable thing is that there have been so few injuries from fighting.

"But guys have gotten hurt, and the players should be made aware of that," said Fitch. "I would get a picture of Rudy Tomjanovich lying in the hospital bed after he had been punched by Kermit Washington. Rudy T's face was the ugliest mess I've ever seen in my life. If they published that picture in every player's playbook at the start of the season as a warning of what can happen in a fight, I think it would get noticed. Let the players know that fights can hurt—even end their careers. Then start suspending people for five to ten games. That is how you can keep this stuff under control."

What else can the league do to fight some of society's problems that come into the NBA with its players?

"We have too many kids in the NBA who have no idea how to act like adults," said Wayne Embry. "In high school and college, the coaches or the street agents were always there to make things easy for them, to cover up their mistakes. Most of these kids weren't pushed to do well in the classroom. They had to do enough to stay eligible, and that was it. They had tutors, counselors, everyone under the sun to help them. Then they turn pro and the agent is there to not only handle the contract, but in some cases the agent does everything for a kid—I mean even pay his phone and electric bills. He'll give the player a monthly allowance. Some of these guys get through with a ten-year NBA career and they have no idea what it means to balance a checkbook and pay the bills because they never had to do it before."

Doug Collins sees another problem.

"If an eighteen-year-old wants to play in the NBA, the only way to get there is to go to college," says Collins, who spent a year as an assistant coach at Arizona State. "But many of these kids aren't either academically prepared for college or interested in doing college work. But we put them into an academic environment where they don't want to be and we expect them to be successful. What happens? The coach becomes responsible for educating these kids and keeping them eligible. Suddenly, you have someone writing term papers for these kids, you have them taking cake classes—you are promoting dishonesty, sending all the wrong messages. And if the kid can play, but he flunks out, no big deal, there are fifteen other college coaches waiting to sign the kid. What kind of people come out of this system?"

Often, they are players who aren't very interested in discipline or listening to their coaches.

"It also breeds the desire for immediate gratification," said Collins. "If a high school star enrolls at one college and doesn't play much as a freshman, immediately he is thinking about transferring. An incredible number of players transfer from one school to another these days, and the reason is usually that they want more playing time. School itself has nothing to do with it. In the pros, rookies get upset if they don't play right away, and they get down on the coach. They have never been taught to wait, to pay dues. Instead of saying, 'I'm going to bust my ass in practice and play so well that the coach has to put me on the floor,' kids say, 'The coach doesn't like me, I'm outta here.' Most of the kids coming into the NBA today do not last four years in college. They leave school early because the money is so big. But they are younger and more immature than the players of ten or twenty years ago. When I was in college, most guys played four years. If you were a good college player, you picked up a lot of international experience in the summers, playing on the Pan-American team, in the World Games, and the Olympics. Now they have taken the Olympics away from the college kids. As for the other events, they help a kid mature, and that pays off once the kid comes into the NBA."

The fact that freshmen were ineligible for varsity play until 1972 helped the maturation process and caused them to stay in school longer, since there were no freshmen phenoms.

Then you add in the money factor.

"There are some guys that it doesn't matter if you give them 2 bucks or 20 million, they give you all they have on the court," said Richie Adubato. "But some players are lazy and have spent their lives just living off their basketball talent. Their goal is to get to the NBA. They get there and sign a $20 million contract. Where is their motivation to improve, to bust their ass in the summers? They already have the NBA. They have the contract and they haven't even played a pro game. That is when coaching is tough."

Chuck Daly talks about basketball reflecting society. Some players get hooked on drugs, others on women and wild spending. Some have parents and other relatives who look at them as a meal ticket, and before a player knows it, that multimillion dollar contract doesn't seem so rich because he's making three house payments and bought five cars for the people who were close to him growing up.

"But what we've lost in the pro game is rewarding players for winning," said Daly. "I remember after we won our first title [1989] in Detroit, looking at the guys and realizing that we were one of the lowest paid teams in the league. For all of us—including me—winning that title was the ticket to big money. Now we have MTV basketball. Kids watch TV and see guys tearing down playgrounds and bouncing balls off buildings to make shots. They figure that pro basketball means a big contract, your own shoe commercials, and rap records—all by the time you are twenty-one. Our young players are being taught that they will go to college for a few years, then walk right into the NBA All-Star Game. As a coach, you talk about hard work, blocking out, playing defense, and the young player is thinking that none of that will get him what he wants. Winning doesn't even get him what he wants. He isn't interested in the team. He wants to know what he can get out of the game for himself."

Cotton Fitzsimmons said that you have to be careful of the kind of people you draft.

"If you take a kid from a high school and college program where there was discipline, and if you insist on discipline with this kid at the pro level, you'll be fine," he said. "But if you take a kid from a school where he was allowed to do what he wanted, why would he be any different in the pros?"

Disciplining the modern player is something that every NBA coach discusses and worries about.

"Suppose you have a star player who steps out of line," said Chuck Daly. "The temptation for a coach is just to suspend the guy. But if you do that, you hurt your team on the floor because you are depriving the other players of that star's talent. It makes it harder to win the game. The front office may say that they want discipline, but they see this guy who is making $2 million and they don't want him suspended. They want him earning that money. They want to win. They want to sell tickets. To sell tickets, you have to win and the coach knows that. So it's nice to say that you're going to be a disciplinarian, but it isn't always practical. As a coach, you are usually into crisis management more than discipline."

Teams have to draw a line.

"At some point, we have to tell these kids that we expect them to act like adults," said Embry.

You wonder what would happen if Minnesota's J.R. Rider had been with a team such as Cleveland, Utah, Phoenix, Chicago, or New York—teams where the general managers and the coaches are on the same page when it comes to discipline. During his rookie season with the Timberwolves, Rider averaged 16 points, but he also had an incident with a female bartender. The police report stated that Rider kicked her in the back. He pleaded guilty to fifth-degree assault and disorderly conduct. He was sentenced to thirty-five hours of community service on September 7, 1994. He was supposed to complete them by the end of 1994, and Rider had to miss a Minnesota practice and shootaround in order to work off his sentence during the final week of December at the Mission Care Detox Center in Plymouth, Minnesota. He mostly made beds and filed papers, although he was four hours late for his first session. He found himself under a legal gun to complete his community service term in that last week of 1994, because he would have had to do a day in jail for every hour he failed to work.

The Timberwolves fined him $31,707.02—two days' pay—for missing the two practices. They hoped that Rider would start to get the message that growing up has everything to do with pro basketball, but it was hard to know if he indeed understood. Yes, losing $31,000 should get his attention, but when a twenty-three-year-old is worth over $20 million, who knows? Furthermore, Rider had several other clashes with Minnesota coach Bill Blair in 1994–95, and was suspended twice—but the message never did sink in.

"I can't speak for other teams, but we [the Cavaliers] expect our players to conduct themselves with dignity and maturity on and off the court," said Embry. "I'm not saying that they must be perfect. Everyone makes mistakes. But we as an organization have to let the players know that we stand behind our coach, that we want discipline and we will enforce the rules we have on the team."

Embry proved it when he ran into a problem with Ron Harper in the late 1980s. Harper was the number eight pick in the 1986 draft, and averaged 19 points in his first three seasons with the Cavs. But Embry did not like some of Harper's friends. They were guys Harper grew up with on the mean streets of Dayton, Ohio. Some of them had gravitated into the drug trade and other unsavory activities. Embry warned Harper several times to try to cut the cord with these associates. Harper told Embry that he had no right to dictate who he considered his friends. After several talks with Harper on this subject, Embry traded him and two first-round picks to the L.A. Clippers for the draft rights to Danny Ferry.

Neither Embry nor anyone else ever said Harper used drugs or did anything illegal. Nor did Harper ever show any signs of drug use—being late for practice or behaving erratically.

"But I just didn't want those guys [Harper's friends] around my team," said Embry. "Maybe one guy [Harper] can handle being around those type of people, but I didn't want my other players exposed to them."

It turned out to be a disastrous and expensive deal for the Cavs. While Embry obviously has had doubts about the on-court results, he has never questioned his decision to trade Harper; in his view, it was a matter of keeping discipline on his team.

"Look at our recent champions," said Embry. "The Chicago Bulls had discipline. Michael was the leader of the team. Phil Jackson had the respect of the players. Their guys weren't always getting into scrapes or skipping practice. I didn't like the way the Pistons played, but that team had very strong leadership and internal discipline when they won their titles. Obviously, the Celtics and Lakers of the 1980s were class acts, and more recently Houston believes in discipline. Look how the Rockets handled Vernon Maxwell."

Another team that has all the right values is Utah. In their entire careers, Karl Malone and John Stockton have missed a grand total of eight games. These guys show up when they are told, work hard, and are nice to their fans. They never went to team owner Larry Miller and demanded to be traded, even though Salt Lake City is the smallest NBA market, and both Dream Teamers would have received far more endorsement contracts and media attention elsewhere. These guys each said they wanted the small-town atmosphere for their families.

So what happens? Derrick Coleman, a career underachiever, calls Malone "an Uncle Tom . . . a fake." Of course, Malone is everything Coleman should be, on the court and off. Instead of trying to learn from that example, Coleman attacked one the NBA's true role models by insisting he sells out to the white man. It is a situation faced by excellent students in inner-city schools every day, where they are ridiculed simply because they achieve and follow the rules.

"I find it humorous when I turn on ESPN and someone is whining about the lack of discipline in the NBA," said Hubie Brown. "It's like they've just noticed it now. No kidding. We've been building up to this for years. For a while, they thought anyone could coach in this league. They thought that the coaches who believed in discipline were out of touch, and a lot of the disciplinarian coaches found themselves out of jobs. Well, you try coaching these guys and keeping discipline. You see how tough it is. The teams that have tried to keep discipline are the ones that have been winning."

Pat Riley brought discipline to the Knicks in the early 1990s. He wasn't afraid to suspend John Starks or Anthony Mason when the two headstrong stars stepped out of line. He also benched them and other players for failing to play and to practice according to Riley's team concept. That discipline helped the Knicks come to within one game of the 1994 title, even though they certainly weren't the second most talented team in the NBA.

Orlando is a rising power not just because Shaquille O'Neal and Penny Hardaway are great players, but they appear to be good guys. They show up for practice on time, work hard, and have managed to stay out of trouble. And that is why the Magic have become an elite team.

Embry and others in the NBA talk about demanding that their players follow a higher standard of conduct than some of them had to adhere to in high school and college. It is almost a page out of Shelby Steele's fine book *The Content of Our Character*. Steele is an English professor at San Jose State. In one of his essays, he states that the reason blacks have been able to compete (and often beat) whites in athletics is that the black athletes are held to high standards—just as high, or in some cases higher than whites—by their coaches. This is not an affirmative action or quota situation. It was athletic Darwinism, and the strongest survived. He points to the NBA and the fact that over 70 percent of the players are black as an example of how blacks can succeed and are willing to pay the price for that success.

But this isn't as much a racial issue as it is a human one. The Timberwolves had problems with Rider, who is black. They have also had trouble with Christian Laettner, who is white. Laettner has verbally attacked his teammates as being selfish and his coaches as being incompetent. Both players need the same thing: discipline from the coach and a front office that tells them that the coach is boss.

"I don't like the situation, but I don't think it is hopeless," said Embry. "I just believe that we have to make more demands, and make sure the players know that we are serious about discipline. These kids want to play. They have made sacrifices to get to the NBA. If you build your team with good people and have a strong coach, the message goes out that you expect your players to act the right way. This is not the easiest way to build a team because sometimes you pass on a talented player you know might help you. But to me, it's the right way to run a team."

5 When the Players Run the Show

The year was 1987, and Harry Weltman was interviewing for a job as the general manager of the New Jersey Nets.

"I spoke to the guys who were the seven main owners," said Weltman. "I mentioned my philosophy for rebuilding the franchise. I told them that there was hardly any talent, and it would take four to five years to turn the franchise into a contender. This was a team with Darryl Dawkins, Micheal Ray Richardson, Albert King, Otis Birdsong, Orlando Woolridge—guys who were either old, injured, or had other personal problems. I said we needed to get some young players and build a nucleus for the future, and I discussed my approach to the draft, trades, and free agents. I spoke for several hours."

Then Weltman asked if anyone had a question.

No one said a word.

Weltman asked, "You sure that everything is clear? You don't have any questions?"

Finally one of the owners asked, "Would you trade Buck Williams for Ralph Sampson?"

Weltman was a bit stunned, because this was the kind of thing you would have expected to hear when Angelo from Fort Lee called WFAN.

"I'll get to that later," Weltman said. "For now, I want to confine this discussion to philosophy and the basic strategy for building this team."

No one else had any other questions; Buck Williams for Ralph Sampson was it. Weltman walked out of that room having no idea if he would be hired as the next general manager. He had held that job with the Spirits of St. Louis of the old American Basketball Association, and with the Cleveland Cavaliers from 1982 to 1986.

Unfortunately for Weltman, he was hired.

"Ralph Sampson," said Al Menendez, shaking his head. "I know exactly who asked that question. It was Bernie Mann. He was one of the owners, and every other day he was asking us when we were going to trade for Ralph Sampson. He thought that Sampson would solve all our problems."

Menendez was the Nets' player personnel director from 1979 to 1988. Like Weltman, he discovered that the Nets had lots of own-ers—and lots of opinions.

"There were seven owners," said Weltman. "They all had their friends, relatives, and whomever they talked to about the team and the kind of job the general manager and coach were doing. Each owner seemed to have a friend or relative 'who really knows the game.' Furthermore, this 'expert' wasn't even going to charge us for the advice. One owner tells you one thing, another owner tells you, 'Don't worry, we're with you. Don't listen to the other owner.' You couldn't even take votes at the meetings with the owners, because they all had different shares in the team. You'd find a guy who spoke with a loud voice and had a strong person-ality, and you'd think that he had a lot of clout. Then you'd be told that the guy owned only three percent of the team, so don't listen to him. Some of the owners didn't get along with each other. After a while, you found you couldn't get them to agree on anything—even when to have the next meeting."

There are some special reasons why the New Jersey Nets are an NBA punchline. Consider the fact that they have given serious thought to changing their name to the Swamp Dragons, because that's where they play—in the Meadowlands in a swamp across the George Washington Bridge from Manhattan.

Long, long ago, the Nets were a highly successful franchise in the ABA. They played on Long Island, were known as the New York Nets, and won ABA titles in 1974 and 1976. But when the ABA-NBA merger came after the 1975–76 season, the Nets had to sell Julius Erving to Philadelphia to help pay their $3 million ad-mission fee to the NBA.

The franchise has never recovered.

"New York is so close and the Knicks' hold on the basketball fans in that area is so strong, it is really difficult for the Nets to have their own identity," said Weltman. "There is no city or core area from which to draw your fans. There are just a bunch of towns in the general area, and each one has its own mayor, police, and fire department. They view themselves as separate entities. And you're sure not going to get the fans from New York City; they are already going to Knicks games."

But the real problem is ownership—namely, the owners' refusal to give a basketball man full command of the team.

"Several of the owners in New Jersey wanted to schmooze with the players," said Weltman. "Some of them were nothing but fans, and they were just out to get the ears of a player or coach. Sometimes, we had more friends and relatives of the own- ers in our locker room after a game than we had fans in the stands."

According to several men who have been in the meetings they would sound like this:

OWNER No. 1: "I think we need to promote. We've got to reach out into the community and let people know we're here."

OWNER 2: "Which community? New York or New Jersey? I don't think we should promote at all. We should save the money."

OWNER No 1. "No, you've got to spend money to make money."

OWNER 3: "Well, if we're going to spend money, let's spend it to get some players and win some games."

OWNER No. 4: "No, we should save the money, go young, and build through the draft."

OWNER No. 1: "I don't care what we do with the players, I'm just saying we should promote."

OWNER No. 4: "Can we wrap this up? I got a meeting in ten minutes."

GENERAL MANAGER: "I just want to make this clear that we talk about our plan for rebuilding this team, and we agreed that it is going to take at least four years—"

OWNER NO. 3: "Four years? We can't be that patient. Let's do it now in case we want to sell the team."

OWNER NO. 5: "Who wants to sell the team?"

OWNER NO. 3: "I just said in case we might want to sell the team."

OWNER NO. 6: "I don't want to sell."

GENERAL MANAGER: "I thought we were talking about what we could do to help the team."

OWNER NO. 7: "Any thoughts about Ralph Sampson?"

"The owners refused to follow a chain of command, and that is why the eternal question that hangs over the Nets is 'How the hell did we get into this mess?' " said Weltman. "It took me two years of dealing with the owners to figure out whose word could be trusted, who meant what he said, and who really understood the situation. We'd have meetings and waste hours on something that just wasn't going to happen, like hiring Rick Pitino as coach. The meeting would degenerate into me telling them why Pitino wouldn't take the job in the first place, and could we please discuss something that was relevant to the team?"

Since entering the NBA in 1977–78, the Nets have had only six winning seasons—none of which reached as high as fifty wins. Only once, in 1984, did the Nets ever win a round in the play-offs—and then they lost in the second round. Some big names have coached the team: Kevin Loughery, Stan Albeck, Bill Fitch, Willis Reed, Chuck Daly, and Larry Brown. Only Fitch and Loughery survived more than two full seasons. In their nineteen NBA seasons, they have had eleven coaches.

"You look at all this futility and you're amazed that the Nets are still in New Jersey," said Menendez. "But the owners are Jersey guys who at least can agree upon the fact that they are very proud of their state. They are tied to a strong long-term lease at the Meadowlands, which makes it hard for them to move. But when you come down to it, those guys just like owning a basketball team."

When Weltman was hired in 1987, he inherited a 24-58 team that was coached by Dave Wohl. Some of the owners wanted to keep Wohl; others wanted him fired. The Nets started 2-13, and Weltman replaced Wohl with veteran scout Bob McKinnon as he searched for a new coach. McKinnon's record was 10-29 when he gladly handed over the team to Willis Reed.

"I thought I had prepared myself to coach," said Reed. "I'd played in the league [with the Knicks] and won a championship. I coached the Knicks into the playoffs in my first year. I coached in college at Creighton and I had been an assistant under Mike Fratello with the Atlanta Hawks. But when I came to the Nets, I just didn't have the same fire after a while. I coached part of one season (7-21 in 1987–88) and all of the next year (26-56 in 1988–89). Then I talked to the owners about maybe moving into the front office and helping to build the organization that way. They offered me a five-year contract to work with Harry Weltman. I didn't know if I'd last the whole five years, but I knew that they had to pay me for five years and I could use the security."

So Weltman and Reed went coach hunting and settled on Bill Fitch right before the 1989–90 season.

"Bill had left Houston and had been out of basketball for a year," said Weltman. "I went to Bill because I wanted someone with experience, someone who had helped build a team—as he did in Cleveland and Houston—and someone who could teach young players. I also needed someone who could handle the losing and handle the toughest situation in the NBA without going crazy."

In 1989–90, most of the Nets' main players were injured, rookie Dennis Hopson turned out to be a bust, and Weltman was fired at the end of the season, taking the fall for the 17-65 record.

Reed was elevated to general manager. Fitch returned as coach, and the team's record improved to 26-56. Some of the moves made by Weltman—such as trading for Mookie Blaylock and Sam Bowie—were helping to build a decent team. Reed was able to draft Derrick Coleman and acquire Drazen Petrovic and Terry Mills in shrewd deals. As the 1991–92 season began, the Nets—or at least their owners—were talking playoffs. The Nets made Kenny Anderson the number two pick in the draft, against the advice of Fitch, who wanted almost anyone but Anderson; he liked Larry Johnson, Dikembe Mutombo, and Billy Owens. Reed seemed to favor Owens and Mutombo. Both basketball men believed their point guard situation was solid with the emerging Blaylock, so why use such a high pick on Anderson? But minority owner Joe Taub convinced his brethren that Anderson was just the guy the Nets needed. Yes, he was leaving Georgia Tech after his sophomore year and was frail and young, but he was a New York native and would bring flash and attention to the franchise. So the Nets took Anderson, who held out for all of training camp and the first two weeks of the regular season. After signing a five-year, $14 million contract, he showed up out of shape. Fitch was not about to hand the kid the point guard job, and the gritty Blaylock certainly wasn't yielding to the rookie. So Anderson sat.

Fitch also clashed with Derrick Coleman, who didn't think he needed to practice hard, or even to show up on time. The Nets started at 7-18, and Taub and some other owners decided they needed a new coach. He had lunch with Jimmy Valvano, the former N.C. State coach who was then working for ESPN. Taub offered Valvano a five-year, $3 million deal to take over the Nets. Word leaked out to the New York area newspapers, and reports said that Valvano would take over the team after the Nets returned from a four-game road trip.

"Why doesn't Jimmy do it now?" asked Fitch. "Let him go on the road for these four games and get a taste of what this league is really like."

While Taub was one of the Nets' main owners in the early 1980s, his share of the team had diminished to five percent by 1991. While he liked Valvano, it was unclear if he was speaking for the other owners when he offered Valvano the job—which turned out not to be a real offer after all.

Fitch then made a decision.

"I was going to get the Nets into the playoffs and then I was going to quit," he said. "Because of the structure of the front office, I couldn't discipline players the way I normally would. Fines and suspensions just weren't going to work [because the owners wouldn't back him]. I was going to be out of there at the end of the season anyway, so if I suspended a talented player, what would I gain? Nothing. I realized that I was in a new era of coaching."

Fitch called a team meeting. He announced that players would not be fined or suspended.

"Practice is at ten in the morning," Fitch told the team. "If you guys all show up at ten, then we'll start. If some people are missing, fine, we'll wait. If we have to wait until two in the afternoon, we'll wait until two in the afternoon. I've got all day."

Some days, practices started at ten. Other days, they began at eleven. By the end of the season, the players were on time for most practices.

With six weeks to go in the season, there was a game where Fitch ordered Derrick Coleman to return to action. Coleman refused to leave the bench. After the game, Fitch calmly told reporters that Coleman had elected not to reenter the game. It made headlines the next day in the area papers, and Coleman was battered on the local talk shows.

The Nets were winning, but the heat on Coleman was so intense that Fitch decided he needed to offer some relief.

"There was a game where we were being blown out with ninety seconds left," said Fitch. "I went over to [starting small forward] Chris Morris, who was on the bench and figuring he was done for the night. The game was over for all practical purposes. But I told Chris that I wanted him to go back in for the last ninety seconds. I knew he wouldn't go. I didn't even want him in the game. I just wanted him to do the same thing as Derrick, so he'd take some of the pressure off Derrick."

Morris stared at Fitch as if the fifty-seven-year-old coach had lost his mind. He told Fitch to forget it. He didn't move.

Once again, Fitch just mentioned to reporters in passing that Morris didn't feel like playing in the last ninety seconds.

More headlines. More heat.

"I got Morris on the same list with Coleman in the eyes of the media and fans," said Fitch. "I didn't have to get on their ass; the media and fans did a better job of that than I ever could. For the rest of the year, those guys set the tone. They busted their butts for me and led us into the playoffs."

The Nets were 33-24 after that 7-18 start and the Valvano rumors. They faced Cleveland in the first round, losing in four competitive games.

When the playoffs ended, Fitch met with the front office.

"I had the satisfaction of getting a team into the playoffs when no one else thought we'd do it," he said. "It was the most unorthodox coaching job of my life. In my three years, we went from 17 to 26 to 40 wins. I believe they wanted me back, but I chose to leave [because of how he was treated during the Valvano rumors]."

Fitch quit, and the Nets paid him $400,000 for the final year of his contract.

On paper, it seemed like a great idea: If anyone could control the Nets, it would be Chuck Daly. After all, he was ringmaster of the Bad Boys in Detroit, and had a remarkable nine-year tenure with the Pistons.

Why would Daly sign with the Nets?

He said it was the challenge.

More than likely, it was the chance to earn over $1 million a year. Daly has been driven as much by money as by victories, and the Nets offered him a chance at both. Like every other coach who accepted the Nets job, he figured he could handle the owners. He agreed to turn the point guard job over to Anderson, and he didn't mind Blaylock being traded—though he thought GM Willis Reed could have received more than Rumeal Robinson in return, and he said so publicly.

In 1992–93, Daly's first Nets team had a 42-29 record when he lost Kenny Anderson, Chris Dudley, and Sam Bowie to injuries. The team limped into the playoffs, losing ten of its last eleven games. The Nets then lost to Cleveland in five games in the first round of the playoffs.

Daly came back for more. He wasn't thrilled when the Nets failed to re-sign free agent forward Terry Mills. He was shattered when twenty-point scorer Drazen Petrovic was killed in an auto accident in Europe. He told the front office that he was concerned about Sam Bowie's health, but he was stunned when Bowie was traded for Benoit Benjamin. Yes, Benjamin was healthy, but he often just stood on the court as if he were lost. Daly asked the

160-pound Anderson to go on a weight program. Anderson wasn't interested. "Kenny doesn't buy into doing weights," Daly explained, shaking his head.

One of his reserve forwards, Jayson Williams, was questioned by police for allegedly shooting at tires in the Meadowlands parking lot. In another incident, Williams and Coleman had an encounter with rowdy teenagers outside a nightclub at 3 A.M. after the Nets had lost to the Knicks in a playoff game. Coleman was charged with third-degree assault, but the charges were dismissed. Instead of asking why his players were out at three in the morning after a playoff game, GM Reed defended them by wondering why the teenagers' parents allowed their sons to be away from home so late.

Coleman was a constant test. In the words of Hall of Famer Tom Heinsohn, "Coleman could be the greatest power forward to ever play the game. The best ever. But he doesn't have the drive of a guy like Karl Malone. He is a guy who has been paid for potential, not production."

Even Charles Barkley said, "Coleman has more talent than I did in my prime with Philadelphia." But Coleman has yet to demonstrate that he can rival Barkley anywhere except at the bank. He had the audacity to turn down an eight-year, $69 million contract extension from the Nets in 1994, and to complain publicly about the paltry offer. He finally did sign a five-year, $37 million contract, and made it seem as if he were doing the fans a big favor.

It's no wonder Daly said, "With this group, I had to pretend I didn't hear things—a lot."

Daly resigned at the end of the 1993–94 season after his team lost in four games to the Knicks in the playoffs.

"That was nothing about the team, just about me," said Daly a year after leaving the job. "I was sixty-three years old. I thoroughly enjoyed coaching in New Jersey. I just decided to do something else."

That's Daly's version, but others had doubts.

"I wasn't surprised that Chuck quit," said Fitch. "He wasn't having any fun. He wasn't in the greatest of health. He had nothing to gain. He was already in the Hall of Fame and had coached the Olympic team to a gold medal. Now he can make as many speeches and appearances as he wants. He doesn't have to show up and battle Coleman every day. He got as tired [of some of the players] as the next guy."

"No one was shocked by Chuck leaving," said Menendez. "He didn't seem happy in New Jersey. Coleman is your modern player. So is Anderson, to a lesser extent. Morris is out in left field."

"You look at New Jersey and you see a disciplinarian coach like Bill Fitch, who had guys yelling at him in practice and not going into games, and you know the problem is not Bill Fitch," said Phil Jackson. "Then you see what happened to a great coach like Chuck Daly there. It has to make you wonder."

But the one guy ambushed by Daly's decision was Willis Reed.

"I was turkey hunting in upstate New York and I wasn't even near a phone," he said. "I went to a friend's house. He had been mountain lion hunting, and he wanted to show me [the lion he'd shot]. Then I left his house and went to sleep in my hunting camp, deep in the woods. My friend had a phone in his house, and a few hours later he came to get me, waking me up. He said, 'Your wife just called and your owners are looking for you.' At that point, I had no idea what had happened. I drove to town, used a pay phone and called one of the owners. He said Chuck was resigning. All I could think was, 'Oh no, I've got to find a new coach again!' Chuck had been going back and forth about coaching another year. One day he wanted to stay, the next he was going to quit. But that's just Chuck's personality. I figured he'd be back."

Reed mentioned that Daly said his health was an issue, that the coach had missed a game in Atlanta and ended up in the hospital for a day because of dehydration and exhausion.

Not knowing what to do next, the owners asked Reed if he wanted to coach the Nets. He knew better than that.

"They did the same thing when Bill Fitch left," said Reed. "I told them again that I had absolutely no interest in coaching."

Reed began compiling a list of coaches. He said he contacted a prominent college coach, whom he doesn't wish to name because the coach declined to interview.

"My five candidates were Paul Silas, Bill Blair, Bob Hill, Brendan Suhr, and Butch Beard," he said. "If Mike Fratello were available, I'd have hired him in a second. I worked with Mike in Atlanta and I consider him a great coach. But Mike was with Cleveland. I didn't want to hire a guy whose experience was strictly college, after seeing what happened to Jerry Tarkanian in San Antonio. So I looked at guys who had a lot of experience as NBA assistant coaches."

He settled on Beard.

"He'd played in the NBA for nine years," said Reed. "He was an All-Star player once. He had been an assistant with the Knicks for four years. He was an assistant with us in New Jersey for two years. He also coached college at Howard University. He had a lot of experience, he knew what hard work was about."

Beard signed a two-year guaranteed contract for $400,000 and $425,000. One of the owners, David Gerstein, said, "This team should win 50 games, sure. We're in it for the [championship] ring."

Well, the fifty part was sort of right—the Nets lost 52 games in 1994–95.

Coleman was a problem. Once again, he was not in the best of shape when training camp began. Beard asked all the players to wear a sports jacket to all the games. The penalty was a $500 fine per game. Coleman refused. He handed the front office a blank check and told them to write in the amount for the entire season. He also missed a shootaround the morning of a game in Detroit, his hometown where he owns a house. Coleman said that the roads were icy, his 1970 Nova wouldn't start, and he didn't want to drive his 1957 Buick in the snow. Here is a guy making $3 million, and he's driving a 1970 Nova?

"Don't worry about Derrick," Coleman told the New York media. "Derrick takes care of Derrick. Derrick goes out and gets the job done night after night. I'm not responsible for anyone else. My missing practices and shootarounds doesn't make us lose a game. . . . I don't worry about getting fined. If they fine me or they don't, I don't care one way or the other."

This reasoning is so twisted that it defies comment. It is galling that Coleman sincerely believes the Nets don't grant him enough respect when he gives them none. He was upset they didn't ask him what he thought of Beard before Beard was hired as coach. He also thought he should have been consulted on the new team dress code, so he flaunted it by declaring that his money can buy his way out of it. To him, it was worth it to pay $40,000 not to wear a jacket. This is what happens when a guy who has won nothing makes $5 million a year. Coleman missed 28 games in 1994–95 due to various injuries. He averaged 20 points and 11 rebounds, but shot only 42 percent and had twice as many turnovers as blocked shots.

Meanwhile, Kenny Anderson sulked about the changes Beard made in the offense. He skipped a practice to protest having been benched in the fourth quarter of a game the night before. When he should have been working on his game, Anderson said he "had some personal [things] to take care of," but was spotted in a local "gentleman's club" called Scores. This came only two months after Anderson told reporters he had cleaned up his life and cut down on the party scene.

Coming to the defense of his teammate, Coleman asked the media, "Where were you guys when Dwayne Schintzius skipped practice? Everyone misses practice. Jayson Williams misses practice. I miss practice. Even the coaches miss practice sometimes. Whoop-de-damn-do. I don't feel Kenny owes an apology to anybody."

Like every other Nets coach, Beard had heard about the problems before he took the job, but nothing had prepared him for what he encountered in the swamp by the Meadowlands. He told reporters how these players "are a different animal from when I played." He said, "If I could just get them to concentrate on their job for two hours a night."

Instead, they think of other things.

Before the 1994–95 season opened, Anderson said that he really didn't want to renegotiate his contract; he had three years and $10 million left. But he also said that some of his friends had been telling him about the new deals other players had signed—players whom Anderson considered less productive than himself—and so maybe he did deserve a new deal.

"Mentally, there are a few of us who can play for Bellevue," said Nets forward Jayson Williams. "I don't think Jesus can coach this team."

Beard probably thought the same thing when Chris Morris showed up at practice one day with his shoelaces untied—a strange way of expressing his belief that he wasn't getting enough minutes or shots. Reed usually finds himself in the middle. He seems weary from all the balls he must keep in the air—the owners' ever-changing opinions, the coaches leaving, and the players and their antics and the owners' willingness to indulge the players.

"Life changes, people change, and the world changes," said Reed. "You can't cry because things aren't what they used to be. I know that players are different today than when I played, although we had our share of screw-ups, too. You have to take the players as they are. If you can't accept the fact that the players and the world have changed, you should get another job."

But other teams demand that their players grow up, that they follow rules and act like adults. Not that these teams are prison camps, but the successful teams are careful to populate their rosters with solid and reliable people, and they let it be known that certain misbehavior will not be tolerated. That has never been the case in New Jersey.

"Because the tail has been allowed to wag the dog, you are losing quality coaches like Chuck Daly," said Bob Cousy. "With some of these teams and players, Hubie Brown and Red Auerbach would be anachronisms. They want their coaches to be hand-holders, or the players run upstairs [to the general manager and owner] to complain. As a coach, you have to be able to deliver an ultimatum and carry it out. But with some teams, a coach does that and the players have at them."

New Jersey is one of those teams, and it's why the NBA has been laughing at the Nets for years.

COACHES

6 The Voices of Coaches

W̄ho has to deal with the modern player?
The man on the front line is the coach. He is supposed to keep
the players happy . . . keep his bosses in the front office happy . . .
keep the media and fans happy. Most of all, he has to win games,
or he's out of work. Even the crusty old-timers who are reluctant
to admit that anything is harder today than what they endured in
the NBA are willing to concede that coaching is now more challenging than it ever was before. Don't think so? Just listen in:

CHUCK DALY: To me, a coach is like the CEO of a major company.
Once Toronto and Vancouver come into the league, there will
be only twenty-nine of these jobs, and the average salary will be
about $700,000. That's a CEO kind of pay. But then you look
at the men who are coaching. Their eyes are red and there are
black circles under those eyes. They are physically exhausted.
They are mentally drained. They look awful because they feel
awful. Then you talk to them—and they sound even worse than
they look. It's funny for me to talk about it now because I'm not
coaching, but when I was there it was pretty hard to laugh.

FRANK LAYDEN: After a while, coaches become intellectual cripples.
It goes back to that word, survival. They ask themselves, "What
if I get fired? No one is going to pay me what I'm making now.
What will I do? There are only so many of these jobs, and guys
are lined up to get them. So I better work my ass off." That's
what happens, the coach becomes a workaholic. That is usually
their nature, anyway. A tremendous work ethic and a great imag-

ination is what got them the job in the first place, so what do they do when the pressure is on? They work even harder, and after a while, that's not healthy.

CHUCK DALY: That's because you take the losing personally. You ask yourself, "What can I do to make it better? What am I doing wrong? Is it me? Is it them? Is there something the front office can do?" You dwell on those questions. Even after I won a world title and had spent my entire life in coaching, I was still scared to death of losing. The fear of failure can overwhelm you as a coach. It's always in the back of your mind.

DOUG COLLINS: Coaching tears up most people. If I were an NBA coach right now, I would be incapable of having this kind of conversation. I could talk to you, but my mind would be somewhere else. I'd be thinking about what players we should bring to our summer league team, what skills I could get certain players to work on in the off season, what free agents might help us. Frank is right, you become an intellectual and emotional cripple. You go to bed, but you can't shut off your brain. You are thinking about what kind of fast break would be best for your team, or what you should do on defense. So you toss and turn for a couple of hours, then you finally get up because you know you can't sleep and then you turn on the videotape and go to work all night. By morning, you may have caught a couple of hours of sleep, but you're still exhausted.

CHUCK DALY: Seldom is a CEO fired during his first five years on the job. But in our business, coaches are lucky to last three years in one place. They may tell you that you have five years to turn it around, but you know that you better be playing very well by the third year or you're gone. CEOs don't have fans and talk shows, where the customers think they know everything about every player you have and how he should be used. In basketball, the average guy is the absolute authority on your job, and that's not true in other businesses outside of sports.

RICHIE ADUBATO: Most of the time, a coach needs five years to turn around a losing situation and make it into a solid contender. But you don't get five years, like Dallas gave Dick Motta when he took over their expansion team. You are lucky to get three years. When I was in the rebuilding phase at Dallas [in the early 1990s], the front office told me that I'd be lucky to win 15 games because we had a CBA roster and we were playing for a high lottery pick. They told me not to let the losing eat me up, just do the best I could with the players. Keep them hustling. They understood. But I had to stand out there and take the losses, and no coach is trained to take losing lightly. After a game, I'd go out with my assistants for something to eat. We'd talk about the game. Then I'd get home about 1 A.M., and I'd put a tape of the game into the VCR. I'd sit there, taking notes until I finally fell asleep about four in the morning. I'd wake up in the chair with the notebook in my lap and the VCR still on. Usually, I'd watch those last four minutes. Then I'd have something to eat and go to practice. You do even more coaching with a bad team than you do with a good one.

DOUG COLLINS: The coaches in our business are supposed to be obsessed with their jobs. If you leave your office at three in the afternoon on an off day, some people will wonder why you're not there until nine at night—or even midnight. Other coaches do that. We've created this coaching mentality in the NBA where if you're not killing yourself, then you're not doing a good job. It's not important enough to you. Coaching has ripped up so many marriages. It gives you this tunnel vision. Nothing else is happening around you. You are at your daughter's play, and you sit there, staring. You see it but you don't see it. Your mind is somewhere else. Your son is telling you what happened in school, and you look right at him as if you are listening—but you're not. Your mind is on your team. It's insidious because you don't even realize what coaching is doing to you and your life until you are in very deep. That is why I've always admired Lenny Wilkens, and how he has kept his perspective. He is a rare one.

LENNY WILKENS: The danger in coaching is to let how your team is playing define you as a person. If you are losing, that doesn't make you a bad person or mean that you are doing something wrong in life. I do know that there are things in this life that are out of your control, and you control what you can. I love coaching. I love working with young people. I love close games. I believe that I can do something in the huddle in the final minute of a game—draw up a play or make a substitution—that will help us win. I've never been intimidated by the other coach, because I am confident in myself as a coach. I hate to lose. There are maybe a half-dozen times a year where we will lose a game and I'll have trouble sleeping that night. But most of the time, I am able to go home and be myself.

When I was a young coach in Seattle, my son Randy came up to me right in the middle of a game. He wanted a dollar for a hot dog. It was a great wake-up call for me. It reminded me that while I was a coach, I also was a father. I gave him the dollar and went back to coaching. In my life, my faith and my family come first. Then comes my coaching. I watch tape, but I don't have to watch a game five or six times to know what happened. I know that there are times in your life when you just have to turn off the coaching, and be a husband and a father because those are the most important things.

DOUG COLLINS: Everything Lenny says is true and most coaches know that, but most coaches also push their families aside, especially during the season. That's why I turned down several jobs after I left the Bulls [Collins was fired after the 1989–90 season]. I wanted to see my son play in high school and at Duke. I knew that I had to be there for my wife and my other children. I had to quit being selfish, and coaching makes you selfish.

FRANK LAYDEN: That's because most coaches are scared to death of being fired.

CHUCK DALY: That's especially true if you've been fired once. You find out that the phone stops ringing. You go from being on this roller coaster where there are never enough hours in the day, to having all the time in the world and nothing to fill it. You feel very alone.

DOUG COLLINS: When I took the Bulls job, I was very aware that they had had nine coaches in the previous ten years. Why would

I be any different? But still, when I got fired, it was the only time in my life that I was told I wasn't needed. I had never been cut from a team. I had never been traded. When I retired from basketball, it was because all my injuries caught up with me. So getting fired was very painful. For the first year, I seldom left the house. I was embarrassed. I lived in Chicago, and that made it worse because the team was doing great. I'd read some of the things the players said in the papers [about the coaching] and it would hurt. It is a real blow to your ego. It can flatten you.

RICHIE ADUBATO: Anyone who says they pull for the team that fired them is a liar. I got fired [in 1992–93] after 29 games [and a 2-27 record]. I lived in Dallas and I continued to watch the games on TV because I figured that eventually I'd get a chance to coach or scout again, and I wanted to be ready. I was lucky, because my friends from the Five-Star camps called me a lot, guys like Mike Fratello, Hubie Brown, Dick Vitale, and Dick Versace. We all know that it can happen to any of us. Chuck Daly reminded me of how he was 9-32 in Cleveland. Don Chaney was the coach of the year one year in Houston, and got fired a year later. The worst thing is if the team wins after you get fired. Then you really start to say, "It must have been me." That can really shake you. In my case, the Mavericks were 22-113 in the two years after I was fired. But you still wonder if you'll get back into the league, and if you do—will you ever get another head coaching job?

FRANK LAYDEN: After a guy is fired, then gets a second job, he usually is more cautious. A little of the bravado is gone because the guy thinks, "Hey, I can get fired again." It happened once and it's something he'll never, ever forget. It changed him. It also makes the coach more distrustful, and a little paranoid. If he starts to lose again, he'll blame the refs, the media, the general manager, the players—he'll start to think that they are all against him. That makes him less effective as a person and a coach, and it usually leads to him getting fired a second time. The problem is that we are a country of sore losers. Vince Lombardi's "Winning is the only thing," is bullcrap. There is only one team every year that doesn't lose its last game. I don't want to get too carried away on this, but for years we blamed our soldiers for losing in Vietnam. And too many parents blame their kids for losing in little league or high school. Coaches never prepare themselves for losing. When it comes, they are devastated. But when they win, they aren't happy so much as they are relieved because they didn't lose.

After we lost to the Lakers in the 1988 playoffs, I went through our locker room and hugged every player. I told some guys, "That was better than winning because you guys were great, you gave me everything you had." Our owner [Larry Miller] understood what I meant, but most owners would not. They are bottom-line guys. If you lose, then there must be something wrong with the coach and the team.

WILLIS REED: You are only viewed on your record. When I was a young coach with the Knicks [in 1977–78], we had a winning record in my first season. It was their first winning record in four years. We went to the playoffs for the first time in three years. Everybody said I did a great job. But when I coached New Jersey [1988–89], I was a much better coach. I had gone from the Knicks to Creighton. I was older, more mature, and had more experience. But I lost in New Jersey, and people said I wasn't even as good a coach as I was with the Knicks. The only thing people care about is your record.

CHUCK DALY: Players are not really held responsible for winning or losing. They are judged by the statistics, how many points they scored or rebounds they grabbed. There are no Ws and Ls next to anyone's name but the coach's. That is why we take the losses harder and why we have to live with them for the rest of our lives.

The toughest part of coaching is dealing with the personalities on your team. You are juggling the egos, the work ethics, and the different agendas. These guys are not exactly the most objective judges of their own games. As a coach, you are primarily interested in winning. As players, they are mostly interested in minutes, shots, and what's in it for them—other than the winning.

PHIL JACKSON: A big issue is money. Some player will look at a low-paid coach and say, "He's making less than the lowest-paid player on our team. What kind of credibility does he have?" On a team, it gets to be a world measured by the dollar. Player X will be upset because he believes he's a better player than Player Y, but Player Y is making $100,000 more than Player X. As a coach, there are times when you have to sit a guy in favor of a player making less money. For example, Stacey King was a lottery pick and signed a big contract out of school, but I played several guys [making less] over him. King thought he should play, partly because he was well paid. Some of the other guys on the team saw him sitting there—and they see him making all that money—and it doesn't sit well with them. In Cleveland, it was the same situation with Danny Ferry.

LENNY WILKENS: As a coach, you can't let contracts make out your lineup. It wasn't my fault that Danny Ferry didn't turn out to be the kind of player [the front office] thought he'd be when they signed him. My credibility as a coach comes from playing the best guys—the guys that I believe will help us win. If that meant playing Mike Sanders over Danny Ferry, I did it. The players know. You can't con them. They see who is kicking ass in practice and whose ass is getting kicked. If you are playing someone simply because of the money he makes, the players know and they don't respect the guy or respect you for playing him.

CHUCK DALY: I never addressed the money part of it. It does rear its head because players are worried about what each other makes. But as a coach, you can't do anything about what they make. At the end in Detroit, after we won the championships, money became a bigger issue than it ever was before. The guys had won the titles, now they wanted something else. But most of the time, a coach deals with basketball problems—guys wanting playing time and statistics. Bill Laimbeer used to walk by the stat sheet at halftime, look at it upside down and immediately be able to read how many rebounds he had. Other guys can actually keep track of their points and rebounds in their head as they are playing the game. I don't know how they do it, but they do.

LENNY WILKENS: As a coach, my method of imposing discipline is that I control the minutes. No matter how much money these guys make, they all want to play. If they know that the coach—

and only the coach—determines who plays, then the coach can get a player to do what he wants. I tell my guys that I'll be fair with them. If I put them out there and they don't get back on defense, they are coming out of the game. If they are selfish, they're coming out. I treat them like men and I expect them to respond like men.

PHIL JACKSON: Players are very aware of the circumstances under which a coach is hired. When you bring in a Lenny Wilkens or a Chuck Daly, and the players see that he has a big contract for something like five years, they know that this guy is going to be around for a while. They know that he is being paid a lot of money, so the front office is serious about him as a coach. They are less likely to challenge that guy than they would the coach on a one-year contract where he's not even making the [players'] minimum salary. Part of the reason Chuck Daly brought some order to New Jersey a few years ago was that the players knew he was being paid more than any coach had ever been paid before. The front office was telling the players, "This guy is *not* being fired to make you guys happy. We are *not* going to bite the bullet on this contract. We are very serious about this guy being the coach of the team."

FRANK LAYDEN: Look at what happened to poor Bill Fitch in New Jersey. There were seven owners there and a couple of them were always out there trying to hire their own coach. There were rumors of a new coach in the papers all the time. What does that do to Fitch's authority? The players figure out that the authority figure is not on the bench. He's not the GM. The authority is coming from some of the seven owners, so the players go over the heads of the coach and GM to the owners. Derrick Coleman gets the message that they aren't going to come down on him. If he doesn't like Fitch as the coach, they'll go get a new coach to keep Derrick happy. When the players see that situation, you as a coach have no chance. Your team won't win.

When I was approached by Sam Battistone to coach the Jazz in 1979, I told him that the only way I'd take the job and the only way we could turn the team around was if the coach had total control. A big reason for the Celtics' success was that Red Auerbach had total control. Whitey Herzog had it in baseball when he turned the Cardinals around in the 1980s. In Utah, I was GM and coach. I signed the checks. I wanted the guys to get their checks and notice my name, so they knew I was in charge. I was not a better coach than Hubie Brown, Pat Riley, Jack Ramsay, Chuck Daly, or a lot of other guys. But what helped me in Utah was having control, and the players knowing it. Then the players know that they can't pull a stunt like refusing to go in a game, like Chris Morris and Coleman did to Fitch in New Jersey. The players know that they can't be late for practice. A coach can bring a team together when he has the authority to tell the players, "I want you to be successful, because if you're successful then you will help me win games. If you win games, then you're going to make more money, become All-Stars, and receive more recognition. We need to be like a family, to fight and claw for each other and realize that there are a lot of peripheral foes, as Pat Riley calls them. I can't see you criticizing me in the papers, and I won't criticize you in the papers. As corny as it sounds, we are in this together."

But then the coach has to have the authority to make it his team. If Chris Laettner or one of these guys comes to you and says, "I can't go to practice tomorrow because I have to make a commercial for Nike," the coach needs the clout to say, "Well, then get a job with Nike, because you just retired, baby." You have to know that Laettner can't go behind your back to the general manager or owner and plead his case. You have to know that the owner won't come to you and say, "Let the guy skip practice because we need Laettner." You don't become a dictator. You talk to the guy. If he's been a good guy for you, you maybe can change practice time so he could make his commercial, collect his $100,000 and then come to practice. But you can't let him undercut your authority.

One time, I had a problem with Adrian Dantley. He was a great player for me, but he wanted to miss a practice. The next day, we had a very important game against Dallas.

I said, "Adrian, you miss practice, you can't play in the game."

He said, "I have a good reason."

I said, "What's the reason?"

He said, "I can't tell you."

I said, "Then it's not a good enough reason."

He said, "Well, you let Mark Eaton have a day off in training camp. He missed an exhibition game!"

I said, "Adrian, you know why he missed that game? His sister was getting married. I thought that was more important than an exhibition game, so I let him go."

He said, "Well, I have an important reason, too."

But he wouldn't tell me what it was. It turned out that he had ordered a Rolls-Royce and wanted to go pick it up somewhere because it was being delivered. You know, if he had just told me that, I probably would have let him go, because it was just a practice, not a game. But he wouldn't tell me, and we had a problem over that. As a coach, you want total control, but you also have to be reasonable.

It comes down to this: if a guy pushes you too far—as Dantley did with me on a number of issues—you have to take a "My way or the highway" approach, even if the guy is the leading scorer in the league, as Dantley was. He wouldn't go along with the rules that the entire team had set—my players helped set the rules—so we traded him.

DICK MOTTA: We go through stages in hiring coaches. In the 1970s, it was the college coaches who had a real impact on the NBA, guys like Bill Fitch, Hubie Brown, Jack Ramsay, Cotton Fitzsimmons, and myself. Lately, we went to the ex-players who were supposed to be able to better communicate with today's athletes. But just because a guy was a player doesn't mean he'll make a good coach. When Dallas hired Quinn Buckner, it was an absolute insult to coaching. This is the best basketball league in the world and we're supposed to have the best coaches—and they bring a guy in with no coaching background whatsoever? It was terrible. It's an insult to all the professional coaches who paid all the dues over the years from driving buses to taping ankles. When [Dallas owner] Donald Carter wanted a coach to replace Buckner, I gave him names of three guys: Phil Johnson, Garfield Heard, and Matt Guokas. All had experience. But Donald asked me to take over the team.

RICHIE ADUBATO: Quinn tried to be a very disciplined coach, but he didn't have the credibility. Instead, he alienated everyone. He went after Derek Harper, and Derek Harper is one of the best guys in the league. You don't need to push him around just to show you're boss. Quinn was telling people that Harper wasn't his type of point guard. But Harper was his one veteran. The other eleven players in the clubhouse worshipped the guy. Harper is a good guy. If you have a problem with a player of that caliber, you resolve it, you don't declare war on him. A player like that can control your destiny.

FRANK LAYDEN: Every good coach has had discipline on his team. Why do you think Pat Riley closes his practices to the media? Because he yells at his players and he doesn't want the media to know it. What's wrong with a coach who yells at his players? Nothing. But a lot of owners don't like that. In some cases, owners listened to players or listened to the media when they said this coach was too hard, and suddenly the league lost a great coach like Hubie Brown and some others. If I were to start a franchise today, I'd hire a Hubie Brown, a Dick Motta, or some other coach who was a disciplinarian.

CHUCK DALY: The feeling was that the dictator-coach was out. The players are making so much money now that they aren't afraid of losing their jobs. Even if they are cut, they still make millions. They never think they will be out of work and broke at thirty-five, which some players are even after all the money they've made. So a number of the disciplinarians were suddenly out of coaching, and that wasn't necessarily good for the league.

BILL FITCH: But I see the pendulum swinging back in our direction. The league knows it needs some discipline. Pat Riley is a very disciplined coach. Who did Dallas turn to when they needed a coach for those great kids they have? Dick Motta. I'm back in the league with the Clippers, which is a very young team. Hey, maybe us dinosaurs can help straighten this thing out.

DOUG COLLINS: An NBA coach is out on an island. A college coach recruits his own players and has a major say in his schedule. In the NBA, the schedule comes from the league office. With most NBA teams, the general manager is going to have the final say on drafts and trades. The real conflict usually comes after the draft, when the rookie is struggling.

You end up with a situation like this:

The GM says: "Why aren't you playing the kid?"

The coach says, "The kid's not ready to play."

The GM says, "He just needs experience. What are you trying to do? Are you trying to show me up or what?"

The coach says, "I'm just trying to win some games."

All of a sudden, you have the two main basketball men in your organization butting heads. The GM has an owner asking him why they paid the number one pick $20 million and he's on the bench. Then the GM says that the coach won't play him. Unless you have a deal like Don Nelson where you are the GM and coach, eventually there is going to be a conflict. I don't care if you are talking about very successful teams, it happens. It happened between Jerry West and Pat Riley with the Lakers. It happened between Wayne Embry and Lenny Wilkens in Cleveland. It happened between Jack McCloskey and Chuck Daly in Detroit. It happened between Jerry Krause and myself with the Bulls. If the issue is major, it eventually forces some very talented people to separate.

FRANK LAYDEN: It is amazing, but some teams just don't think that the coach is really important. One executive told me, "When a major college such as Notre Dame loses a coach, they go on a nationwide search to hire a replacement. When it happens in the NBA, they hire the announcer." And sometimes it even works out, because we have some very talented basketball men broadcasting games who used to be coaches. Or else they bring in a former-player-turned-broadcaster as a coach. It worked for a while in Denver with Dan Issel. The classic example was Pat Riley with the Lakers. Pat was sitting there next to Chick Hearn. He got the job, and even though he'd never coached before, he had a team with Magic Johnson and Kareem. He stayed out of the way and didn't screw it up. He learned how to coach along the way. Now, he's a great coach. But I don't think anyone is born to be a coach any more than a guy is born to be a dentist.

CHUCK DALY: Coaches are viewed as being very replaceable. Part of the thing is that you can't fire most of the players. That is especially true in this age of multimillion-dollar contracts, so that makes the coach even more vulnerable. It's cheaper to get rid of him than the players.

DOUG COLLINS: In the last five years [1989–94], there have been an average of nine coaching changes. One year, thirteen of the twenty-seven coaches were fired. The salary cap is partly behind this. The cap makes it so hard to change your team. You can't just cut guys and eat their contracts. If you make a mistake on a high draft choice and pay him $10 million, you can't trade him. Even if a team might be willing to take a chance on the guy, they probably can't make room for him on their cap, so the deal falls through. How can the owner and GM show the fans that they want to shake things up? They fire the coach. He is the disposable commodity.

RICHIE ADUBATO: I was in Dallas and we were in a building situation. We depleted our roster of our veterans so we could get younger and draft higher. But for a couple of years, we ended up with a lot of CBA guys. We made a mistake on a couple of draft picks like Randy White and Doug Smith, but I had to play them anyway. I was playing guys twenty-five to thirty minutes a night who didn't deserve it, and that bothered me. Even if the front office tells you that they don't expect to win many games, you just get tired of losing all the time. You realize that you're not getting a fair shot, and by the time they do turn this thing around, you're not going to be there—and that's exactly what happened to me in Dallas.

DOUG COLLINS: This probably will never happen, but if I were an owner, I'd tell my general manager this: "Whoever you hire as a coach is your coach. You guys are a package deal. If you hire this guy to coach, you better make it work because if you don't, both of you are gone." This should eliminate the fighting between a coach and a GM to get an owner's ear, which exists in some organizations. When I was with the Bulls, I understood that by the middle of my second year, there was always going to be conflict between Jerry Krause and myself. Jerry is a very hands-on guy. I'm not going to rehash the whole thing, but I don't work well in situations where I feel that someone is hovering over me all the time. That situation with Jerry made me realize that it was just a matter of time [until a new coach was hired]. But in an ideal world, the coach and GM know that their futures are tied together. The GM can't just dump the coach at the first sign of trouble, and the coach can't try to go over the GM's head to the owner. So when they talk about draft picks and trades, they do it from the point of view of what is best for both of them—and that will make it best for the team.

That is why I had to take the offer from the Detroit Pistons. I've been given a chance to be both the general manager and the coach. I hire my own people, and have final say over player personnel moves. It is a great opportunity for me to try out some of the theories I have about coaching. This time, I know that I'll rise or fall depending upon how I perform. It should keep the politics to a minimum. Really, it's an ideal setup.

BILL FITCH: I came back to coach the Clippers when I was sixty. But I didn't feel sixty. I have a great place to live in Houston. I can look out my window and see a lake. It's peaceful and it's beautiful. But I know that I can do that anytime. I only have so many years left that I could coach. I didn't want to sit behind a desk. I wanted to be at practice, in the locker room, and at the games. I was out of the NBA for two years, and I missed being part of a group that was busting its ass to try and do something. When I took the Clippers job, a lot of people thought I was crazy. Some said that I needed good luck. I told them, "No, I need good players."

Others said that they'll cheer for me. I said, "No, pray for me."

No one put a gun to my head and made me take this job. I wanted it. I'm a teacher and a basketball man and I missed the game terribly the two years that I was out.

CHUCK DALY: Basketball is a love affair. Coaches are not artistic in the traditional sense, but we do see Picassos and Monets when certain things happen out on the court. When you see something happen on offense and defense, and it works like you practiced it—that's one of the greatest feelings in the world. It's one of the reasons you keep coaching.

WILLIS REED: I enjoyed coaching, but it takes a certain ego that I found out I didn't have. A great coach believes he can come up with an offense or a defense that no one has ever seen before. Or he thinks he can get something out of a group of players that no one else can. When I started coaching, I believed that. But after a while, I saw all my limitations, and I didn't think I could come up with that special play. But those who are coaching lifers, they never lose that feeling.

JOHN HAVLICEK: Over the years, I have been approached about coaching. But I knew I could never deal with the personalities. I was a very dedicated and disciplined player. To me, there was a right way and a wrong way to do things, and I don't think many players today would be willing to sacrifice as much as I did when I played. You can talk to Jerry West, and he'll tell you that the worst years of his life were when he was a head coach in the NBA. I know I'd feel the same way.

FRANK LAYDEN: I quit coaching [17 games into the 1988–89 season with an 11-6 record] because I was fifty-seven years old and the job was taking up so much time and getting tougher every year. In Utah, I knew we'd have a good team for years because Karl Malone and John Stockton were both young players. I had been training [assistant] Jerry Sloan and I wanted him to get off to a good start. I spent a lot of years coaching in Catholic school and not making any money. In my last year coaching at Niagara, I made $20,000. I left to take a job as an assistant coach with Hubie Brown in Atlanta for $30,000 [in 1976]. Hubie was making $75,000. I got a car and I made enough money to put my kids through college. I got a chance to coach Utah, and I really enjoyed it. But you know, I never loved the game the way a Dick Motta, a Bill Fitch, or a Chuck Daly did. That is why I was able to walk away when I did.

DICK MOTTA: I didn't plan to coach Dallas one more time, but when Donald Carter asked me to come back [in 1994–95], I didn't feel sixty-three. I felt a lot younger because we had these good young players who were good kids. I thought to myself, "I've been coaching for forty years. I can teach these kids something. Why waste all that experience?" It still gnaws at me when we lose a close game, but coming back one more time—it reminds me of how much I missed it the couple of years that I was out.

BILL FITCH: As a coach, I've never been bored. I like challenges. I looked at the Clippers job where so many other guys had failed and I thought, "You know, there is a mountain no one has managed to climb. Maybe I can be the guy."

CHUCK DALY: It's an addictive form of life. You put yourself on the line every time your team takes the floor. You get an immediate result. You know if you won or lost. When you stop coaching, what you miss is the action. It's really hard to get that out of your system.

7 Stranglers on the Sidelines

When Bob Cousy talks about today's NBA games, he can sound like Professor Kingsfield from *The Paper Chase*.

"What can today's basketball players do better than the players that came before?" he asks.

Okay, what?

"Run, jump, and finish on the fast break," says the Hall of Fame guard. "These kids play higher above the rim than anyone ever has."

No argument there.

"So what kind of offenses do most teams use?" asks Cousy.

Okay, what kind?

"They slow the game down," he says.

So?

"So what are the major weaknesses of the modern player?" he asks.

Okay, what?

"Dribbling, passing, and shooting from the outside," says Cousy. "And what are the primary skills you need to play walk-it-up-the-floor, half-court basketball?"

Dribbling, passing, and shooting?

"Exactly," says Cousy. "None of it makes any sense. These kids are far more equipped physically to play the running game than the players were in my era, yet we ran the ball more than almost every team today. I watch some games and it drives me crazy. You see these kids trying to throw four or five passes in a half-court set. They aren't confident handling the ball. Other players don't like to move without the ball—which is a key to a successful half-court offense. Most teams are simply playing the game wrong."

Really?

"Just think about it," says Cousy. "More than ever, teams should run. But they probably are running less than at any time since the coming of the 24-second clock [in the 1954–55 season]. You tell me why."

Okay, why?

"The coaches," says Cousy. "I swear, some of these guys are strangling the game."

Dr. Cousy is not alone in this charge. Another Hoopologist, Rod Thorn, agrees. Thorn is a former NBA player, coach, and general manager. He is now the director of NBA Operations, which means he is second in command to commissioner David Stern. Stern considers Thorn to be his "basketball expert."

Thorn watches the game and sees the same problems as Cousy—and he points the finger of blame in the same direction.

"What we need to do is get the media and coaches out of the mind-set that losing an 85–80 game is somehow better than losing 115–110," said Thorn. "The coach that plays games in the 80-point range is trying to sell you on the fact that his guys play tough. They play defense and he gets them to hustle. Well, maybe they do in some cases, but in a lot of instances the coach is having his own team hold on to the ball for most of the 24-second clock. He is cutting down on the number of shots and the number of possessions. He isn't keeping the score down by playing great defense, he's doing it by not playing much offense. But most people don't understand that."

Yet most coaches like things exactly the way they are.

"That's because most coaches want to be known for their defense," said Chuck Daly.

Why?

"No one wants to be known for coaching a finesse team," said Daly. "That makes it sound as if your team is soft, and if the team is soft, then the coach must be soft. Or at least that is how the reasoning goes."

What Daly means is that the coach must be tough enough to get his guys to defend, to rebound, to "win the war in the trenches." The last part sounds like a football phrase, and it is. But a number of today's basketball coaches admire football coaches. Football coaches are organized. Football coaches are "generals" and "in command."

When the Indiana Pacers faced New York in the 1994 Eastern Conference Finals, coach Larry Brown didn't even consider trying to run against the Knicks. Granted, Brown also had a strong, physical team with Dale Davis and Antonio Davis—but they weren't the wide-bodied thugs that the Knicks could put on the court in the persons of Charles Oakley and Anthony Mason. In Derrick McKey, Reggie Miller, Byron Scott, Vern Fleming, and even the unheralded Haywoode Workman, Brown had better, faster athletes than New York.

But what did he say about the series? He vowed that the Knicks would not intimidate his team. He said his Pacers wouldn't back down, that they could match up with the Knicks or any other team under the basket. If the game was hand-to-hand combat, they were men enough to handle it.

"I was listening to Larry say all this and I nearly gagged," said veteran basketball writer Bob Ryan. "I wondered why he didn't just say that he was going to let Reggie Miller loose, let him fire some three-pointers off the break and take the tempo away from the Knicks. Why let them set up to guard Reggie? And in a couple of games where the Pacers did win, it was because Reggie just took over the game by himself, running and firing away. But Larry didn't want to play that style game, for whatever reason."

The reason is exactly what Daly said: macho.

When the Knicks and Pacers met again in the 1995 playoffs, it was only a little better. They played some close games, and two that may have been great games because of their fantastic finishes. But the Knicks were able to control the tempo. The Pacers averaged 93 points in winning the 7-game series, the Knicks were slightly under 95. Both teams only broke 100 points in the opening game—and neither did it in the next six contests. Yes, the Pacers beat the Knicks—thanks to Patrick Ewing blowing a layup at the buzzer—but you have to wonder why Brown just didn't force the issue and push the ball up the court.

But maybe saying you wanted to run the Knicks off the floor

might be considered an admission that you aren't tough enough to beat them at their own game. It was why some critics challenged the heart of a young Cassius Clay; they said that all he did was dance around and jab, instead of standing in there and slugging it out. But why slug it out with a great puncher unless you have no other choice?

The problem is that coaches have limited their own choices.

"In the back of every coach's head is the thinking that you can't run in the playoffs," said Daly.

So many of them don't even try.

Larry Bird knew that the playoff pace was slower and the fast breaks could be fewer, but he still encouraged the Celtics to run whenever possible. Why sacrifice the easiest way to score points? Bird would ask.

In Boston's 1986 season—their last banner year—the Celtics averaged 114 points in the regular season—and 108 points in beating Houston in six games in the Finals—with the Rockets and their Twin Towers of Ralph Sampson and Hakeem Olajuwon trying to slow things down. In their entire playoff run, Boston was under 100 points only twice in 18 games.

"You still can run if you really want to and if the coaches will simply let the players do it," said Cousy. "But a lot of them are really control freaks. That is why they don't like the running game. They don't want to give up any of that control. They want to call every play from the sidelines. It drives me crazy."

It also drives the scores down.

When Houston beat New York in seven games to win the 1994 title, playoff records were set for the fewest points and fewest field goal attempts in a seven-game series. It was the first time in a seven-game series that neither team could manage 100 points.

Houston won the series averaging 89 points and shooting 43 percent. The Knicks averaged 86 points and shot 41 percent.

In the entire 1994 Eastern Conference playoffs, there were only two games where both teams scored over 100 points. In the 1992–93 regular season, only three teams averaged fewer than 101 points—Detroit, Dallas, and Minnesota. But in 1993–94, there were a dozen.

The NBA began crunching numbers and discovered the following:

- In 1985–86, the Celtics' final championship season, there were an average of 219 points scored in an NBA game.
- In 1990–91, Chicago's first title, it was down to 212 points—a drop of 7, but not really alarming.
- In 1993–94, the year of the Rockets-Knicks, the average game saw 202 points. That was a 17-point drop in nine years—or ten points in just three seasons.

The Knicks allowed only 91 points per game, the lowest total since the advent of the 24-second clock in 1954–55. Shooting percentage had sunk to .466—down from the all-time high of .492 in 1983–84. That .466 mark was the lowest in twenty-seven years.

But even worse than the numbers are what the games look like.

"They are ugly," said Pacers general manager Donnie Walsh. "There is a general feeling throughout the league that this isn't how basketball is supposed to be played."

A lot of people blamed Pat Riley and the Knicks. Others blamed the Pistons for winning this way—although Detroit usually scored over 100—and Riley for copying the Pistons' style. A few people even blamed Dick Harter, noting that he was an assistant in Detroit during the Bad Boys era, then he joined Riley in New York, supposedly bringing his bag of dirty defensive tricks with him. The Harter theory seems like a very serious stretch.

Riley just wants it known that it's not his fault.

"Blame the NBA," he told writers at the 1994 Finals. "All the one-on-one macho dunking. All the In Your Face stuff. The NBA sells these things, and the game has evolved into this."

Still, how does that explain the Rockets and Knicks walking off the court with the halftime scoreboard reading 32–31 in Game 1? What does all the posturing have to do with the two teams combining for only 28 points in the fourth quarter?

"Want to know how bad the 1994 playoffs were?" asked veteran NBA scout Al Menendez. "What most people will remember is Reggie Miller talking trash to Spike Lee, and that didn't even happen in the Finals. The year before, we had John Starks head-butting Miller. What kind of crap is that? Or maybe that is what the league wants, if we are supposed to be tailoring our game to the MTV generation."

Menendez is right. The only thing that did bring the NBA some attention—other than the moaning about the terrible games—was Miller making jumper after jumper, then running down the court and grabbing his throat while staring at Lee. Of course, Miller will say that Lee started it by first yelling at Reggie that he was going to choke.

But that was also an exciting game. Miller scored 25 points in the fourth quarter in that fifth game at Madison Square Garden, going 5 for 5 on three-pointers. The Pacers came from 19 points down to beat the Knicks 93–86, Miller finishing with 39 points. Yet purists came away shaking their heads, wondering how Miller's incredible shooting had become a sideshow to an NBA All-Star talking trash to a movie director who happened to be sitting court-side.

By putting in some tight rules about trash talking, the NBA cut down on many incidents in 1994–95—although no provision was made for players and celebrity fans going jaw-to-jaw, or, in the case of Miller and Lee, gesture-to-gesture.

"But a bigger problem [than fighting and trash talk] is how the game is being played," said Menendez. "Everyone wants their team to play great defense, climb the boards for rebounds, and hit the floor for loose balls. They want intensity. No one has a problem with hard, clean fouls. But all the throwing of elbows, the second and third hits they give a guy after he's already been fouled, all the low-life crap is going to drag the game down. It kills the beauty of basketball."

The fans didn't like it, as ratings for the 1994 NBA Finals were down over 20 percent from 1993. David Stern blamed it on markets, pointing out that the ratings for 1993 were inflated by the presence in the Finals of superstars Charles Barkley and Michael Jordan. But the last time anyone checked, New York did happen to be the biggest market in the country, and the Knicks were in the 1994 Finals.

"Come on, it was the games," said Doug Collins. "Unless you lived in one of the two cities and had a rooting interest, it was hard to watch those games. When they broke into Game 5 for the O. J. Simpson car chase, most fans were probably happy to watch something else. If you had done that in a Lakers-Celtics Finals or a Bulls-Lakers Finals, the TV switchboards would have been flooded with calls from fans who were mad. But hardly anyone complained in 1994, and that tells you something."

Phil Jackson agrees.

"Given the way the league is going, what I'm going to say sounds like a faint protest," said the Bulls coach. "Most games (in 1994) were not good to watch because of how they were being played. I would not use the kind of defense you see many teams use today. I can't see myself bending to that level of coaching. I can remember when Pat Riley's team faced the Celtics in the playoffs, and he claimed Boston was brutalizing his Lakers. This was in the middle 1980s. Those games were nothing compared to the physical play you see today. Maybe, one day I will have to be like Riley. I'll have to join the fray, eat my words. There is a real feeling [among coaches] of, 'If you can't beat 'em, join 'em.' But I can't stand watching some of these games. The Knicks play ugly. People say that if I had his team, I'd coach the same way. I don't think so. That is just not how you play the game. I look at how Pat's Laker teams played . . . how the Celtics of the 1980s played . . . how the Bulls played in the 1990s . . . I mean, basketball is a game of movement, both of the ball and the players. I don't believe in winning at all costs and playing that type of basketball."

Jackson offered another theory.

"Why couldn't Houston and the Knicks have played a running game?" he asked. "I don't care what they say, they had the players. Look at Houston with guys like [Kenny] Smith, [Vernon] Maxwell, [Robert] Horry, and Hakeem Olajuwon. Aren't those guys athletes? You mean to tell me that they couldn't run? As for the Knicks, when you look at [Charles] Smith, [John] Starks, [Derek] Harper, Greg Anthony, and even [Patrick] Ewing. They have average team speed. To me, it was a complete fallacy that those teams couldn't win other than by a slow, physical game. What we really saw was control basketball at the ultimate level."

Now we fast-forward to 1995. The NBA caught a break when the Knicks were eliminated in the second round. But guess what? The teams that were winning featured coaches with guts enough to let their players run. Paul Westphal did it all year in Phoenix as the Suns and Orlando topped the NBA in scoring at 110 points per game. When Houston faced the Suns in the Western Conference semifinals, Rockets coach Rudy Tomjanovich allowed his athletes to play a wide-open game. The Rockets won the series in seven games, and they did it averaging 109 points. Yes, this was basically the same team (with the key addition of Clyde Drexler) that was held to 89 points in the 1994 Finals against the Knicks.

Look at some of the other series in 1995. The Pacers tried to slow down Orlando, but the Magic relied on the fast break in the regular season and stayed with the game plan in the playoffs. In Game 7 against Indiana, the Magic ran the Pacers off the court, 105-81. The score would have been higher, but most of the second half was garbage time. By refusing to play it safe, by trusting the talent of his players and challenging them to be aggressive and fast break against a team that wanted to apply the brakes, Orlando showed you can run and win in the postseason.

Then in the Finals, the Magic continued to run, and Houston ran even faster. The Rockets averaged 114 points in sweeping Orlando. They averaged 107 points in their playoff run. All of this shatters the theory that you have to play low-scoring, mud-slinging games to win a title. Consider this: the Rockets scored more and ran far more than they did in the regular season, when they only averaged 103 points per game.

Deciding how to play is in the hands and egos of the coaches. Will most coaches look at teams such as Orlando and Houston and then say, "Hey, we can't run with those guys, let's slow it down?" That's more likely than their deciding to check out some old tapes of the Celtic fast break. It seemed that far more NBA coaches were impressed by Mike Fratello's Cavaliers—who averaged only 90 points per game, gave up only 89 and played hard but very boring basketball—than they were with teams such as the Magic, Suns and others who ran. The Cavaliers were considered Fratello's team; Tomjanovich and Brian Hill were referred to as guys who just let their players play.

Regular season scoring dropped last year—and probably will continue to drop—despite the closer 3-point line, and even though the crackdown on hand-checking meant that the average team scored 31 more points at the foul line in 1994–95 than in 1993–94.

But TV should tell the NBA something else. Until Jordan's return, the regular season ratings staggered along. But in the playoffs, when the most entertaining teams prevailed, ratings were up. In 1994, the problem was indeed the games—and the coaches. In the 1995 playoffs, the games were better because the coaches allowed their players some freedom. Such freedom is anathema to some of the NBA's most highly regarded coaches.

"Since he became the Knicks coach, I've never heard Pat Riley say one word about his offense," said Willis Reed, general manager of the New Jersey Nets, who pays very close attention to what is being said by the Knicks. "All he ever talks about is defense. If his team loses, it's because they didn't defend or rebound. It's never because they didn't run or score enough points. He has taken his entire focus away from the offense."

"You know what the Knicks do from day one of training camp?" said Cotton Fitzsimmons. "It's all hit, block out, bump the guys cutting to the basket—no one gets a layup. It's pound, pound, pound. That is how they're coached and it's how they play—because teams play the style the coach wants them to."

Even Isiah Thomas was stunned by some of New York's stunts.

"We [the Pistons' Bad Boys] still averaged 103 points," he said. "We had some athletes and more quickness than New York. We could move our feet. But the Knicks, they just try to beat you with brute strength."

Brutal is the proper word for it.

"You take athletes who are bigger now than they ever were," said Doug Collins. "Then you put them in the weight room and you tell them to get as big and strong as they can—and don't worry about the quickness—because in basketball, you are now allowed to hold people. You take the guys who were the great power forwards in the 1970s, guys like Maurice Lucas. Well, Maurice Lucas was 6-foot-9, 220 pounds. If you weighed 220, you were big. Today, these guys have bulked themselves up to 250, 260 pounds. Look at Derrick Coleman, Charles Oakley, Karl Malone. They are huge and they just slam people around. Maurice Lucas is downright frail compared to these guys, and he was an enforcer in the 1970s and early 1980s. By encouraging all this physical play, you also are encouraging a bigger, meaner player. That's why basketball often looks so much like wrestling. We have huge people with that kind of mind-set."

Cavs player personnel director Gary Fitzsimmons said that the defense—especially half-court defense—is better now than ever because of the athletes.

"If you can get a bunch of big, strong, and quick guys to bust their ass and defend, you can smother a team," he said. "You can get big guys double-teaming a man at the low post. You can get them playing what amounts to a zone and shutting down the middle. All of these kids love to dunk, but their next favorite thing to do is to block someone else's dunk, so you can convince them to block shots. Today's athlete prides himself on being tough and being able to jump, and a good coach can sell that kid on defense. Now, everyone gets their players to double-team the ball near the basket and then zone away from the ball. Coaches know that shooting skills have gone to hell, so they use their athletes to cut off the inside game and dare the offense to beat them from the outside. Even if the shot is worth three points, the percentages of making a jumper from twenty-two feet are a lot less than a guy making a shot from twenty-two inches."

Virtually every coach will tell you that he believes in fast break basketball, that he wants his team to run.

As men such as Jackson and Cousy keep saying, there actually was a time in the NBA—through most of the 1980s—when most coaches even practiced what they preached. Their teams rebounded, passed the ball, and then tried to get their butts down the court before the defense could set up.

Then came the Pistons.

Detroit did more than bring the World Wrestling Federation into the NBA; it made ugly, stuck-in-mud, beat-the-hell-out-of-each-other basketball popular—at least with the coaches.

Chuck Daly knows this. Daly coached the Bad Boys, and the fighting never bothered him. Neither did the 90-point games or the criticism from fans and media in other cities outside Detroit. He didn't worry about the spirit of the NBA, or how the game should be played.

"If you are a coach in this league, the name of the game is winning," said Daly. "Defense wins. Defense travels. You win on the road with defense. There are nights when you are in New York and you left your jump shot back in Detroit. That happens. But a good team will take its defense with them onto the court every night, eighty-two nights a year."

All of that sounds fine. But there is something else. The Pistons redefined what is meant by playing defense in the NBA.

"It used to be that you could run, pressure people, and play a wide-open game and still be considered a good defensive team," said Cotton Fitzsimmons. "The great Boston teams with Bill Russell were like that. Magic Johnson's Lakers loved to run. People who understood the game realized that those Laker teams were very good defensively. But the Pistons made a different kind of defense fashionable. It's an ugly game where you get as many big centers and power forwards as you can and you clog up the middle. You manhandle people. You walk the ball up the court, you bring the game to a crawl. Some coaches may think that's great defense, but I don't buy it. I don't think the fans will, either, at least not in the long run."

The success of the Pistons and now the Knicks further reinforces the ways in which basketball skills have declined. It's a style that won't work against a diversified offense: good jump shooting will shred it, and so will an effective running game, because it requires the big men to get back on defense and set up in the middle. It's a style of play that would never have beaten the dynastic Celtics of the 1950s and 1960s, or the open-man Knicks of the early 1970s, or the Showtime Lakers of the 1980s. It works because it's trying to win the championship in an already diminished league.

Daly is one of the few coaches willing to be honest. He says that he intentionally slowed down the game, that he wasn't interested in the fast break. If you didn't like it, tough.

"When I coached the great Detroit teams, our goal was to get a good shot every time down the floor," he said. "I know that's a trite expression, but in this league, it works. Why run ninety-four feet and then not get a good shot? I had one of the greatest point guards in history in Isiah Thomas, but I consistently told him to just stay with our offense, get us a good shot. If we do that, we'll win the majority of our games."

Early in his career with the Pistons, Daly let his players run loose, and Detroit was among the top five scoring teams in the league. But it went nowhere in the playoffs.

"Other teams slowed us down and forced us to play a half-court style offense," said Daly. "After watching that for a few years, I figured why not just do it in the regular season so you can play the same way all year? Any coach with intelligence would realize that. To win in the playoffs you must have a tremendous half-court game. I mean, one that is absolutely *terrific*. And you are going to have to stop people. So why not just play that way all year?"

Actually, it was Hubie Brown who first suggested this theory around 1980. He said that teams that averaged 115–120 points in the regular season, but dropped to about 100 points in the play-offs—well, those teams were in trouble and were never going to win a championship.

"You cannot have a huge point differential between the regular season and the playoffs and expect to play for a title," said Brown. "That shows there is something wrong with your offense. Then comes playoff time and teams find a way to stop it."

But let's look at Daly's record:

- His 1983–84 Pistons averaged 117 points per game, third highest in the NBA. But the Pistons still averaged 110 points in losing to New York in the second round.
- His 1984–85 Pistons averaged 116 points—again, third highest in the NBA. They were eliminated by Boston in the second round, and still averaged 110 points.
- His 1985–86 Pistons were knocked out by Atlanta in the first round. They averaged 114 points in the regular season, *116* in the playoffs.

So despite Daly's and Brown's theories, the Pistons' scores weren't that much lower at all in the playoffs compared to the regular season. The real story was that Daly discovered he could not run with the better teams, so he decided to change the game. He would slow *them* down. It was Daly who helped influence the entire philosophy of playoff basketball.

So what happened to the offense?

"We've gotten very predictable in what we do," said Daly. "You throw the ball to the low post. If the guy in the low post isn't double-teamed, he shoots. If he is double-teamed, he passes the ball back out and someone takes a three-pointer. Or else, you just run a pick-and-roll play. Just three things."

Basketball man after basketball man will tell you the same thing: today's offenses are boring. The offenses do three things:

1. Try to score near the basket from the low post.
2. If the low post is covered, throw the ball back out and launch a three-pointer.
3. Run a pick-and-roll play.

Larry Brown said before the 1994–95 season that even if the NBA's new handchecking rule and closer three-point line did add more points to the board, they would still make offensive basketball even more boring. "With the officials barely letting you touch a guy outside, coaches will just run a lot of isolation plays. They will put their best athlete on the wing, clear out and let him go one-on-one. Michael Jordan might score 100 points with these rules and he'll live at the foul line."

One of the reasons Chicago Bulls general manager Jerry Krause gave for firing Doug Collins was that Collins ran too many isolation plays for Jordan. He wanted more motion in the offense with all the players involved. Under Phil Jackson, the Bulls are one of the few teams that actually have a system where the ball and players constantly move. It is the Triangle Offense, designed by Tex Winter—the venerable Bulls assistant.

Jordan didn't especially like it, but he learned to live and win with it. One of his complaints was that it created too many jump shots and not enough room for an athletic player to go one-on-one.

Neither Collins nor Krause want to dig up this old debate. But Collins looks at today's game and sees defenses that are way ahead of the offense.

"They guard the man dribbling the ball full court," Collins said. "They make you chew up the 24-second clock, and by the time you get it past half court, there are only sixteen seconds left. Then by the time you get into your offense, you have maybe ten seconds. Everyone is so well scouted that they almost always take away the first and second options of a play. Soon, the shot clock is about to expire and someone throws up a desperation shot. The greatness of the Bulls came from Michael Jordan's ability to beat the 24-second clock. Both he and Scottie Pippen could go off on their own, improvise, and get their own shots. Coaches call it 'beating them off the dribble.' It means rather than run a structured play, you set up an offense that gives a Jordan room to operate and let him do his thing."

That's also called isolation, and Larry Brown deplores it.

"It can be the death of team basketball," he said. "What is more boring than having two guys on one side of the court, and three others on the opposite side? The three guys are maybe thirty-some feet from the basket. They are just standing there, watching. They have nothing to do. They aren't even decoys. The only reason they are there is to occupy three defensive players. Because of the illegal-defense rules, you have to guard those three guys with three of your own men, even though everyone in the building knows that those three guys are not a part of the offense. The whole thing is crazy."

Larry Brown even made it a moral issue.

"They thought the new handchecking rules would create more movement for the offense, but I just see it creating more opportunities for one-on-one basketball," he said. "As a coach, I hate to play that way. But the rules may force you to eventually do just that. You have to tell one of your players, 'I love your game and I love you, but I want you to stand thirty-five feet from the basket and not touch the ball.' How am I supposed to tell my players that?"

A lot of people insist that you can still play a motion offense.

"We've had some great offensive coaches in this league," said Phil Jackson. "Larry Brown is one. Doug Moe was another. There are some others. But when coaches get together and talk about that, they'll say, 'Sure, those teams were sweet teams to watch, but what have they ever won in the playoffs? If we have to, we can slow them down.' In our championship years with the Bulls, that was somewhat of a threat to us, but we believed that we could run or play a half-court game. We were good enough to beat you either way."

But other coaches said, "That's fine for Jackson, he had Jordan." Or they said, "Phoenix could run because they had Kevin Johnson. Portland tried to run, but they couldn't get past Detroit or Chicago in the Finals."

As Jackson said, "For many coaches, the comfort zone now is simply not to run."

*   *   *

It doesn't have to be this way.

"I won't join the mob," said Phoenix Suns owner Jerry Colangelo. "I refuse to let my team play the slow-down game. It's not entertaining, and we are still in the entertainment business. I want our fans to see our players' talents, to see them run and make the spectacular plays that built this league. When I hire a coach, I hire a guy who also wants the running game. All coaches tell you they'll run, but you have to check their records. When we rebuilt the Suns [in the late 1980s], I asked Cotton Fitzsimmons to be my coach because I knew he'd put a running team on the floor."

Fitzsimmons asked a very elementary question: "When you are putting together your team, why not say, 'Let's get some guys who can run and some guys who can shoot. Let's make it fun. What is wrong with giving fans the kind of basketball they enjoy?' That is Jerry Colangelo's philosophy and that is my philosophy."

It also became the Phoenix Suns of Kevin Johnson, Danny Ainge, Dan Majerle, Eddie Johnson, Tom Chambers, and the rest who averaged 113 points during the early 1990s.

"You get guys like that and then you really coach the running game, from the first day of practice," said Fitzsimmons. "Everything is push, push, PUSH THE BALL . . . run, run, RUN! Then take good shots off the break, figure out where the players like to get the ball on the run. While Pat Riley is yelling 'Rebound! Block out! Kill! Kill! Kill!' we are concentrating on getting the ball down the floor before the defense can set up and try to kill us. Look, I admire what Riley did with the Knicks. He could take those guys in the gym at 8 P.M. and they could play until 8 A.M. and they still couldn't score 100 points against each other. In my opinion, Pat can't like the way his team plays. It's not his style of basketball."

But when a high-profile coach such as Riley switches from Showtime to Slowtime—and wins both ways—it just enhances his reputation. It encourages other coaches to do the same.

When he was with the Lakers, Riley seldom called a play. Magic Johnson ran the team. But now, we are in the era where coaches love to leave their fingerprints on every aspect of their team in most sports. Baseball managers continually change pitchers and try to play the percentages. Football coaches have staffs larger than the

Pentagon. They seem to rotate three to four players in and out on every play. Joe Montana is one of the greatest and smartest quarterbacks of all time, yet coaches refuse to let him call his own plays—unless he changes them at the line of scrimmage. Why wouldn't Montana know what would work better than some assistant coach in a press box a hundred miles above the field?

Basketball has become the same way. Coaches call out different offenses and defenses.

"When I coached in the middle 1960s, we didn't have any assistants," said Dolph Schayes. "I'm not saying that no assistants is the way to go, because a head coach needs someone to help him. But now, I see four or five guys in suits, and I think that maybe the NBA should commission a study to determine just what four assistant coaches do all day."

"If I see one more coach whip out a clipboard and spend the whole timeout during a crucial part of the game on Xs and Os, I'll scream," said Cousy. "I mean, this is a very emotional moment in the game. The guys in the huddle are sweating, out of breath, and feeling all these external pressures. If you put something new on the blackboard and expect them to execute it, that's unrealistic. This clipboard business all started with Al Attles at Golden State, when the Warriors swept [Washington's] K. C. Jones in the 1975 Finals. Well, K. C. didn't use a clipboard, and people jumped all over that. Now, all the coaches use clipboards when what you really need is just a couple of key plays that the players know by heart that you can use in crucial situations. Don't try to reinvent the game."

Cousy is now in the TV business as an analyst for Celtics games. He says that coaches know they are on camera during timeouts, and all that has done is inflate their egos and make them believe they are the stars, not the players.

"Now, too many coaches are afraid to experiment," he said. "They figure if they go by the book and screw up . . . well, no one can really second-guess them. But if they give their players some freedom and they throw the ball all over the gym, suddenly the coach feels exposed and thinks he'll be blamed for the loss. When we had the great teams in Boston, Red Auerbach had only six plays for us. Our goal was to run the break so well that we'd never have to call any of the plays. I don't care what anyone says, the best way to play basketball is still the transition game."

Or as Phil Jackson said, "Sometimes, you just have to give the horse his reins and let him run. He is closer to the ground and may know the track better than you do."

Those who believe in the running game are convinced that it is needed more now than ever.

"The half-court defenses are better than when I played," said Cousy. "So is the scouting. If you were going to play just a half-court game, you'd need more than Auerbach's six plays. Teams also spend a lot more time working on their defenses. When we got behind in a game, Auerbach would call timeout and say, 'Damn it, pick 'em up all over the court.' We would sort of set up our own press. Now, these teams have a million different defenses. But because of those things, you *must* run. Why walk the ball up the court right into the gut of that defense? Instead of letting the defense dictate your game, you can control the game by running on offense."

Doug Collins said that today's coaches "are perfectionists in an imperfect game." He said that one of the greatest attributes of players is to "play through their mistakes. It's a game of missed shots, of turnovers and blown assignments. You try to cut down on the mental errors especially, but a coach has to realize that it is an imperfect game today. It was imperfect twenty years ago and it will be imperfect 200 years from now. If you get too negative, you just ruin the game for the players and yourself."

That is exactly what many coaches are doing.

"The biggest myth now is that the NBA is a player's game," said Bob Ryan. "It is off the court with all the lunacy going on. But on the court in the last few years, the coaches have been trying to strangle the game to death."

8 Coaching Lines

There is a story about Jerry Tarkanian that may or may not be true, but NBA people tell it to demonstrate what a college coach faces when he becomes a head coach in the NBA. It was during the exhibition season of 1992. Tark had just been hired to coach the San Antonio Spurs. He found himself in an elevator with New York Knicks forward Anthony Mason. Mason was excited to see Tark and began talking to the league's newest coach. Tark stared at Mason as if he were some obscure high school recruit. He may have heard the name before, but he didn't know the face—or any particular reason he should be aware of Anthony Mason.

Of course, any NBA coach would tell you not just that Mason is a bullish rebounder with a quick temper and trashy mouth, but that he is a pure left-handed player who handles the ball with remarkable grace for a man who weighs 250.

"Before I went into the league, I knew the players," Tark insisted recently.

Maybe he did. Maybe the story isn't true. But no matter what Tark says, he was no more prepared for the NBA than a Trappist monk would be for a backroom, high-stakes poker game at Harrah's Casino.

That's how Richie Adubato felt when he came into the NBA in 1978 as an assistant under Dick Vitale with the Detroit Pistons.

"Both of us were straight out of college," said Adubato. "We really didn't know the players, at least not the guys on the bench. One night, we played Phoenix, and Garfield Heard came into the game. Dick looked at me. All I had was a scouting report that said

Heard liked to take a baseline jumper. Neither one of us would have known Garfield Heard if he was sitting next to us on the bench. Heard beat us that night. Now, after fifteen years in the league, I can give you the life history of every twelfth man. But back then, we were often flying blind."

Until P. J. Carlesimo was hired straight out of Seton Hall to coach Portland for the 1994–95 season, the last two college coaches without pro experience to take over NBA teams were Tarkanian in 1992 and Vitale in 1978. Tarkanian lasted 20 games; Vitale went one season and 12 games.

"I got into trouble a few years ago when I said that [Pistons trainer] Mike Abdenour was better equipped to coach in the NBA than a college coach," said Chuck Daly.

He was talking about Duke's Mike Krzyzewski being courted by the Boston Celtics to replace Chris Ford.

"Some guys like Dean Smith thought I was putting down college coaches," said Daly. "Look, some of those people are brilliant, but this is a different game in the NBA. The clock, the mentality of the players, the travel, and the grind of the schedule— none of that is like college and you can't understand it until you experience it every day."

Jerry Tarkanian got to see that firsthand, which explains why he's now coaching Fresno State instead of the San Antonio Spurs.

"I never talked to Jerry Tarkanian in my life until the day after Larry Brown left as our coach," said Spurs owner Red McCombs. "Then Tark called me out of the blue. He said that he saw that [general manager] Bob Bass was named interim coach, and if I needed a coach for next year, he was interested. He told me, 'This is my last year an UNLV. I've always been interested in coaching in the NBA and I really like your team.' We struck up a relationship and Tark called me a lot after that."

It's very likely that Tarkanian and McCombs were hustling each other. McCombs made his money selling cars, and he appreciates a man who can sell himself. Tark had made a career out of recruiting. He could entice mothers who otherwise wouldn't set foot in Las Vegas even if someone put a gun to their heads to allow their sons to attend UNLV—all because Tark and his wife, Lois, would be there to take care of their boys. He perfected the Father Flanagan image, a nickname given him by Dick Vitale.

Tarkanian and McCombs continued to talk. Tarkanian said he'd never coached a great center before, and couldn't wait to work with David Robinson. McCombs was impressed by Tarkanian's desire, and he signed Tark to a three-year, $1.2 million contract. Tark was sixty-two years old and had the hangdog look of a man who had just seen his last friend in the world walk out the door, never to come back. It was those deep-set Armenian eyes as much as his trademark towel that made Tarkanian perhaps the most recognizable basketball coach in America, pro or college. In twenty-five years at Long Beach State and Nevada–Las Vegas, he had compiled the highest winning percentage of any Division I college coach—ever. He also had attracted more attention from the NCAA investigators than any other coach—ever. Finally, his stay in Vegas was played out: the school was facing two years' probation, and Tarkanian was under pressure from university president Bob Maxson to resign. No college would touch him, not wanting to bring the NCAA sheriffs to their gym door. The only place left for Tark was the NBA.

Even before training camp began, Tarkanian had to be in a state of shock over several aspects of NBA life:

1. In college, he played nearly 70 percent of his games at home. He personally made out his nonconference schedule. And UNLV played in the Big West. There aren't any teams like Pacific and the California-Irvine Anteaters in the NBA. Nor are there any Christmas tournaments at Hawaii-Hilo. The NBA schedule is forty-one at home, forty-one on the road. If you don't like it, tough.

2. In college, Tarkanian was general manager and coach. He picked the players and he started whomever he wished. In the NBA, the general manager drafts and makes trades, and the coach—especially a new coach—takes the talent given him. Tark's college background made it hard for him to understand why the front office would lose Rod Strickland to Portland via free agency.

3. He was not king. Most of the players made more money than he did. The owner and general manager had more experience in the NBA than he did.

4. There was no salary cap at UNLV, and Tark could have a entire team of redshirts sitting out for next season. He seldom had players transfer out, as Strickland in essence did when he left the Spurs for Portland. Rather, he continually received calls from college players who wanted to leave their schools and play for UNLV. That doesn't happen in the NBA.

"The game itself also is so different," said Hubie Brown. "It doesn't matter how much film you watch or how you're told that this game revolves around the matchups, the college coach has no idea what you are talking about. I know. I went from Duke to Larry Costello and the Milwaukee Bucks. I was not prepared for the athleticism of the NBA, or the physical duress under which the game is played. Nothing in college compares to what a player must go through simply to get a good low-post position in the NBA. A college coach can't comprehend the strength or the jumping ability of the pros. He can't understand how all this talent gives pro players the ability to erase their own mistakes because they play the game a foot above the rim."

Tarkanian's first training camp went reasonably well, and the Spurs were 6-2 in the exhibition season. Tark was good for a few laughs when he tried to call a twenty-second timeout, but instead of touching both of his shoulders with his hands, he sort of touched his head and stood on one foot. That began the talk, "How the hell can Tark coach in this league when he doesn't even know how to call a twenty-second timeout?"

Tarkanian insists his team would have been fine "if the owner had just left us alone." He said that he was stuck with Vinny Del Negro at point guard because the Spurs didn't retain Strickland. He didn't have his starting power forward because Antoine Carr was hurt, and he had to play Sidney Green and Larry Smith. Of course, he also had three good players by the names of David Robinson, Dale Ellis, and Sean Elliott. Tarkanian failed to comprehend that most pro coaches are glorified supervisors on an assembly line. They don't hire the workers. They don't pay the workers. Often, they can't even change the workers. Their job is to make them work productively. But Tark kept trying to act like a GM, making calls about trades and telling anyone with a notebook or a microphone how the Spurs needed to get another point guard.

"Tark made the point guard issue a cause célèbre," said veteran

San Antonio sportswriter Kevin O'Keefe. "And with Red Mc-
Combs, you can tell him something once, maybe twice, but that's
it. He doesn't want to hear it every day."

"He had a decent point guard sitting there in Avery Johnson,"
said McCombs. "But Tark wouldn't use the kid."

McCombs wasn't the only one saying this; David Robinson was
telling Tark the same thing. Yes, Robinson and Johnson were close
friends, but Robinson also knew that the little left-handed point
man was one of the quickest guards in the NBA.

"What really got to Tark was the losing," said McCombs. "I
never saw a coach take losing harder. He was devastated."

According to Lois Tarkanian, Tark would sit in a chair and moan
all night after a loss at UNLV, "as if someone was stabbing him in
the back, over and over." Tark will never look like the life of the
party, but after a loss his face would turn gray and his eyes red, and
he would walk around looking like a man who had lost his last
quarter in a slot machine. After all, his teams seldom lost more
than five games a year in college. Suddenly, he was 1-4, 3-5, and
players such as Sean Elliott were putting their arm around him and
saying, "Coach, it will be all right. Come on, we have another
game tomorrow night."

Tarkanian was having chest pains. He may have been having
doubts about himself as a pro coach, although he probably would
never admit that. He had to be homesick for UNLV, where he
owned the town and ran the team. In the words of Kevin O'Keefe,
"Tark often walked around looking as if someone had just hit him
in the face with a frying pan."

McCombs invited Tark to his ranch, bought the coach some
cowboy boots and tried to cheer him up. "What killed Tark was all
the damn advice he was getting from people he thought were his
friends," said McCombs. "There are some real snakes in this league
and you have to be careful who you listen to."

"That's one of Jerry's weaknesses," said Al Menendez. "Often,
everybody's opinion has equal weight with Tark. For example, one
of the guys he was listening to was Larry Brown. Now Brown had
just been fired by Red McCombs, so Larry wasn't going to have
very nice things to say about the Spurs."

"Tark kept telling me that these guys were his friends," said
McCombs. "I said, 'Well, them sumbitches are going to cut your

nuts off.' During his 20 games, his attitude turned so damn negative. They just killed him by telling him how bad the team was, how he'd never win. I told him that this was easier than coaching in college. He didn't have to worry about keeping kids eligible. All he had to do was motivate them and coach them like he would another team, but all of Tark's supposed friends convinced him that he had to reinvent the wheel."

The Spurs were 9-11 after losing to Houston on December 17. Tarkanian headed home for a meeting with McCombs the next day.

"I had no intention of firing Jerry when we met after the Houston game," said McCombs. "But he started talking about his point guards. Then he said, 'You misled me. You said this was a good team. Well, it can't even play .500 ball.' I asked him why he thought that, given the fact that we had won a lot of games in the previous three years. Jerry said his friends told him that his team wasn't even as good as some .500 clubs in the league."

As Tarkanian spoke, McCombs sighed, leaned back in his chair, and told Jerry to wait. Then McCombs left his office. He went into Bob Bass's office and discussed Tarkanian's negative attitude.

"Red, you can't fire another coach," said Bass.

"Bob, he doesn't believe that he can coach," said McCombs.

Then McCombs asked Bass to telephone John Lucas. McCombs wanted to hear if Lucas thought the Spurs were better than a .500 team.

"I am a recovering alcoholic," said McCombs. "I had been friends with John Lucas for a long time. I respected what he did with his life, and I've never been afraid to take a chance."

Bass and Lucas also were good friends; they usually had lunch together whenever Bass was in Houston, where Lucas's rehabilitation center is located. Today, both Bass and McCombs claim it was their idea to hire Lucas, and both say they first suggested Lucas to each other. No matter, the Spurs did have a coach on hold.

McCombs went back in to talk with Tarkanian. Once again, Tark was bleak about the team's prospects. According to McCombs, the conversation went like this:

"Jerry, I don't have time to educate you," said McCombs. "If you believe all this bullshit that your friends are telling you, well, it's over."

"What do you mean?" asked Tarkanian. "Am I fired?"

"Jerry, you don't believe you can win with these guys, so I'll get me a coach who thinks he can."

"You can't do that," said Tarkanian.

"I just did," said McCombs.

Tarkanian sat there, stunned. He was sixty-two years old and had never been fired from any job before. His history with the NCAA made him think that no college would hire him. He was done as a pro coach after 20 games, and who else in the NBA would give him a chance?

"I never dreamed I'd get fired that day," said Tarkanian. "There wasn't anything in the papers or anything to tip me off. They pulled the plug on me too quickly. It probably killed my chances to coach in the NBA again, although I'd love the chance."

Two years after he was fired, Tarkanian still sounded like a guy who was hit by a truck but wanted the license plate number. Making matters worse for Tarkanian was that after Lucas took over the team, he started Avery Johnson and the Spurs immediately won 24 of their next 28 games. Where Tarkanian was like a man at a perpetual funeral, Lucas was Mr. Sunshine. It was the perfect personality transplant. The Spurs finished the season with a 39-22 record under Lucas and made it to the second round of the play-offs. NBA types saw the situation as an indictment of college coaches. Lucas was a former all-pro point guard. He had coached the minor-league Miami Tropics of the United States Basketball League. When it came to the pro game, he had a clue of what to do.

So where do NBA coaches come from? NBA general managers struggle with that question every year.

"It's very hard to find people to coach your team," said Cavs general manager Wayne Embry. "The job is so complex. You need to handle the players, deal with the media, know the Xs and Os."

Embry will tell you that it's difficult to turn over what amounts to a $100 million business to a guy who has never been a head coach before.

"Now that the salaries are higher, the owners expect quicker results," said Embry. "Some of them don't want to train a coach."

But if you don't try something new, you end up with a sixty-three-year-old Bill Fitch joining the L.A. Clippers for one last ride in 1994. Or you hire Don Chaney, who has coached nine years in the NBA with a career record 117 games under .500—this despite winning a Coach of the Year Award—and has never taken one of his teams past the first round of the playoffs.

"Finding coaches is a problem," said Hubie Brown. "There is no one formula that works. It's like going into the city and trying to find the neighborhood with the cop who has the respect of people on the street. Or going into an inner-city high school and looking at the teachers. In one class, you'll see a young, big guy who's 6-foot-5 and the kids are tearing down the lights and throwing erasers at him. Across the hall is this ninety-eight-pound, gray-haired lady teaching English, and her kids are silent, taking notes, hanging on her every word. Go figure that one. It's the same in coaching."

Indeed it is.

How does Dick Motta last forever—when Motta never even played high school basketball? And why wasn't Bob Weiss a success? Weiss was a 12-year pro, a hard-nosed guard and a smart player. He later was an assistant for eight years, including six in Dallas under Motta. It would seem that he had the ideal résumé for a head coach, but Weiss was handed three head coaching jobs, and he flopped in San Antonio, in Atlanta, and with the Clippers.

"A lot of times, you just don't know who will do the job until you put him in charge," said Embry. "We don't have a system for training NBA coaches."

It wasn't always that way.

"For a while, the colleges were farm systems for coaches just like they are for players," said Phoenix Suns president Jerry Colangelo. "When I came into the NBA [in the late 1960s], I was appalled by how awful the coaching was. Usually, a former NBA star was the coach, and his idea of practice was to roll out the ball. While he smoked a cigarette and drank coffee, his players scrimmaged."

Colangelo broke into the league as a scout with the Chicago Bulls. He not only looked for players, he watched the coaches. One who impressed him was a guy in Ogden, Utah. John Richard Motta spent six years at Weber State, winning 78 percent of his games. He was thirty-seven years old and already a polished coach.

The Bulls were looking for someone to replace Johnny Kerr, who fit Colangelo's profile of the typical 1960s pro coach: Kerr was a great guy, he knew the league and understood the game, and he had been an All-Star center. But he'd never had to teach basketball, and he went directly from playing in the NBA to becoming a head coach.

But wasn't Johnny Kerr the NBA Coach of the Year in 1966–67 when he led the expansion Chicago Bulls into the playoffs? Yes, he was, but the Bulls' record was just 33-48, pretty meager for a Coach of the Year candidate. Furthermore, Kerr would be the first to tell you that his main job was selling the Bulls to the media and community; it was his assistant, Al Bianchi, who did most of the Xs and Os. The following year, after Bianchi was hired to coach in Seattle, the Bulls record dropped to 29-53 as Kerr coached the team himself without an assistant. Kerr was fired after the second season.

Before leaving the Bulls to take over the expansion Phoenix Suns, Colangelo suggested that Dick Motta be the new Chicago coach. The Bulls hired Motta, and he was there for the next eight years—winning 50 games in four different seasons. He won the 1978 title with Washington, and then had a long career coaching in Dallas.

Ironically, Colangelo hired Kerr to be his first coach of the Suns. But he knew that public relations and fan appeal were as important as the on-court coaching in the first years of a new team. Kerr is a wonderful after-dinner speaker, a tireless promoter, and the kind of redheaded nice guy people simply enjoy having around.

Kerr coached the Suns for one and a half seasons.

"I would have been around a little longer if we had called heads," he said. "Then we would have had Kareem Abdul-Jabbar. Instead, we lost the coin flip [in the 1969 draft] and got Neal Walk."

When Colangelo fired Kerr as a coach, he made Kerr a broadcaster, which turned out to be Kerr's true meal ticket. Colangelo coached the Suns himself for a half season, compiling a 24-20 record after Kerr's 15-23 start. Then Colangelo again needed a coach.

This time, he found Lowell Cotton Fitzsimmons in Manhattan, Kansas. Fitzsimmons was thirty-nine years old. He was 5-foot-7.

He played three years of basketball at a place called Midwestern State, then he coached nine years at Moberly Junior College, followed by two years at Kansas State. In his last season at Kansas State, Fitzsimmons's team had a 20-8 record and won the Big Eight title.

"My understanding is that after the season the Suns owners told Jerry that he could be coach or general manager, but not both," said Fitzsimmons. "So Jerry went shopping for a coach. I know that he talked to Bob Knight, who was at Army back then. Knight turned him down. He interviewed a couple of other well-known coaches, but all they did was take Jerry's offer back to their universities and use it as leverage to get better deals out of their athletic directors. One day, I got a call from Jerry, and for forty-five minutes we talked about the players in the NBA draft. I figured he was just another NBA executive doing his homework. Then he mentioned that he was looking for a coach and did I have any ideas about that. I suggested five names, and I remember two of them being Tex Winter and Norm Stewart. Jerry then said, 'How would you like this job?' I told him that I was always interested in the NBA."

The Suns went 48-34 in Fitzsimmons's first season, even with Neal Walk instead of Kareem Abdul-Jabbar at center, and even though it was only the third year in the history of the Phoenix franchise. Fitzsimmons lasted only two years with the Suns before moving on to Atlanta. Colangelo then hired Butch van Breda Kolff, who had spent five years coaching the Lakers and Pistons. But he fired van Breda Kolff after only seven games and a 3-4 record.

"To be honest, I don't think Jerry had coaching completely out of his system," said Fitzsimmons. "But by the end of that year where he took over for Butch, I believe that Jerry saw that being general manager was a much better job."

In Colangelo's second stint, the Suns were 35-40. He then went coach shopping again, this time stopping in Norman, Oklahoma, where he found thirty-six-year-old John MacLeod. At Oklahoma University, MacLeod had an 80-79 record in six seasons, his best being 18-8 in his final year. His own basketball career was spent as a benchwarmer at little Bellarmine College in Louisville, Kentucky.

MacLeod started slowly, with 30-52 and 32-50 records in his first two seasons. But in his third year, Colangelo suggested that MacLeod hire Al Bianchi as an assistant. Colangelo had seen how Bianchi had helped Johnny Kerr with the Bulls, and the veteran NBA player and coach became the adviser MacLeod needed. Colangelo was also revamping the roster, and in 1975–76 the Suns were 42-40 in the regular season, then got hot in the playoffs and went all the way to the Finals, where they lost in six games to Boston.

Colangelo was named the 1976 Executive of the Year. MacLeod established himself as an NBA coach and survived thirteen and a half seasons with the Suns.

Fitzsimmons, Motta, and MacLeod have to be considered three of the most successful coaches in NBA history. What do they have in common?

1. All were discovered by Jerry Colangelo.
2. None came from a high-profile college program. (Big Eight basketball was a football afterthought until the 1980s.)
3. None were stars at a major college.
4. All were in their late thirties when they were hired.
5. None would be hired by an NBA team today.

"That's because the stakes and the dollars are so much higher now," said Richie Adubato. "Put it this way: Suppose you needed heart surgery tomorrow. Are you going to let the bright kid straight out of medical school do it, or will you hire a guy who has been through 300 procedures and can show you the record of his success rate?"

"But this is basketball, not heart surgery," said Fitzsimmons. "I'm not saying that it's easy for a college coach to come straight into the NBA, but it isn't impossible. A guy can learn, and if he surrounds himself with the right assistants, he can make the adjustment more easily. A lot of pro coaches just flatter themselves by saying a trainer would do better coaching in the NBA than a top college coach; that just doesn't make any sense. The problem is that a lot of teams don't want to take a chance on a college guy."

At the start of the 1994–95 season, twelve of the twenty-seven NBA coaches had had college experience. Some had been pro players who later coached in college, then returned to the NBA; others, like Larry Brown, have coached everywhere. Only Portland's P. J. Carlesimo had come straight from college to a head coaching spot in the NBA.

"A lot of college coaches would have a tough time dealing with the NBA because they don't have the control in the pros that they do in college," said Doug Collins, who was an all-pro guard, then an assistant at Arizona State for a year before taking over the Chicago Bulls in 1986–87. "It can be little things, like the coach being called by his first name in the NBA, but in college he is always Coach so-and-so. Then there are all the aspects of the game such as the clock, the substitution patterns, and all that."

Another factor is money.

"Many of these college coaches have million-dollar deals when you add in their TV shows, shoe contracts, and summer camps," said Wayne Embry. "It isn't worth their while to go into the NBA and risk being fired."

That is especially true with such established coaches as Dean Smith or Bob Knight. What could the NBA do for these men other than ruin their reputations? Portland Trail Blazers owner Paul Allen went after Duke's Mike Krzyzewski and told Coach K., "Write your own ticket." Over the years, Miami and Boston have also offered Krzyzewski chances to coach in the NBA. He turned them all down. Dean Smith said he turned down several NBA offers in the late 1970s and 1980s, including one from the Knicks. In the summer of 1993, Arkansas's Nolan Richardson interviewed with the Atlanta Hawks, then returned to Arkansas and won the national title. Even if the feeler from the Hawks didn't mean more money for Richardson, it certainly helped his prestige, and the Hawks hardly suffered because they hired Lenny Wilkens, who won 57 games in Atlanta and became the 1994 Coach of the Year.

"Our problem may be that we keep going after the elite college coaches," said Colangelo. "Those guys just aren't going to move. Maybe we should look at some of the young guys in the second tier of coaches."

That would include people such as Cincinnati's Bob Huggins,

Florida's Lon Kruger, and Mike Jarvis at George Washington. It is a mystery why Clem Haskins isn't in the NBA; a nine-year pro, Haskins went back to school to learn to coach and has been very successful at Western Kentucky and now Minnesota.

"But even some of these guys in lesser Division I programs have very good deals," said Embry. "The ideal thing to do would be to hire them as an assistant for a couple of years so they could learn the league, but assistants [making $100,000 to $150,000] earn far less than a lot of these younger Division I coaches. The coaches ask, 'Why should I take a pay cut to go into the NBA and be an assistant?' It's a good question."

In the middle 1960s, Jack Ramsay left St. Joseph's College in Philadelphia to serve as the Sixers' player personnel director for two years—after which he took over as coach and became one of the most successful in NBA history. But those two years in the front office were critical to his early success. Then again, Ramsay wasn't even making $40,000 at St. Joseph's, so he didn't have much to lose by moving to the NBA.

Now, NBA executives also have to ask themselves, "Why should I risk turning my team over to some college guy who may need three years to figure out the NBA? I don't need someone to do on-the-job training at my expense."

So what do many of these teams do? They hire Kevin Loughery, Don Chaney, or someone else who has proven to be an average pro coach—at best. They settle for a sure thing—even if it's boring—rather than try to gamble and break out a coach who might become the next Ramsay, Motta, or Fitzsimmons.

Here is another list of coaches, men who never played in the NBA. What do these guys have in common?

Richie Adubato.
Mike Fratello.
Bob Hill.
Brian Hill.
Frank Layden.
Brendan Malone.
Rick Pitino.
Ron Rothstein.

None of them would have become head coaches in the NBA if it weren't for Hubie Brown. If there is a stable of pro coaches, it comes from Brown and the Five-Star summer basketball camps in New Jersey.

For a while, it was Don Nelson's assistants who were being hired as head coaches—Mike Schuler and Garry St. Jean. Before that, there was the Jack Ramsay clique from Philadelphia, the main characters being Paul Westhead, Jack McKinney, and Jimmy Lynam. Some place Chuck Daly with the Five-Stars; others trace his roots back to the Ramsay camp because Daly was a coach at Penn.

But Hubie Brown has had more of his disciples become head coaches than anyone else in recent NBA history. And disciples is the proper word, because most of these guys take what Brown says as gospel. Even if they don't use every one of his theories, they'll tell you that in a perfect world they probably would. That's because there is so much truth in most of what Brown says.

According to Brown, coaches are coaches, be it in junior high school or the NBA. Naturally, a coach adjusts to his talent and the maturity of his players, but at heart he is still a disciplinarian and a teacher.

"If there is one piece of advice I give coaches, it is to stay within your own personality," said Brown. "That's what the great ones do. But even at the NBA level, you find coaches who try to be someone else. The players look right through those guys. Your presence is the key. You have to be honest with yourself and the players. You have to be able to tell them, 'Are we going to be tough on you? Yes. Are we going to criticize you, but also be constructive? Yes. Are we going to be consistent? Absolutely, Yes! By the end of the year, we are going to push you to reach your potential and make you a better player.' That sounds so easy, but at the pro level, these guys are going to *fight you*. And some of them, well, you're just not going to like them at all because they are jerks and morons. But a player will allow you to be tough on him as long as you're fair, constructive, and consistent. He'll take all the crap you dish out if he knows that you won't carry it over to tomorrow. That's a key, holding no grudges."

But some NBA people do hold a grudge against Brown and the

coaches who have come into the league under him. They say that he just hires his buddies from New Jersey . . . and they hire their buddies . . . and it's one big club of guys who never played in the NBA, but believe that they invented the game.

"I don't worry about what people say," said Brown. "All I know is that eight of my assistants have become head coaches in this league. I want someone else to match that." The eight are Stan Albeck, Brendan Malone, Layden, Fratello, Pitino, Adubato, Rothstein, and Bob Hill. Albeck is the only one who was a pro coach before he was hired by Brown.

Most of today's NBA fans know Brown for his excellent work on TNT's NBA telecasts. Some say that he loses them when he becomes too technical, so they're aware that he coached somewhere. But Brown hasn't coached in the NBA since he was fired 16 games into the 1986–87 season by the New York Knicks. His career record in the NBA is 341-400. In nine-plus seasons with Atlanta and the Knicks, he never reached the Finals and survived the first round of the playoffs only three times. His best season as a coach—at least in terms of record—was in 1975 when he took the Kentucky Colonels to the ABA title in his rookie year as a pro head coach.

Brown's critics throw this record back at him. They ask, what has this guy ever won? And what have most of his assistants done when they became head coaches? Only Pitino and Fratello have been consistent winners—and Pitino seems far more comfortable in the college ranks.

"He [Brown] is overrated," Doug Moe told *Sports Illustrated* in 1983. "He's everybody's conception of what a good coach should be, but what has he done? Hubie is very insecure and an average coach who happens to be great at promoting himself. Plus, I defy anyone to say his teams aren't boring."

Yet just as those who owe the beginnings of their careers to Brown can sometimes overstate his influence, Brown's critics are too quick to dismiss him and his impact on the league.

"I was a veteran player with Kentucky when Hubie was hired to coach the Colonels," said Gene Littles, a veteran NBA assistant. "None of us had ever heard or seen anything like the guy. He came in talking about deflections, converting on a certain percentage of fast break opportunities, and all kinds of stats we had never heard of. It was like the guy was a mad professor of basketball. He mesmerized us and made us look at the game differently than we had before."

Brown grew up poor in Elizabeth, New Jersey, and attended Niagara University on an athletic scholarship.

"Larry Costello, Hubie, and I were on the baseball team," said Frank Layden. "We were very close, but we had no idea that all of us would end up in the NBA. Larry talked about going to dental school and later became an excellent guard in the NBA. Hubie and I just wanted to coach, and we went right to the bottom and worked our way up."

Layden played a grand total of 18 games of college basketball, averaging 2 points for Niagara. He then coached in junior high for three years, and spent seven more winters as a high school basketball coach.

Brown was a starting point guard in his last two years at Niagara. He seldom shot, but he played hard and smart—the typical profile of an undertalented, overachieving athlete who later becomes a coach. Brown did a two-year hitch in the army and didn't begin his coaching career until 1959. He was already twenty-six years old. He coached at a few New Jersey high schools; in one of his leagues, the other coaches included Rollie Massimino, Dick Vitale, and Richie Adubato.

One player in that league was Mike Fratello, a 5-foot-7 guard at Hackensack High. Fratello was Brown's kind of player, a 150-pound center and noseguard in football who played basketball with the same frightening tenacity. After a game in which Brown's team beat Hackensack, Brown noticed that Fratello was limping on a badly sprained ankle. He took Fratello home and treated the ankle, and a friendship was born that would eventually lead Fratello to the NBA.

But the central experience for what would become the Hubie Brown line of coaches was the Five-Star Camp. Started by Howard Garfinkel in 1966, this summer camp was designed so the best high school players in the New York–New Jersey area could play against each other and receive instruction from the top high school and small-college coaches in the area. It quickly became like honey to college coaches, who swarmed around to evaluate the talent and make contacts. Garfinkel began his own college scouting service, rating high school players with one to five stars; a player given five stars was supposed to be a future pro.

Over the years, the Five-Star camp was held at several spots in New Jersey and Pennsylvania. Later, other camps would follow the formula, the most famous being those run by the Nike and Adidas shoe companies. But the Five-Star Camp remains the king. In 1994, 419 high school seniors each paid $375 to attend. According to Garfinkel, 202 of his campers eventually played in the NBA, including Michael Jordan and Patrick Ewing. NCAA rules bar Division I college coaches from running clinics or doing any personal instruction with the players; that teaching is left to high school and small-college coaches, and Brown was one of the first guest lecturers.

"After a day of coaching and speaking, the coaches themselves would get together," said Adubato. "I can remember a group of us—Chuck Daly, Dick Vitale, Fratello, Brendan Malone, and Brendan Suhr—talking basketball with Hubie until three or four in the morning. That kind of thing happened all the time."

The coaches got to know each other. They also invited other coaches they knew to the camp.

"What you find are the coaches who are willing to put basketball in front of everything else," said Adubato. "Hubie was at the center of it. We picked his brain to death. He was just so far ahead of everyone else. He had thought about things that other coaches never did. He could explain a complicated point to you in very clear, concise terms."

Brown had both substance and style. He didn't speak in sentences, he uttered proclamations. He could tell you how to grill a steak and make it sound as if he'd just presented you with the secret to the theory of relativity. Brown would become so *intense* and make it seem that his subject was so *important* to him, that you made it important to you. It was why he was often a candidate for Teacher of the Year during his different high school stints. When he discusses the ninety-eight-pound English teacher who can keep a room of tough kids in their seats and their attention riveted on her words, that is exactly how Brown's friends and admirers talk about him.

*   *   *

In 1967, Brown left Fairlawn High to become an assistant at William and Mary. He took a pay cut from nearly $20,000 to $7,000. His next stop was as an assistant at Duke, where he still was making $7,000. He spent four years at Duke under Vic Bubas. Brown wanted a head coaching job at a major college, but in 1972 he was hired as an assistant by Larry Costello in Milwaukee.

"That was the old Niagara connection," said Layden. "When Hubie became a head coach in Atlanta, he hired me as his assistant. While I had lectured occasionally at the Five-Star camps, I wasn't one of the guys like Fratello, Rothstein, and Adubato. I was the head coach at Niagara when Hubie hired me with the Hawks."

That's really where Hubie's Men began to infiltrate the NBA, when he was named coach of the Atlanta Hawks in 1976.

Here's the family tree:

1. Brown hired Layden. Then Layden left the Hawks to become the head coach in Utah. Brown hired Fratello and Brendan Suhr as his assistants.
2. Vitale became the head coach of the Detroit Pistons in 1978, and he hired Five-Star friend Adubato. Vitale was fired as head coach, then Adubato took over—and he was later fired by the Pistons.
3. When Brown moved to the New York Knicks in 1982, he had several assistants—Adubato, Ron Rothstein, Bob Hill, and Rick Pitino. Brown knew Pitino because Pitino had been a player at the Five-Star camps.
4. Fratello became the head coach of the Atlanta Hawks, partly because of Brown's recommendation. He hired Rothstein as an assistant. When Rothstein moved to Detroit to be an assistant under Chuck Daly, Fratello turned to Brian Hill, a friend from New Jersey who also was in Fratello's wedding party.
5. When Fratello became Cleveland's head coach in 1993, he hired Adubato and Rothstein as his assistants.
6. Brian Hill became Orlando's head coach in 1993. When he needed a top assistant in the fall of 1994, he hired Adubato away from the Cavs.

There is more, but you get the idea—these guys keep hiring each other. That is one of the complaints from those who don't like the Five-Star Gang. The other is that none of these guys were star players at a major college, none were head coaches at a major college, and nearly all of them are from the New York–New Jersey–Eastern Pennsylvania area.

"When I hired a guy, it's because he was a teacher first," said Brown. "I didn't care what kind of talent they had as a high school or college player. But I did care about how they reacted with talented basketball players—that is crucial to coaching. To me, the best place to watch coaches teach was at the Five-Star camps. I'd see them grow from high school coaches into college coaches. In the camps, I'd see them coach a team in practice, and then in game situations. By the time I hired them, I knew these guys very well."

Brown's critics, particularly the ex-players who have become coaches, still ask, "Just who are these guys?" Lord knows, their résumés prior to their entering the NBA were unimpressive to say the least:

- Fratello played only one year of college basketball at little Montclair State in New Jersey. He then helped scout for Brown's high school team in Fairlawn. He later was an assistant at James Madison, Rhode Island, and Villanova (under Rollie Massimino). Brown brought him to the NBA in 1978. He was never a head coach anywhere until he took over the Hawks in 1983.
- Adubato played basketball at William Paterson College in New Jersey. He was a high school coach in Brown's league, then later the head coach at Division III Upsala College, where his record was 100-62. He went from Upsala to the NBA thanks to Vitale. Adubato was an assistant under Brown, and later was a head coach with the Pistons and Dallas.
- Rothstein played three years of college ball at Rhode Island, where he averaged 5.3 points. He coached high school ball in New York for nineteen years, and also spent a year as an assistant under Adubato at Upsala College. He later scouted for the Hawks and Knicks when Brown was the head coach, then was hired as a full-time NBA assistant by Fratello in Atlanta. He has been a head coach in Miami and Detroit.
- Brian Hill played basketball at Kennedy College in Nebraska. He

was an assistant at Montclair State—Fratello's alma mater. He also was a head coach at Lehigh (a 75-131 record in eight years) before being hired as an assistant by Fratello in Atlanta in 1987. He became the head coach of Orlando in 1993.

- Bob Hill averaged 2.2 points per game in three years at Bowling Green. He was an assistant at several universities, including Pittsburgh and Kansas, before Brown hired him as an assistant in New York in 1985. He replaced Brown as interim coach with the Knicks in 1986—his first head coaching job anywhere. Hill later became the head coach at Indiana and San Antonio. He also was an assistant under Brian Hill in Orlando in 1993–94.
- Rick Pitino was a star player at St. Dominic's High in Oyster Bay, New York, and captain of the basketball team at U. Mass. He was an assistant at Hawaii and Syracuse and the head coach at Boston University, where he had a 91-51 record. Brown first knew him as a high school player, and he hired Pitino to be an assistant with the Knicks in 1983. Pitino later became an exceptional coach with Providence, the Knicks (for two years), and the University of Kentucky.
- Brendan Malone played basketball at Iona University in New York, but was hardly considered a star. He was the head coach for 10 years at New York City's Power Memorial High, then spent six years as an assistant under Jim Boeheim at Syracuse. He also was the head coach at Rhode Island for two years before Hubie Brown brought Malone to the NBA as an assistant with the Knicks in 1986. He moved to the Pistons as an assistant in 1988, and stayed there until Isiah Thomas became an honorary Five-Star by hiring Malone to coach Thomas's expansion Toronto franchise.

"The Five-Star guys network like crazy and help each other out," said Cotton Fitzsimmons. "They are very proud of it."

Longtime NBA assistant Gene Littles said, "What the Five-Star guys do is take care of each other. When one of them gets fired, there is another one there to hire him as an assistant. It gives them a great chance to get back on their feet. That's a tremendous advantage when you are trying to survive in this league."

But while other coaches are rather suspicious, they often hire their own, too.

"In Utah, one of my assistants was Scott Layden," said Frank Layden. "My connection with him was that I married his mother."

Cotton Fitzsimmons, Don Nelson, and Dick Motta all hired their sons as assistants at some point in their NBA careers. But that was usually as far as it went.

"What some people resent is the fact that the Five-Star people probably put in more hours, watch more tape, and simply give more of themselves to the game than anyone else in the NBA," said Adubato.

No, what a lot of NBA people don't like is that the Five-Star guys will tell you how hard they work, with the egotistical implication that no one else works as hard.

There is something else that must be said for them: they take the time to train each other to become head coaches. And that began with Brown.

"I told my assistants that I would allow them to have an identity," said Brown. "When I went to Milwaukee, Larry Costello gave me that chance [by permitting Brown to coach the defense]. There were some intimidating guys on that team, with Oscar Robertson, Kareem [Abdul-Jabbar], and Bobby Dandridge. I came to them as an assistant coach from Duke, and Larry Costello knew that the players had to see me work to gain any respect for me. He gave me that chance, and it was something I never forgot. When I was the head coach, my assistants also were out there coaching. I might have one group of players with me at one end of the floor, and an assistant would be at the other end with some players. Or I'd have my two assistants divide up the team and work with them while I'd oversee the whole thing. An assistant must develop a real relationship with the players. He must have some clashes with them in order to gain their respect."

Since none of his assistants other than Albeck had pro experience, Brown also had to teach them the NBA game.

"I was hired by Hubie [in 1978] after being an assistant at Villanova," said Fratello. "I was really nervous, but Hubie kept telling me to just watch and listen. I kept a pack of index cards with me during practice, and I'd write down things he said during practice. Then I'd take them back to my room and study them at night. After our first day of double-session practices, Hubie told Frank Layden and me that he had to give a clinic the next day in St. Louis and he wanted us to run practice. I was in a complete state of panic, and I asked him what we should do. He said to do the same things we did the first day. In fact, he wanted me to run the practice. I was thinking to myself, 'When I blow the whistle, I wonder if the guys will stop and listen.' Hubie read my mind. He told me, 'Michael, you have been a coach all your life. Now go out there and coach. Don't worry about it.' He was throwing me into the fire just so I'd know that I could do it."

But Brown also gave his coaches speeches about how the NBA game is different because the twelfth guy on the team is probably better than the best guy you coached in college. He'd tell his assistants about how they have to adjust to the talent, how this is really the only place where the game is played above the rim—and what that means in terms of putting together an offense and a defense. He would tell them that they'd spend the first month or two "in absolute shock" because of the talent level.

"In my first year, I'd sometimes scrimmage with the Hawks when we were down to nine guys in practice because of injuries," said Fratello. "It was a tremendous experience for me as a way to understand the kind of athletes I was now coaching. Forget trying to get off a shot; that was impossible. It was nearly impossible for me to get free even to catch a pass forty feet from the basket."

Of course, the players had to be amused by having the 5-foot-7, 150-pound Fratello on the same court with them. Brown knew this, but he also was aware that this was a dramatic way for Fratello to get a message about the ability of NBA players.

"The truth is that there has never been a college coach who has stepped into this league and knocked it on its ass in his first season," said Brown. "When it comes to some of these guys, they only know that a basket is worth two points—that's it. So we start from page one and work from there. The inexperience of my assistants didn't bother me because I knew that they were smart guys who worked hard. They'd learn the idiosyncrasies of the pro game. They'd learn the referees, the matchups, the shot clock, and the different coaches and their styles."

But there was more.

"When I was an assistant in Milwaukee, Wayne Embry was the

general manager, and he allowed me and my wife to attend the All-Star Game," said Brown. "That was a way to meet people for your next job. My assistants all had it in their contracts that the team would pay for them and their wives to go to the All-Star Game. Why the wives, too? Because she may meet the wife of a general manager. When the GM has fired his coach, his wife may say, 'You know, I met so-and-so's wife and she is really a nice person.' Wives become friends and they can help their husbands get head coaching jobs."

There's even more.

"Everyone used to laugh at how we charted things," said Brown. "Now, everyone charts during games. I started the charts when I was coaching in Kentucky, and it grew into a four-page form. We not only keep track of how we score on certain plays, but how we score on fast breaks, second shots, side out-of-bounds plays, under-the-basket out-of-bounds plays, half-court traps . . . virtually everything that goes on during a game. Then we condense it and use it at halftime and after games."

And there's more.

"We put up the rosters of every NBA team on our office walls," he said. "Then we had a list of all the top college players, the best CBA players, and the best players in Europe. All of that was on the wall, too. We did that so we always knew what players were where in case we needed to put our finger on someone."

Yes, there's even more.

"When my assistants finally did get a chance to coach their own team, they would know an offense and a defense that worked in the regular season, and also an offense and defense that worked at playoff time—not everything you do in the regular season will work in the playoffs. Furthermore, the coach will have a complete understanding of these offenses and defenses and be able to teach them. They don't have to use everything, but I wanted to give them a foundation to be a pro coach—a crash course in the NBA."

This is all reminiscent of the line Jim Finks, the general manager of the Chicago Bears, had about the Dallas Cowboys: "I don't know if they were the first team to use a computer [to compile draft information], but they definitely were the first to brag about it." Still, it has worked for men such as Pitino, Bob Hill, and Fratello.

"If you think about it, the only way I was going to get a head coaching job in the NBA would have been if my father had bought a team," said Fratello. "Or some team had to be willing to take a chance. In this case, it was Ted Turner and Stan Kasten in Atlanta. They knew me from being Hubie's assistant with the Hawks, and that helped convince them that I deserved a shot."

Fratello coached the Hawks for seven years, winning at least 50 games four times. His NBA record is even better than Brown's. Other than Pitino, he is the most successful of the Five-Star Gang.

What kind of coach was Brown?

Doug Moe labeled him an egotist whose teams were boring. Others agreed, especially if they were talking about the Hubie Brown who coached in New York in the middle 1980s. They said his offense was a snoozer: Pound the ball inside. Power left. Power right. The Woody Hayes of basketball. Keep the ball on the ground, chew up the clock, and grind it out. They say Brown made the game ugly, and each possession was like life and death as he called every play from the sidelines.

There are elements of truth in this. In his first two years in Atlanta, his teams averaged slightly over 100 points—near the bottom of the league. But in the next two years, the Hawks were in the middle of the pack. They were not afraid to run once Brown assembled some athletic players.

But Brown also was innovative in his use of the roster. In his five years with the Hawks, he played ten players almost every quarter.

"When I was an assistant in Milwaukee, we had an eight-man rotation," said Brown. "That meant there were four players every night who were unhappy because they didn't get into the game. I mean, we had one of the best records in the league and there were still four guys who were pissed off. So I promised myself that when I got my own team, I'd try to use at least ten guys."

Hawks owner Ted Turner hired Brown in 1976. The Hawks were a mess with a 29-53 record, and Turner wanted to unload most of the team's high-salaried and experienced players. Within two years under Brown, the Hawks had the NBA's youngest team—and one that was fun to watch.

"When you are young and have a low payroll, the only way to

win is with energy," said Brown. "You know that you are going to shoot a low percentage, so you have to get more shots than the other team. To create more shots, you have to press and trap, force the other team to turn the ball over and then score off their mistakes. In the three years in Atlanta, we were one of the worst shooting percentage teams in the league, but we were near the top in forcing turnovers and attempting shots."

He told his team inspirational stories. One of them was about Dick Cunningham, a backup center with the Milwaukee Bucks.

"We called him the Cement Mixer because he was 6-foot-10, 255 pounds," said Brown. "He never got in a game because Kareem was playing over forty-six minutes a night. We practiced two hours a day, seven days a week. In my two years with the Bucks, we never had a day off. It was amazing how hard we practiced. Oscar, Kareem, and those guys didn't like it, but they practiced anyway. After every practice, the Cement Mixer would do his sprints, running the length of the court and back. Then he would sprint to the top of the old Milwaukee arena, right up all those stairs. It was incredible, this guy's energy. In my two years there, Kareem was always fighting migraines, and there were nine games where he couldn't play because of those migraines. Well, the Cement Mixer started those nine games, and we were 9-0. I mean, here was a guy playing two minutes most nights, but when Kareem was out—nine times he was able to play all forty-eight minutes—we won all those games. That tells you that your twelfth man has to be in as good shape as your starters. It also tells you that you never know when your time is coming, but it is."

If Brown led the league in parables, he also broke the sound barrier with his screams. Players were morons, cement heads, cinder heads, idiots.

"You know, some people said to my players, 'How could you play for that guy?' I said, what do they know?" said Brown. "Were they in the gym and the locker room with me and my players every day? They didn't see what I was doing for a guy's career. They didn't see how I'd put some jerk into a game every night for sixteen to thirty-two minutes, and I'd have to argue and fight with him to get him to do things so that he could be on the floor for those sixteen to thirty-two minutes."

But some coaches are effective by not yelling.

"I know that," said Brown. "God gave those coaches that kind of personality, and some are very good coaches."

Atlanta was the perfect laboratory for a basketball professor like Brown. He cleaned out the malcontents and the stubborn veterans; "sending a message" is what he called it. This was in the late 1970s when there was no salary cap, so it was easy to turn over a roster. Then Brown was able to assemble a group of young players and mold—some would say pound—them into his own image.

"After a few years in Atlanta, we had three guys on the All-Star team—John Drew, Eddie Johnson, and Dan Roundfield," said Brown. "You see, players will put up with a lot if they see you are helping their games."

While Brown's Hawks never went further than the second round of the playoffs, they steadily improved from 31 to 41 to 46 and finally 50 victories in 1979–80. But the next season, several of his players—including stars Drew and Johnson—developed drug problems, and the experiment blew up in Brown's face. He won only 32 games and was fired late in the season. Brown landed in New York the following year, and had some success with the Knicks in his first two seasons. He inherited a team that won 33 games and pushed them to 44 and 47 victories. But then he had conflicts with management, massive injuries, and not all of his players bought his philosophy. Brown was fired after a 4-12 start in the 1986–87 season. He has had chances to coach other NBA teams, but seems happier doing his television work and his clinics.

Hubie Brown is just the most visible symbol of the long-standing division between the former NBA players turned coaches and the coaches who came from the colleges.

"I came into the league in 1973–74," said Brown, "and that was the height of the influx of college coaches with guys such as Fitch, Motta, Fitzsimmons, MacLeod, and Ramsay. The coaches would socialize, and you'd see all the ex-pros at one table. You knew that some of them were looking at the college coaches and saying, 'What the hell do they know? They never played the game.' Meanwhile, the college coaches were together at the other table."

While Brown didn't say it, the college coaches were saying,

"What do those guys know about Xs and Os and organization? All they did was play. They never paid any dues to earn the right to coach in the NBA."

As Brown said, "It took a lot of years for that to break down, but it did for the college guys who proved their worth by standing the test of time."

Some NBA people will tell you that another faction is the Five-Star Gang. They have their own approach to the game, and many in the NBA don't like it.

"I've just never been a big fan of theirs," said Motta. "They always have all the answers."

"I know that the Five-Star guys chart everything," said Cotton Fitzsimmons. "That's fine for them. But I didn't need a chart to tell me that my team gave up 15 fast breaks, and 10 of those led to baskets. I didn't need a chart to tell me that my team was getting run out of the gym or killed on the boards. They can say that I'm not coaching. Fine. I can say they are overcoaching, just trying to keep up with the Joneses."

Many NBA players-turned-coaches insist that basketball is an art. It's jazz, not a symphony, and every note cannot be captured on paper. They say that the Five-Stars want to attach a number to every facet of the game, and that they reject anyone who doesn't follow their scientific approach. Some ex-players now coaching also say that the Five-Stars often don't understand players. Because the Five-Stars didn't play in the NBA, they don't comprehend injuries, fatigue, and other human failings that players have.

Brown and his disciples have done more than their part to strangle the game by slowing it down and over-coaching. But give credit to Brian Hill for letting his Orlando Magic team run. There are some people who will blame Brown for everything they hate about the NBA. Others genuflect at the mention of his name. Somewhere in the middle is the truth.

Like him or not, Brown must be admired for the fact that he is always thinking about the game. He was the first to suggest that a team should play the same style of offense in the regular season as in the playoffs—if there is a huge drop in the points scored from the season to the playoffs, that team is in trouble. It was Chuck Daly who later made that theory popular with the

Pistons' Bad Boys. Brown also was innovative defensively, in terms of pressing and double-teaming men in the low post from different directions. Finally, Brown must be given credit for taking the time to train other coaches to run an NBA team. That is more than most coaches are willing to do, and it's something this league desperately needs.

9 The Worst Job in the NBA

Gene Littles knows what they will write on his tombstone: INTERIM COACH, RIP.

The trouble is that no interim coach ever rests in peace—and very few of them survive the job.

"I've been there three times," said Littles. "After the first two times, I promised myself that I'd never do it again."

As the 1994–95 season opened, Littles was on the Denver bench. It was his third season next to head coach Dan Issel, his sixteenth in the NBA.

"At one time, I wanted to be a head coach very much," he said. "But after what I had been through, as I went into the [1994–95] season, I wasn't sure if I wanted to be a head coach anymore unless there were ideal circumstances. I knew for sure that I didn't want to be an interim coach. I figured with Dan Issel in Denver, as popular as he was and as good as our team seemed, that would never be an issue."

Littles figured wrong.

Issel quit the Nuggets 34 games into the regular season. They had an 18-16 record, and he was under no pressure from the fans or media. In fact, Issel is a Denver icon, having been a Hall of Fame player for the Nuggets and a respected broadcaster before taking over as coach in 1992–93. He had never been a coach at any level when he was hired by the Nuggets.

"Before Dan accepted the Denver job, he called me," said Littles. "I was working in the front office for the Hornets. I had been their interim coach, and then they put me upstairs. I wasn't doing much in the way of basketball. Dan told me about his offer from the Nuggets and wanted to know if I'd go with him as his top assistant. He knew I had been a coach in the league for a long time, and he thought my experience would help him."

This was a lifeline to Littles, who was buried in the Hornets front office. He thought that he had received a raw deal in Charlotte. He had been an assistant under Dick Harter for the first one and a half seasons of the expansion franchise, then took over for Harter as an interim coach, finishing 11-31 in 1989–90. He was given the Hornets for the entire 1990–91 season, improving their record to 26-56.

"The next year, we were ready to draft Larry Johnson," said Littles. "I was going to start getting some players to work with, but then they made a change."

Allan Bristow had been the general manager. While deciding to draft Larry Johnson, Bristow also decided that he'd like to coach the star forward from UNLV.

"The Denver offer was super," said Littles. "I had played with Dan with the old Kentucky Colonels [of the American Basketball Association in 1974–75]. We are good friends. The general manager [Bernie Bickerstaff] is someone I respect. It sounded like it would be fun."

For two years, it was.

Issel replaced Paul Westhead, and the Nuggets went from a 24-58 record to 36-46 in 1992–93. In 1993–94, the Nuggets were 42-40, but more importantly, they came from an 0–2 deficit to beat Seattle in a five-game series in the playoffs. The Nuggets became the first eighth-seeded team in NBA history to knock out a top seed.

"At that time, we thought that was great," said Littles. "But it might not have been the best thing for our young team. Maybe we would have been better off if we had lost to Seattle in five games."

Why?

"Because our young players came into camp the next year really thinking that they had won something," said Littles. "It became harder for us to convince them to play together. The expectations around the team had increased, but the guys weren't mature enough to handle it. That really bothered Dan."

Littles said that in their first year together, "Dan would tell us to have fun. I'd get on a guy during a timeout for taking a bad shot, and Dan would tell me to let it go. Let the guys relax and grow. But in our third year, I was the one telling Dan to relax and not jump all over guys in the huddle. You could tell, coaching had changed him."

Issel became reclusive on the road. After a game, he went directly to his room, usually calling his wife.

"You knew that he was replaying the game in his head, over and over," said Littles. "In his first couple of years, officials didn't get to him like they did in that last season. Suddenly, he would turn red and get so upset—I thought he was going to break a blood vessel somewhere. I don't know how many times I had to grab Dan before he ended up chasing the officials down the floor."

Issel talked to Littles and his other assistant, Mike Evans, about how the players didn't seem to be responding like they had in the 1994 playoffs. He wondered why the players weren't preparing themselves for the games in the same way they had a few years ago.

"Once in a while, Dan would tell us, 'I don't need this,' " said Littles. "But every coach says that during the season. What I did notice was that he no longer enjoyed the wins, and the losses were tearing him up. He had a few guys bitching about their playing time. We had a rookie in Jalen Rose, who really is a good kid. But Jalen just couldn't understand why he wasn't getting a lot of minutes. We'd tell him about how he had to work his way in, how he could watch and learn things from the bench—but he just couldn't understand that. He'd never sat before in his life and didn't think the players we had were any better than him. As I said, he is a good kid. But it was tough to coach him."

Issel kept asking Littles why the team didn't seem to be as hungry as it was the year before.

"That bothered him," said Littles. "This is what happens, especially to an inexperienced coach. It is so hard for them to accept the fact that maybe their team just isn't as good as they thought it was—or as good as other people think it should be. The coach takes it personally. He wonders why he can't turn the key to get things going."

Littles thought that Issel had to be tormenting himself in those long nights in hotel rooms. He'd invite Issel to the coffee shop for a sandwich or to the hotel bar for a beer. Issel rarely accepted the offer.

Sometimes, Issel told Littles how he wanted to play everybody, but how was he supposed to find enough minutes for twelve guys? And how come the players didn't understand that it was impossible to play twelve guys?

"Once in a while Dan would say, 'These guys are killing me,' " said Littles.

But the coaches would laugh. Coaches in every locker room from CYO ball to the NBA have been known to utter that sentence.

"Despite all that, I never thought he'd resign," said Littles. "Okay, we weren't playing as well as we thought we could, but we were still 18-16. We also were without LaPhonso Ellis [due to knee surgery], and he probably was our best player. I saw how Dan's personality had changed, but I had seen how coaching changed other guys I knew, and they never quit."

On January 14, 1995, the Nuggets beat Houston.

"It was one of our best games of the year," said Littles. "Dan said he wanted to meet with Mike Evans and me after the game. We knew that there had been some trade talks going on, so we wondered if Dan had something he wanted to discuss with us about the players."

When Littles and Evans walked into Issel's office, the coach was there along with general manager Bernie Bickerstaff. The meeting went like this:

ISSEL: "Guys, I'm outta here."
(The assistant coaches began to laugh until they saw the grave look on Issel's face.)

LITTLES: "What do you mean, you're outta here?"

ISSEL: "I'm gone."

LITTLES: "You're what?"

ISSEL: "I told Bernie earlier in the day that I'm gonna resign. Now, I'm telling you guys, I just can't take this anymore."
(Suddenly, Evans and Littles knew that Issel was serious. They looked at Bickerstaff, who hadn't said a word.)

BICKERSTAFF: "I'm not going to take it [the coaching job]."
  (Bickerstaff had been the coach of the Seattle Supersonics in the
  late 1980s and had to quit because of bleeding ulcers.)

ISSEL: "I told Bernie that you guys can handle the team for the rest
  of the year."

BICKERSTAFF: "Gene, I'd like you to finish the year with the team.
  And Mike, you've got to really help Gene. We need you guys."

Reluctantly, Littles agreed to coach the team for the rest of the
year.

When Littles walked out of the room, he realized that he was an
interim coach for the third time—believed to be a dubious NBA
record.

"I didn't sleep that night," said Littles. "In fact, I hardly slept
for a week. I had already been having a tough year. I had just gone
through a divorce. About a week before Dan quit, I had been
hospitalized for a day. They found that my blood sugar was way
down and that I was dehydrated. I had never been sick in my life
like that. Now, I was the head coach."

Littles took the job for a couple of reasons: He had healthy
respect for both Issel and Bickerstaff. He was grateful because the
two men gave him a chance to get back on the bench.

"I also had four years left on my contract and I had assurances
that I would be around in some capacity if they decided to hire
another coach," said Littles. "That was important to me, because
both times I was an interim coach before, all that happened was
that my ass ended up out the door."

After meeting with his assistant coaches following that victory
over Houston, Issel went home. The next morning at practice, he
called the players together and told them that he was resigning.

"The players all looked at each other and said, 'Jeez, he quit,' "
said Littles. "They were like us the night before. They couldn't
believe it. Guys were shaking their heads and mumbling, 'The big
guy quit on us.' They had no idea what to make of it."

"When Dan said he was resigning, I thought he was kidding,"
Dikembe Mutombo told reporters. "Then instantly, there was silence. There was nothing anyone could say. The last few days, I

could look at his face and see that something was wrong. But I never thought he'd do this."

A few days before he quit, Issel had an argument with Jalen Rose over playing time. Mutombo had been complaining that he wanted more shots. Reggie Williams was worried about his minutes, especially after the Nuggets signed free agent Dale Ellis and were working him into the rotation at small forward. There was a practice where Issel said nothing, he just sat in the corner and left Littles and Evans in charge. But he also had two years left on his contract; no one thought he'd quit.

"Dan talked about how he just couldn't get the guys to play hard every night," said Littles.

After informing the players of his decision, Issel held a press conference and told the media exactly what he had said to Bickerstaff a few days earlier: "I can't handle this, I don't like the person I've become. I'm not having fun. I need to make this decision for my own good and the good of my family. I don't want to coach anymore."

Issel said he'd never envisioned himself as a "coaching lifer." He didn't know if he had "coaching burnout" because he had never been a coach before. Over and over, he just said that coaching was making him into a person that he didn't want to be.

"I admire Dan because he was able to see himself changing and he realized that he didn't need this job," said Littles. "Some guys, their entire identity is tied up in coaching. They'd never quit under any circumstances. I give Dan a lot of credit for caring about what the job was doing to him and his family."

Littles took over and discovered that the team was in a coma. They lost seven of their first eight games.

"They were in shock," Littles said. "They were hung up on the fact that 'The Big Guy quit on us.' They had no emotion."

It sounded as if the players were using Issel's resignation as an excuse to no longer care about the team. When Littles cut Reggie Williams's playing time, Williams stood up and said he was resigning as co-captain. The team's other captain—Mutombo—was saying that the NBA "could go to hell" because he wasn't voted to the All-Star team. But Littles wasn't upset by Mutombo.

"I love Dikembe," he said. "He plays so hard. He's very emotional and he says what he thinks. I'll tell you, I respect him because he doesn't just care about himself, he cares about the team, too. He'll get on other guys for being selfish or not playing hard— Dikembe practices as hard as anyone on the team—but the other guys don't listen to him. I wish they would."

Another problem for Littles was that his stint as coach overlapped with the Muslim holiday of Ramadan. Muslims spend the month-long holiday fasting from sunup to sundown. This meant that Nuggets guard Mahmoud Abdul-Rauf, one of the team's top scoring threats, could never quite schedule a meal early enough to be ready for a 7:30 game. Since he wasn't eating anything until after the games, he was weak, and his performance suffered.

Littles was puzzled by the Nuggets' mood immediately after Issel's resignation.

"I'm not sure exactly what it was," said Littles. "I just know that we were flat night after night. I had a meeting with the guys. I told them that we were the last team to make the playoffs last year. Nothing is guaranteed. It is easy to drop right out [of the playoffs]. I talked about playing hard and playing together."

The players also had some meetings during the losing streak. Mutombo spoke, but the players pretty much ignored him. Their attitude was, "What did he ever win? He's a young guy just like us." Cliff Levingston talked about his days with the championship Chicago Bulls and the attitude on that winning team—and how the Nuggets should try to capture that championship mind-set.

"The problem was that these young guys don't remember how well Cliff played for the Bulls in some of those playoff games," said Littles. "All they knew was that Michael Jordan was on those teams, and Cliff wasn't Michael Jordan. Some of our players thought that Cliff was just another guy on the bench."

Littles said that the Nuggets needed a veteran player with credibility to help tell the facts of life to this young team. "We needed a role model for our players," said Littles.

The players weren't interested in Levingston, because he was at the end of his career and playing little. Mutombo was "one of them," so it was hard to take his harsh words seriously. Williams was supposed to be a co-captain, but he is a shy man by nature and he quit as captain anyway because his playing time was cut—and that's not exactly the ideal "team-first" message.

So the leadership of the team fell upon Littles—and the players knew that he was nothing more than an interim coach, a guy keeping the chair warm until the real coach was hired.

In a couple of cases since 1980, being an interim coach has led to a championship. When Magic Johnson clashed with Paul Westhead, and Westhead was fired after a 7-4 start in 1981–82, Pat Riley came down from the broadcasting booth to take over the team. He won the 1982 title—his first of four with the Lakers.

Don Chaney was the NBA Coach of the Year in 1991 with the Houston Rockets. But he opened the 1991–92 season with a 26-26 record, and the Rockets decided to put longtime Houston assistant Rudy Tomjanovich in charge.

"I didn't want to take it," said Tomjanovich. "If I stayed as the assistant, I knew I was pretty safe. I had spent twenty-four years with the Rockets as a player and assistant coach. What if I became the head coach and we lost? Then I'd be fired. I'd have to move my family. It looked like a real gamble."

Tomjanovich had done everything but be a head coach. He was a five-time All-Star. He had scouted on the road. He had helped run practices at home for coaches such as Bill Fitch, Del Harris, and Chaney. He had broken down films. He had taken an active part in the college draft. But he had never been a head coach, and in Littles's words, "That chance is almost impossible to pass up because you know that the chance may never come again."

Tomjanovich took it. He finished the 1991–92 season with a 16-14 record. Hakeem Olajuwon told the media that Rudy T. was a great guy and the Rockets should make him the full-time coach. The Houston front office didn't have any better ideas, so Rudy T. came back and he delivered back-to-back titles to Houston.

"Riley and Rudy T. had superstars on their teams," said Littles. "The stars worked together with the coaches. But in most instances, when a coach is fired in the middle of the season it's because the team isn't very good—he has no superstar."

Sidney Lowe was an interim coach with the Minnesota Timberwolves. Chaney had that job with the L.A. Clippers. Bob Hill did it twice—once with the Knicks, another time with the Indiana Pacers. Rex Hughes did it twice, his stops being Sacramento and San Antonio. Others who have tried it since 1980 are Richie Adubato, Jerry Reynolds, Fred Carter, Garfield Heard, and Bob McKinnon.

"Sometimes, you get through that first season, and they give you another year," said Littles. "But usually, that's it. The players know that you don't have a long-term contract. The word around the league is that an interim coach is a guy who probably will be fired at the end of the year. Look at the record book. It happens most of the time. You just don't have a lot of clout with the players. Also, if you want to make some major changes in the offense or defense, how are you supposed to do it in the middle of the season when you don't have any real practice time? You pound your head against the wall, asking, 'How do I regroup? How do I start to win?' The front office may even tell you not to worry about winning, just get the guys to play hard. But they really don't mean that. In this league, all that counts is winning, and you've taken over this team that is a mess and you're supposed to straighten it out, and do it NOW! Well, good luck."

When a new coach is hired, why doesn't he keep the interim coach as an assistant?

"Sometimes, the new coach may feel threatened by keeping the guy who was the last head coach on his staff," said Littles. "Or the new coach may just want to hire his own people as assistants."

In Rudy T.'s words, "The danger of being an interim coach is that it's easy to get promoted right out the door."

Most basketball fans have never heard of Gene Littles. He was never a "name" player or coach. He has spent most of his sixteen years in the NBA as an assistant with bad teams, expansion teams, or rebuilding teams.

"Coaches will tell you that there is no substitute for talent, but they like to think they can make a big difference anyway," said Littles. "Well, I'll tell you—there is no substitute for talent. None. It doesn't matter how great a coach you are. Believe me, I've seen enough bad teams to know that you gotta have the players."

Littles was a star guard at little High Point College in North Carolina, where he played well enough to be elected to the NAIA Hall of Fame. He was a guard in the ABA for the Carolina Cougars and Kentucky Colonels, averaging 9 points over six seasons. He decided to become a coach. He spent two years as an assistant under Bobby Cremins at Appalachian State, then he became the head coach at North Carolina A&T, where he inherited a team that had won only three games in the previous season. His record over the next two years was 40-15. Then he was hired by Tom Nissalke—an old friend—to be an assistant with the Utah Jazz in 1979.

He moved to Cleveland as an assistant in 1982. When George Karl was fired after a 25-42 record in 1985–86, Littles was named interim coach for the first time. He was forty-two years old and had fifteen games to show what he could do with the Cavaliers.

"I remember being in the Cleveland locker room and looking at the players," said Littles. "I saw Eddie Johnson, and he was headed to drug rehab at the end of the season. Keith Lee had bad knees and couldn't run. Lonnie Shelton was fat and had bad knees. He couldn't even play. Melvin Turpin . . . poor Melvin . . . he was my center. He was really fat, too. John Bagley was my point guard, and that season he lost all of his confidence. It was like he was just . . . gone. World B. Free was my shooting guard. He had a bad hip or something, and he had been into it with George Karl—World had sort of quit for a while. The best guy I had was Phil Hubbard, who was a real leader, but he wasn't a great player and he didn't have much talent to lead. I stared at those guys and wondered, 'Just what the hell am I supposed to do with these guys in fifteen games?' My very first game, we played the Celtics, who were on their way to the title. We were down by 20 points at the end of the first quarter and they crushed us."

Hubbard and Free played well for Littles, but the Cavs were 4-11 under him. At the end of the season, the Cavs ownership fired general manager Harry Weltman. Littles didn't wait around for a pink slip, he left to become an assistant under Doug Collins, the new Bulls coach who had never been a head coach in the NBA. He spent a year in Chicago, then moved to Charlotte as an assistant.

"When I came to Denver, I thought that this would be a very stable situation," said Littles. "The fans and media loved Dan Issel. I mean, the Big Fella's jersey is hanging right up there in the arena. I remember Dan being a little nervous about coaching, and I told him, 'Dan, half the guys in this league who are coaches don't know as much about the game as you do. You played the game.

You know what it takes to win. Don't worry about the coaching. You've played for guys like Adolph Rupp, Hubie Brown, and Doug Moe. You've picked up a lot over the years. I can help you with the Xs and Os and the matchups. You'll do a great job dealing with the players—and he did."

But in the middle of his third year, he quit.

"Coaching does crazy things to people," said Littles. "I talked to Dan a couple of times after he quit, and he told me that his wife stopped him from watching our games on TV or listening to them on the radio. She saw him turning all red in the face and getting stressed out again—as if he were still coaching the team. He was still beating himself up a couple of weeks after he resigned. I said, 'Big Fella, that's not healthy. Just let it go. I'll handle it.' Then we both laughed."

"They figured you're just there until the next guy came in," said Littles.

The Nuggets were 3-13 under Littles.

Then the Nuggets ownership convinced Bickerstaff to coach the team. They did it by naming him president, general manager, coach, and what amounted to a basketball dictator. They gave him a five-year, $5 million contract extension to hopefully keep those ulcers from bleeding. The Nuggets players saw Bickerstaff and knew that this guy didn't just have a hammer over them, he was walking into the dressing room with a bazooka on his shoulder. He was totally in charge and he could blow anyone out of his way who didn't want to follow.

Furthermore, Littles returned to being the top assistant. He slept better at night, and for once, he had survived a stint as a head coach. When you are an interim coach, this is as close to a happy ending as it gets.

THE
LEAGUE

10 Bad Boy$

It's not fair to blame all the NBA's troubles on Chuck Daly and the Detroit Pistons because the league itself actually promoted the Bad Boy image. But if you want to know when the NBA began to go wrong, you have to look no further than Detroit in the middle 1980s when Daly was hired to coach the team.

In their final season under coach Scotty Robertson, the Pistons averaged nearly 113 points, sixth best in the NBA. But they also allowed 113, and that translated into a 37-45 record. The team Daly inherited was led by Kelly Tripucka (26.5 points), Isiah Thomas (22.9), Vinnie Johnson (15.8), and Bill Laimbeer (13.6).

"When [general manager] Jack McCloskey hired me, he wanted me to do something about the Pistons' defense," said Daly. "Frankly, I wasn't sure what I could do with the team. They had won 39 and 37 games the two years before I got there. I looked at the tapes of those games and I thought Scotty Robertson did a good job. I didn't know how I could improve it. But I had a contract with two guaranteed years and an option for another year, and if they wanted me to work on the defense, I'd work on the defense."

Well, Daly immediately did something right because the Pistons were 49-33 in his first season, losing to New York in a five-game series in the 1984 playoffs.

In Daly's first season, the Pistons averaged 117 points, third in the NBA in scoring. They allowed 113 points—so much for being a defensive coach. All Daly did was rev up an already high-powered offense. But in Daly's first three seasons, the Pistons never went past the second round of the playoffs.

"You can coach defense all you want," said Daly. "But you have to get guys who are willing to play defense, or you are talking to yourself."

At this point in his career, Laimbeer was just another young center trying to find an identity. He had an accurate fifteen-foot jumper and a knack for rebounding in traffic. He was "physical," but he hadn't even approached the stage where he needed to register in hotels under phony names to hide from the harassing phones calls and death threats.

"I looked at our situation and how the game was played in the playoffs," said Daly. "Everyone knows that in the playoffs, the game slows down. The accent is on a half-court offense, a tough defense, and controlling the boards. Well, if you have to play that way in the playoffs, why not just do it in the regular season? Why play one style for 82 games, then change it all around for the playoffs?"

That was the summer of 1986, the time of Daly's epiphany. It also was when the Bad Boys were born. He didn't know about the Bad Boys back then. He couldn't guess that two championships, videos, $32 million in merchandise sales, and his own private clothing contract with a tailor would follow. Nor did he have any idea that his team would become the most despised champion in NBA history.

All Daly knew was that he couldn't win in the playoffs if all his team did was try to outscore the opposition.

"The more I thought about it, the more I knew that slowing down the tempo was the way to go back then," said Daly. "Everyone wanted to run up and down the court and put up big numbers. By slowing it down, we would frustrate the rest of the league. Our identity was going to be our defense. On offense, we wanted to establish a half-court game that could produce about 100 points a night. Our goal was to play every game as if it were a playoff game."

Instead of getting into a nuclear arms race, Daly believed the secret to victory was trench warfare. He convinced Jack McCloskey to trade Tripucka—a soft, jump-shooting forward who couldn't defend a stop sign—for Adrian Dantley. No one ever accused

Dantley of being a defensive forward. He was listed at 6-foot-5, but was much closer to 6-foot-3. No forward that small ever scored as many points as Adrian Delano Dantley of Washington, D.C., and Notre Dame.

Daly saw that Dantley was most deadly in a slow, half-court game where he'd get the ball near the hoop and use a variety of head and ball fakes to make bigger players leave their feet. He was always among the league leaders in free throw attempts, averaging 8 per game.

"A.D. living at the foul line gave us time to set up our defense, and it took away the other team's fast break," said Daly.

By this point, the Pistons had drafted Dennis Rodman, John Salley, and Joe Dumars. They traded for Rick Mahorn. They won 52 games. They still averaged 111 points, but they allowed 107. More importantly, they advanced to the second round of the 1987 playoffs, losing to Boston.

Mahorn came to the Pistons with a gap-tooth sneer. He entered the NBA in 1980, a muscular 6-foot-10, 240-pound forward from little Hampton Institute in Virginia. He averaged 28 points and 15 rebounds in college, but the reason the Washington Bullets took him in the second round was that Mahorn was big, strong, and a little mean. He combined with another 6-foot-10, 240-pounder by the name of Jeff Ruland to give the Bullets a couple of wide bodies who liked to Ping-Pong opposing big men under the basket. An elbow from Mahorn would send Robert Parish flying . . . right into a hip from Ruland. Boston Celtics broadcaster Johnny Most called Mahorn and Ruland, "McFilthy and McNasty."

They lived up to their nicknames, and that was why Daly wanted Mahorn.

"Before the championships, I was just trying to survive as a head coach," said Daly. "I had been fired by Cleveland. In my first few years in Detroit, we did well in the regular season but didn't advance very far in the playoffs. Then we added Dumars, Salley, and Rodman—all kids we got in the draft who would play defense. And Mahorn was a factor because he was so tough mentally."

No, Mahorn was a basketball thug, period.

Laimbeer saw the act and liked it, and Mahorn liked Laimbeer. It was McFilthy and McNasty all over again, only more foul, more repulsive. The Pistons became downright dirty, because players such as Rodman, and to a lesser extent Salley, were willing to follow Mahorn's lead.

"All coaches are into survival," said Frank Layden. "Sometimes, that means doing things they don't believe in, maybe even something they believe is wrong. But a coach can tell himself, 'If I want to make it in this league, then this is what I have to do.' Chuck Daly is a dear friend of mine, and his team took on an image and won. He wanted to win, so maybe he let some things go. When Rodman was a rookie, he did a war dance around Karl Malone. Karl was on the floor, and there was Rodman dancing around him. It was not good. On the way out of that game, I told Jack McCloskey, 'That kid is going to be great, but you have to get him under control.' They never did, and all he did was get worse and worse. Hubie Brown often told me that how you break into the league—and what team you break in with—often determines how it will be for the rest of your career. Well, that's what happened to Rodman, and he was much worse after he left Detroit."

Daly made Isiah Thomas the captain.

"If you're going to coach in the NBA, then you have to get along with the superstar," said Daly. "If you don't, then you won't survive. You may have to give up some of your ego to do it, but if you don't, you have no chance as a coach. In Detroit, I had to have Isiah on my side. That meant giving him a lot of room to try things his way. From the beginning of time, all coaches have had special arrangements with their superstar. But now more than ever, it has to be a cooperative thing. The player has to buy into what you want to be done on the team. It's not going to be smooth, but it can work if the superstar and coach realize that they have to live with each other and that if they want to win, then they have to make it work."

So Daly tolerated Thomas being very close to Pistons owner Bill Davidson. (Thomas and Davidson even took vacations together.) Daly also understood that Thomas would want to express his opinions to the front office about trades and other personnel matters. It was Thomas who first pushed for the Mark Aguirre–Adrian Dantley deal with Dallas. Thomas and Aguirre were both from Chicago. They both had the same agent. Daly and McCloskey listened to Thomas and thought his reasons had merit. They believed that Aguirre could give the Pistons scoring off the bench, that it was time to start either Salley or Rodman, and Dantley would not like losing his spot in the lineup. Thomas also insisted that he would make sure that Aguirre stayed with the program. The trade was made on February 15, 1989. When he arrived in Detroit, Aguirre was taken to dinner by Thomas, Laimbeer, and Mahorn. They laid down the law and told him that they would all personally kick his fat ass if he loafed in practice or whined about playing time and shots. They challenged him, saying that Aguirre had always maintained he was a championship player—well, here was his chance to prove it. And it worked. Aguirre was a potent force off the bench as the Pistons won their first title in 1989.

"Isiah, Laimbeer, and the other guys policed themselves," said Daly. "I never had to make rules about drinking and curfews because they made stricter rules for the team than I ever would. Once the dominant players accept what the coach is selling, they supply the muscle or motivation for the other players. They become the guys willing to practice hard every day no matter how many minutes they played the night before. They are the guys willing to sacrifice their bodies to play defense, or their egos to allow someone else to score. Usually, there are only four or five teams every year that have a legitimate chance to win a title, and if you can get the key players to understand what a rare opportunity it is when you are one of those elite teams, you usually can get them to back you."

Thomas was the unquestioned leader and he embraced the Bad Boys image. He loved to see his big men beat on the other team. Thomas himself had the personality of a guerrilla fighter; other players talked about his "sneak attacks," how he'd run up behind you, jump on your back, and grab you by the neck during a fight. Knowing that Mahorn and the Bad Boys were behind him just made Thomas more willing to incite many of the fights for which his teammates would later be blamed.

How did Daly feel about all this? He liked the standings as the victories piled up. In 1987–88, the Pistons averaged 26,012 fans in the massive Silverdome, leading the NBA in attendance. They still were averaging 109 points but allowing only 104, third fewest in the league. The Pistons had indeed changed their image—defense was their black-and-blue calling card—and the public bought it.

"Not every team can play pretty basketball like Pat Riley's Lakers or Larry Bird's Boston Celtics," said Daly. "I didn't know where all this [Bad Boys stuff] would lead, I just knew it made us a better team."

The Bad Boys became a classic Us Against the World situation, and coaches like that. It brings a team closer together as it fights off real or imagined attacks from the outside. One of their constant critics was Cleveland Cavaliers general manager Wayne Embry, who was appalled by their style of play. Late in the 1988–89 season, the Pistons defeated the Cleveland Cavaliers at the Rich-field Coliseum to clinch the Central Division title. As they walked out of the building, they saw Embry's Lincoln parked in its des-ignated spot on the arena ramp. Thomas spat on the car first. Then Mahorn, Laimbeer, and the rest of the team followed. Daly re-portedly saw it and smiled.

The Bad Boys were born on January 16, 1988. The christening and the official name wouldn't come until later that summer. But on the evening of January 16, 1988, at Chicago Stadium, the Bulls and Pistons were having at it. Michael Jordan was in his fourth NBA season, averaging 35 points. It was Doug Collins's second season as the Bulls' coach, and he knew that if he wanted a third year, he needed a healthy Jordan.

"Michael drove into the lane and the bodies closed around him," said Collins. "I didn't see if it was Mahorn or Laimbeer, but one of those guys just took Michael down, and took him down hard. Charles Oakley was with us, and he was Michael's body-guard. Oakley stepped in the middle of it—this was happening right in front of our bench—and I saw Mahorn coming up behind Oakley. By now, there was a lot of pushing and shoving going on, and I thought Mahorn was going to hit Oakley from behind."

At this point in his life, Collins was thirty-seven years old. That is young for a coach, but old enough to know better.

"I grabbed Mahorn from behind," he said. "I wanted to get him around the arms so he wouldn't throw a punch, but he was so damn big and sweaty, my arms went up and suddenly they were around his neck. I'm sure that Mahorn thought I was going to choke him, so he just threw me over the scorer's table and into the stands as if I were a little kid."

For the record, Collins is 6-foot-6, 185 pounds.

The Pistons were in several fights before this, but never had a coach been flung like a rag doll into the stands. The Pistons had been fined before, but they almost viewed it as the price of victory. They wrote the checks with a smile.

The fight was shown over and over again on ESPN, TNT, CNN, and local sportscasts. It was ugly, scary, and dangerous. The sight of Mahorn flinging away Collins didn't sit well with the NBA office in Manhattan's Olympic Tower. NBA director of operations Rod Thorn suspended Bill Laimbeer. It was the first time he had missed a game in seven years with the Pistons.

The Pistons were outraged.

It was the first time any Piston had been suspended for fighting. And yes, it was Laimbeer who was suspended, not Mahorn, who was just fined as was everyone else in the brawl. Of course, Laimbeer said, "Why me?" He didn't even touch Collins. Of course, he could have ended Jordan's career, but that's not how Laimbeer saw it. He simply was closing the lane to the basket. He was playing "good, tough defense." Other Pistons insisted that the league was protecting Jordan, and that the Bulls were just a bunch of whiners and wimps.

Naturally, Daly supported his players. If it bothered him to see one of his players get nasty with an opposing coach, Daly never admitted it.

"It was a situation like what Pat Riley had with the Knicks," said Daly. "He started off looking at his talent and wanting to have a defensive team. But if you have combative people, they won't just give you one shot. They become almost maniacal about defense."

In other words, the inmates were taking over the asylum, and Daly was not about to bring out the straitjackets—not as long as the team kept winning.

"I liked the macho, tough-minded, intimidating personality that our team was developing," said Daly. "Let's face it, we were very successful with this style."

More alarming is the fact that the NBA marketing wizards loved the Bad Boys.

"The league put out a tape on the 1988 Finals called *The Bad*

Boys," said Pistons public relations director Matt Dobek. "Until then, there had been no nickname for the team. We sort of marketed ourselves as the NBA's Oakland Raiders, with Jack Tatum and those guys, taking on their tough-guy persona. Some of the guys took to wearing black like the Raiders. At the time, it seemed like a fun thing to do."

Detroit was the star of the NBA's highlight film.

"If you see the video today, you'd laugh your ass off because you can't believe that the NBA would sell a team like they did the Bad Boys," said Dobek. "It opens with the song 'Bad to the Bone,' and you see the confrontations. You see Mahorn knocking down Bird. You see Isiah getting ready to take a swing at Robert Parish. You see Laimbeer doing his stuff. Then they show the Oakland Raiders playing football, followed by the Pistons wearing black Oakland Raiders paraphernalia. Then comes the line where they call us 'The NBA's Bad Boys,' and they show Mahorn throwing Doug Collins into the stands. I mean, the first five minutes was nothing but one fight after another. I'd like to think that someone was fired for making a tape like that."

No chance. The image was selling, and soon everyone wanted a piece of the Bad Boys.

"A local businessman came out with an entire line of black Bad Boys clothing featuring a skull and crossbones," said Dobek. "He made over $20 million on all the T-shirts, hats, and stuff."

Dobek even cashed in himself, co-authoring a book called—you guessed it—*Bad Boys*, with Isiah Thomas. It sold over 100,000 copies.

"Like it or not, the nickname became our trademark," said Dobek. "What bothered us was the hypocrisy. On one hand, we had Rod Thorn suspending and fining our players, saying that they didn't want the fighting or that kind of image for the league. But then you had the NBA and the TV networks selling that image to attract fans. We sold out buildings all over the league not just because we were champions, but because we were the Bad Boys. That added some electricity to the games."

Daly agreed.

"When I was hired by Detroit, my daughter wanted a Pistons T-shirt," said Daly. "That was in 1983. I wanted to buy one at the airport—nothing. They had Lions, Tigers, and Red Wings shirts, but no Pistons. Then I went to a mall and a couple of sporting goods stores, same thing—shirts for all the local teams but the Pistons. Five years later, they sold about $32 million worth of Pistons merchandise in a year. Everywhere you went, there were Pistons and Bad Boys shirts. The only thing I regret about this part of the Bad Boys is that I should have gotten a piece of the action for myself."

Actually, Daly did. He had a TV show, a radio show, and made commercials for just about everything from planes and trains to automobiles. He became the first NBA coach to have his own clothing contract. And naturally, there was a Chuck Daly book.

What's so great about the Bad Boys style? It works.

It may not mean a championship. In the NBA with its 24-second clock, you still have to put the ball in the basket to win. But being the Bad Boys, throwing elbows, slamming bodies, karate kicking, and slapping all adds up to having to score fewer points in order to win.

The NBA has always had its hatchet men, its players with more eyes than teeth. Red Auerbach made sure that he had at least one on his roster, be it Bob Brannum, Jim Loscutoff, or Gene Conley.

"Those guys were there to protect Bob Cousy," said Auerbach. "If they did some other things, that was a bonus."

In the 1980s, Marc Iavaroni was Julius Erving's bodyguard on the great Philadelphia teams. The late Wendall Ladner filled that role when Erving was in the ABA with the old New York Nets. Kurt Rambis supplied some muscle on the great Laker teams of the 1980s.

But none of those guys were as belligerent and blatant in their physical attacks on the opposition as Mahorn and Laimbeer.

"I was known as a physical player," said Hall of Fame center Willis Reed. "Maybe I'm getting soft, but we had nothing in my era compared to how the Pistons played. I've talked to a lot of guys I played against and we can't believe that the Pistons were allowed to get away with that."

Seldom did the Pistons start a fight by throwing a punch. In fact, Laimbeer never threw the first punch. But he once elbowed Brad Daugherty in the throat, causing Daugherty to take a swing at

Laimbeer's nose. Daugherty was suspended, Laimbeer was fined heavily and whined about it.

Laimbeer and Mahorn also perfected their World Wrestling Federation routine. They never committed a foul. They never started a fight. They never even touched anyone. Laimbeer led the league in both cheap shots and whining. As Mitch Albom wrote, "You paint a portrait of Laimbeer's career and you get everybody screaming and Laimbeer with that big-eyed look, saying, 'Who? Me?' " His other favorite line was "What? What! What did I do?" Laimbeer comes from a family where they often asked him when he was going to get a job that paid some serious money. Being a spoiled brat probably came naturally, but Laimbeer embraced the character and expanded it to where he became a cartoon with all his silly gestures and faces.

Meanwhile, Mahorn was very scary. Just ask Mark Price. Late in the 1988–89 season, the Cavaliers were in a tight race with Detroit in the Central Division. Price was eating up Thomas to the point where Isiah said, "Mark came into the league as a lamb and now he's a lion." On February 28, 1989, the Cavs were crushing Detroit at the Richfield Coliseum. The ball was in the far corner, and naturally the eyes of the officials and fans were on the ball. Trailing the play—about fifty feet behind the ball—were Price and Mahorn. As they crossed midcourt, Price tried to pass Mahorn, and Mahorn threw out his elbow, catching Price in the side of the head.

Price went down as if he had been hit in the head with a baseball bat. The officials didn't see it, but it was on tape. Mahorn drew a $5,000 fine. Price missed two games with a concussion, and a medical report from Cleveland Clinic said that Price would have had brain damage had the blow been two inches higher.

The Cavs and Wayne Embry were incredulous at what they considered the league's lack of action. Their star had been attacked, and all Mahorn drew was a fine. Meanwhile, the Pistons were just laughing at the fines and the TV networks were sending the Bad Boy image across the country.

"I started to get really concerned in the late 1980s when I saw the Pistons play Chicago in the playoffs," said Cotton Fitzsimmons. "I can remember a couple of instances when Michael Jordan had a clear lane to the basket, and one of the Pistons came from behind, grabbed him by the shoulders and threw him down.

That could have ended Michael's career. That's not physical basketball, that's dirty and it shouldn't be allowed."

"When I coached the Bulls and we faced the Pistons, I told the guys that we knew what they were going to do," said Collins. "If we were ahead late in the game, you can be sure that they would try something to provoke an incident, to get one of our players in a fight and thrown out. They wanted to drag you down to their level. They wanted the game to deteriorate into a wrestling match. I told the guys that when they go up for a shot, draw a foul, and hear the official's whistle—expect the extra hit. I know that Laimbeer would see Michael getting ready to jump, and Laimbeer would stand on Michael's foot. What if Michael jumped anyway and blew out his leg? There is no place in the game for that. I saw Mahorn intentionally try to injure guys. The Pistons will say that they were just being physical, but I don't buy that. Some of the players wanted to hurt you, and they didn't care if they did."

Given the fact that the officials—and the league, because the officials take their marching orders from Rod Thorn's office in New York—allowed the Pistons to be the Bad Boys, Daly was not about to worry about his critics.

Wayne Embry could scream all he wanted about how "the Pistons promote violence. Basketball is physical enough, you don't need guys wanting to be heavyweight champs. You don't have to be ugly to win."

Frank Layden could insist all day that "the Pistons were the first trash-talking team. Guys in the league always talked to each other, but the Pistons said things that were personal, things that would start a fight in any bar. They always took their shirts out of their pants when they came out of the game. They just acted defiant."

Here is what the Bad Boys style did to the other team:

1. It upsets the pyschological balance of the game. Their antics make you want to beat them up rather than beat them on the scoreboard. You feel that the officials won't protect you, so you have to stand up for yourself—and the Pistons were the masters of not throwing the first punch.
2. If five guys are grabbing and shoving on defense, it puts tremendous pressure on the officials. Do they want to call a foul on every play? If they do, the fans will boo. The coaches will

complain. And the league liked its officials to "let the guys play." Do you want a three-hour game with 80 foul shots? Most officials would start out calling the games close, and then simply stop blowing the whistles—bending their wills to the Piston mind-set.

3. In the 1980s, the typical team averaged close to 110 points and wanted to run. By using their Bad Boys tactics to slow the game down, the Pistons controlled the tempo and played at a pace that was more comfortable for Detroit.

4. Suppose you wanted to drive to the basket, but you're worried that Laimbeer might take your head off and send you to the hospital—you may try it once. But once you're down on the court with a trainer putting smelling salts under your nose, you'll say, "Next time, I'm taking a jump shot. It's not worth it."

5. Instead of worrying about the Pistons, you scream at the officials. The officials are human, and they retaliate by giving the Pistons even more latitude to maim.

Rather than force the Pistons to raise the level of their game to acceptable NBA standards, the NBA allowed the league to degenerate to the Pistons style.

The Bad Boys became Chuck Daly's Frankenstein.

"We got to the point where we probably went overboard with it," he said. "The intimidation factor was one of the reasons for our success. But after we won a championship, teams really began to escalate their game against us. It got very, very tough and very physical. We just got into too many fights."

That was part of the reason the Pistons didn't protect Mahorn after winning the 1989 title. Daly said that Mahorn was picking up too many fines, drawing too much attention to his team for all the wrong reasons. He loved Mahorn and knew that Mahorn was at the heart of the Bad Boys. But he also hoped that by exposing Mahorn to the expansion draft he might send out a message that the personality of the team was changing.

"After winning the 1989 title, we went to the White House to meet President Bush," said Matt Dobek. "Isiah presented the president with a Pistons jersey and hat. He also spoke on behalf of the organization when he said, 'This is the end of the Bad Boys era.' In a sense it was, because Mahorn was drafted by Minnesota. Laimbeer was Laimbeer, and he was going to do his crap. But Mahorn was just too . . . I don't know . . . scary. To this day, I look at what he did to Mark Price [the elbow in the head] and some of the other things he did . . ."

For a public relations man and ardent Pistons supporter, Dobek is remarkably candid. Even he knew that Mahorn was out of control. But it was too late. The Pistons had just as many fights en route to the 1990 title. Meanwhile, Mahorn refused to play in Minnesota. He went over to Italy and said he quit, while his team in Rome said he was cut for cussing out the coach and throwing a chair against the dressing room wall. The Pistons won a second championship with Salley and Rodman handling Mahorn's old power forward spot.

"That second title took so much out of us," said Daly. "For three straight years, we went to the Finals. We played over 100 games in each of those seasons, and most of those games were very intense. Because of our style, we had very few blowouts and that meant our main guys played a lot of minutes."

After the 1990 title, Daly sensed that his team would never be the same. There would be no three-peat, and that was why he nearly took an offer to coach the Miami Heat. The general manager was Billy Cunningham, who was the head coach of the Philadelphia 76ers when Daly broke into the league as an assistant. But Daly decided to come back for one last stand with Detroit, passing up a chance to coach one of the better young teams in the league.

"Chuck tried to play down the Bad Boys image," said Dobek. "He thought it detracted from the fact that we had a great team. Also, he believed that the officials were becoming overly conscious of our players. They weren't just calling the game, they were officiating Laimbeer and Rodman differently than they would a Brad Daugherty or a Bill Cartwright."

Of course, Laimbeer and Rodman played a much different game than Daugherty or Cartwright. The only player Daugherty ever punched in his career was Laimbeer. Everyone else in the NBA would say that Daugherty was a highly skilled player, an All-Star but still soft in the pivot. Cartwright was known for being clumsy more than physical. Once, Thomas went ballistic when one of Cartwright's inadvertent elbows nearly broke his nose. The elbow just missed Thomas, but he retaliated, throwing a punch at Cartwright. Unfortunately for Thomas, the punch landed; Cartwright was fined, but Thomas broke his wrist.

The only time Daly worried about the Bad Boys image and tactics was when he thought it was costing him games. Otherwise, whatever the Pistons did was just wonderful. Naturally, the Detroit fans loved the Bad Boys. People will love Atilla the Hun as long as he wins.

"Things began to escalate," said Daly. "Teams would gear up to play us. Every night, you had to gear up and the games just kept getting more and more physical."

Teams were sick of the Pistons pushing them around. Coaches would tell their players to stand up to Detroit. Daly liked the macho style of his team, but the whole league was becoming macho when the opponent was Detroit.

"We had too much fighting the last few years," said Daly. "But it was something we couldn't do anything about. People would attack us. We talked to the players [about not fighting], but it was a style that had been very successful for us so it was very hard to back off."

The Bad Boys died on their home court on Memorial Day in 1991. They were swept by Chicago in four games. In one game, Rodman whacked Bulls backup center Will Perdue three times in the back. Finally, Perdue took a swing at Rodman and both drew technical fouls. In another game, a frustrated Mark Aguirre slammed Horace Grant to the floor at midcourt in full view of the officials and was nailed with a technical. Rodman also undercut Scottie Pippen as the Bulls forward went up for a break-away layup. Pippen got off the floor, stared at Rodman but didn't retaliate.

What the Bulls did—with the help of some veteran officials—was insist that Detroit play basketball in order to remain champions. But the Pistons suddenly discovered that they couldn't score.

"We went so far in our defense and our half-court game that it took away from our offense," said Daly.

Furthermore, the Pistons were aging, tired, and simply couldn't run with the hungry Bulls. Smelling blood after Game 3, Michael

Jordan said that the Pistons weren't worthy to be champions. It was the Bulls and their aggressive but clean style of basketball that was more representative of the NBA. Bulls coach Phil Jackson continually stressed that the Pistons were a dirty team, a not-too-subtle reminder to the officials to keep their eyes open and their whistles ready.

As it was apparent that the Pistons were going down for good in Game 4, Isiah Thomas led the starters off the court with twelve seconds left. There would be no handshakes. Instead, they would lose the same way they won—with no class.

"The stuff that Michael Jordan and Phil Jackson said really bothered our guys," said Dobek. "They believed they received no credit from the Bulls for winning two championships, because they had won 'the wrong way,' as Jordan said. So the players talked among themselves and planned to walk off if they lost that fourth game. It was Isiah and Laimbeer's idea. Chuck Daly knew about it. He tried to talk the guys out of it. They basically said, 'The hell with it, we're doing it our way.' Chuck found himself in a real bind because he didn't like the idea, but he also didn't want to hang his players out there alone."

So Daly stood by his players, for better or worse.

"Walking off became a real black mark against the Pistons," said Dobek. "They paid for it dearly because people then made them out to be bad guys. It was as if the critics were waiting for something like this to happen."

In a 1994 interview with Mitch Albom, Thomas admitted that he would not leave the court early again if he had to do it over.

"If I had known it was going to cause such a stir, I'd have shook his hand for the sportsmanship aspect. When we beat them, he [Jordan] was very honorable about it, he shook hands and everything . . . well, losing never did sit well with me."

Thomas also told Albom that the reason the Bulls won was that Jordan won "the mental game" with Joe Dumars.

"They [Jordan and Dumars] got to be friends and he [Jordan] got inside our inner workings. . . . He got to understand what drove us as people. He was able to use that to divide us. . . . Bird and Magic were never friends. The Celtics and Lakers were never friends. You can't let people know you."

This is a very revealing statement because three years after the fact, Thomas still refuses to admit that Chicago was the better team. Instead, he blames Dumars, the classiest player on the Pistons.

In the years of their decline, the Pistons continued to have fights, and Thomas was in the middle of many of them. He once said, "The losing gets to you and after a while, you don't know what else to do but fight."

On November 16, 1993, he even got into a brawl in practice. Laimbeer set what Thomas considered as an unduly harsh pick on him. Thomas retaliated by coming up and punching Laimbeer in the back of the head. Just like when he attacked Cartwright, Thomas got the worst of it, this time breaking the middle finger on his right hand.

Laimbeer and Thomas quickly resolved their differences. Both understood what had happened. Thomas knew that Laimbeer was a cheap-shot artist, and the pick was a cheap shot. Laimbeer knew that Thomas liked to come up from behind, and he did. But what the heck, that also was how they won two championships.

A month later, Laimbeer retired. Thomas ruptured an Achilles tendon in March of 1994, and his career was over. The Bad Boys were done.

Daly's defense is that the Pistons had to be the Bad Boys if they were going to be champions.

"We had three great guards in Isiah, Joe Dumars, and Vinnie Johnson," said Daly. "They were going to supply most of our offense. We didn't have the guys who could score in the low-post game. The backcourt was going to give us our points, then we had to shut other teams down defensively."

Wait a minute. Were the Pistons actually that bad? Let's reconsider.

Thomas? A Hall of Fame guard.

Dumars? A Hall of Fame guard.

Johnson? One of the greatest sixth men ever, true instant offense off the bench.

"That may have been the greatest backcourt in NBA history, bar none," said the *Boston Globe*'s Bob Ryan, certainly no Pistons fan.

What about Laimbeer?

"Someone had to wear the black hat in this league and I guess it was me," Laimbeer said when he retired.

Why? Why do we need that kind of villain in the NBA? And why did it have to be Laimbeer? Conventional wisdom is that Laimbeer lacked the basic basketball ability to be a success. In Mahorn's words, "He couldn't even jump over a piece of paper, but he was a great rebounder. He would hit you, disrupt you, get you out of your game and while you were trying to hit him back, he'd beat you."

Okay, Laimbeer had no post-up moves, none—and he didn't want any. Rather than learn a little hook shot or other moves near the basket, he spent his summers playing golf.

But the man was one of the best-shooting big men ever. He was automatic from twenty feet. That created major defensive problems. What center wants to be guarding a jump-shooting big man twenty feet from the basket? Thomas and Laimbeer didn't run a pick-and-roll, it was a pick-and-slide with Laimbeer picking for Thomas, sliding sideways and then catching a pass from Thomas, setting up his twenty-footer.

Laimbeer also was an excellent rebounder in his days with Cleveland and his early days with Detroit—long before he was the Western Hemisphere's most hated man in shorts. The point is that when you take a guy who is 6-foot-10, 250 pounds who can rebound like a center and shoot like a guard, you are not talking about the second coming of Henry Finkel. Laimbeer was a very good basketball player.

Mahorn brought the bad-ass attitude to the Pistons, and Laimbeer discovered that it gave him an identity. Acting like a jerk didn't necessarily make Laimbeer a better player, but it gave him attention and an identity, things he craved.

"Laimbeer probably defined the Bad Boys," said Daly. "He could frustrate a player, then play Gandhi and just walk away. I could understand why the guys who played against him hated him, but he was a very special guy. I loved having him on my team because of the leadership he and Isiah supplied."

The Pistons had Rodman, who would become the best defensive player in the NBA. They brought 7-foot-1 James Edwards off the bench. Edwards was good enough to start for most teams and he had an unstoppable and automatic fallaway jumper from the low post. John Salley was a starter in Miami. Even Mahorn could hit an open twelve-footer and was a fine passer for a big man. Aguirre was a 20-point scorer in Dallas before the Pistons brought him off the bench.

Why wouldn't this team have been good enough to win a championship without all the fights and fines? They started Laimbeer, Mahorn, Rodman, Thomas, and Dumars. They came off the bench with Edwards, Johnson, Aguirre, and Salley. They could play big or small. They had tremendous depth. They could put scorers on the court, or defensive-minded players.

But many NBA coaches didn't see it that way. They thought the Pistons won *because* they fought. They thought a Bad Boys persona was a way to hide a lack of talent, when in reality the Pistons had the deepest team in the NBA in the late 1980s.

So many coaches began to copy the Bad Boys style. Walk the ball up the court. Provoke the other team, keep the score down in the 90s—or better yet, in the 80s.

"If you look it up, we scored more points than people thought in the playoffs," said Daly. "Most of the time, we were over 100 points in the Finals, which is an offensive onslaught compared to what you see today."

In their final championship year, the Pistons averaged 104 points during the 1989–90 regular season. In their five-game victory over Portland in the Finals, they scored under 105 points just once. It took them 20 playoff games to win that 1990 title, and they were under 100 points in only 7 of those 20 games. The Pistons put the ball in the basket more than you think. They ran a better, more intricate half-court offense than you imagine. And they had the best pick-and-roll plays in the game because of their guards.

But what did teams copy?

The fighting and mugging. The trash talk and phony, macho posing.

"It went right down into the colleges," said veteran NBA scout Al Menendez. "The Fab Five at Michigan with all their antics were direct descendants of the Pistons—the mouthy attitude and all that. Like the Pistons, some of those kids were really talented and they didn't need all that trash. Then other college and high school kids began copying the Fab Five. A lot of the problems we have in the game today started with the Pistons."

And it was helped along by the NBA, which promoted the Bad Boys until it was too late.

"Kids watch the pros," said Frank Layden. "They saw the Pistons pull their shirts out and cop that tough-guy attitude. They said, 'Wait a minute, that's how you play. You get in people's faces, you beat them up, you abuse fans—whatever it takes to win.' And it spread because the people in charge allowed it to happen. It is still spreading because now it has become acceptable. Until enough people stand up and say this is wrong, nothing is going to change. It will just get worse."

11 The Official Rules

Did you ever watch a game where something amazing happens on the court—say, a guy is decked by another player—and there is no whistle?

One player is on the court, holding his head and bleeding from the nose. Another guy is sheepishly looking up at the ceiling, hoping that no one notices that he nearly committed assault and battery.

There are 20,000 fans screaming and millions more ready to kick in their TV sets—and the officials didn't see a thing.

"Believe me, I know exactly how it can happen," said Jack Madden, who was an NBA official from 1969 to 1994.

All we have to do is go back to the 1987 Eastern Conference Finals between Boston and Detroit.

In Game 4 of the series, it was Larry Bird vs. Bill Laimbeer. When Bird made a move to the basket, and Laimbeer grabbed him and threw him to the court, Bird knew it was no accident. He was convinced that Laimbeer would have loved to see him limp off for the rest of the game—or maybe even the rest of the series, since the Celtics were in front 2–1.

Bird erupted and threw a basketball at Laimbeer. Laimbeer was called for a personal foul while Bird was ejected. When he came into the Celtics dressing room, he found Robert Parish there. The Boston center had left the game early because of an ankle injury.

Bird said he had been ejected.

"Laimbeer," said Parish, without even hearing the details.

The two players laughed, but there was nothing funny about it.

Detroit won the game after Bird was ejected, setting up Game 5 in Boston with the series tied.

In the second quarter, Parish told Laimbeer to keep his elbows to himself. Laimbeer kept his elbows in Parish's stomach and lower back. The two big men went up and down the court a few times and nothing out of order seemed to be taking place. The officials were Jack Madden and Jess Kersey.

"There was a long rebound that bounced out to the corner," said Madden. Kersey was the official under the basket, Madden was trailing the play. This was when the NBA used only two officials.

"Both Jess and I followed the ball into the corner," said Madden. "Suddenly, I heard the crowd, and I turned around and saw Laimbeer flat on the court. It looked to me as if he probably had just fallen down. Laimbeer loved to flop, and I figured he just took a flop."

The Pistons screamed that Parish had fouled Laimbeer. Not only that, the Pistons also thought Parish had punched Laimbeer and he should be ejected. The officials saw it this way: "Detroit is complaining about a cheap shot? Who are they to talk?"

Since the game was in Boston, the fans certainly weren't demanding any justice. They figured that the Chief gave Laimbeer exactly what he deserved.

"Neither Jess or I saw anything, so we let it go," said Madden.

This was the game where Bird stole Isiah Thomas's inbounds pass with five seconds left, then delivered a pass of his own to Dennis Johnson, who made a layup to give Boston a 108–107 victory at the buzzer at Boston Garden.

"I can't remember if it was the alternate official or someone else from the league office, but they came into our room after the game and asked us what happened on the play with Laimbeer and Parish," said Madden. "We said that we didn't see anything. Then we put in a videotape and we saw that Parish decked Laimbeer. We were flabbergasted. I remember saying 'How the hell could we miss that? My God, Parish should have been ejected and we didn't even call a foul.' But honestly, neither one of us saw it."

The play became a major issue inside the NBA.

"Assuming they really didn't see it, it was just hard for us to figure out how they missed it," said NBA director of operations Rod Thorn.

The tape was played over and over. It happened in the middle of the key, and it should have been Kersey's call. He should not have been chasing the ball in the corner. But some viewing the tape believe that Kersey did indeed see it, but he just swallowed his whistle and watched.

In his book, *Drive*, Larry Bird told co-author Bob Ryan, "Out of the corner of my eye, I saw Robert punching Laimbeer and Laimbeer going down. Referee Jess Kersey was standing right there, but he didn't do anything about it."

Was it frontier justice, a couple of veteran officials deciding that Laimbeer simply got what he deserved? Celtics general manager Jan Volk called Laimbeer "the consummate provocateur roaming the hardwoods." Detroit general manager Jack McCloskey verbally attacked Kersey, believing that he protected the Celtics by turning his back on the play. At the very least, the Pistons believed that the officials made assumptions about Laimbeer—as Madden said, "Laimbeer had been flopping all game"—but an official isn't supposed to assume anything about anyone. He should watch the play and call what he sees.

"The NBA really investigated it," said Madden. "In the end, neither Jess nor I were fined. There wasn't much we could say other than we didn't see it. You look at the tape and you wonder how we missed it, but we did."

It would be one more year before the NBA would adopt the three-official system, but this incident was the driving force toward the change.

"Had there been a third official, he would have seen what happened," said Thorn.

"To the fans, this is going to sound crazy," said Madden. "But sometimes, they have a better view of certain plays than we do. For example, if we were sitting in the stands, I'm sure we would have seen what happened to Laimbeer. Goaltending also is easier to call when you are further away from the play. You have a couple of officials on the move—often running while looking back over their shoulders—well, that isn't the best perspective to see every play. By being close to the action, we see things under the basket that the fans never do. But once in a while, something happens and we miss it. There is no other explanation."

We have only Madden's word on this because the NBA does not

allow its active officials to be interviewed and Kersey is still officiating.

The missed call on Laimbeer and Parish wouldn't have been news
twenty-five years earlier.

"That's because there was little TV coverage, no ESPN or CNN
to show the play over and over, and there was no such thing as a
VCR," said Thorn. "Unless you were in the building, you had no
idea what the official called or if he called it right. That is why some
officials really did become laws unto themselves. They could pretty
much do what they wanted, and how was the league office supposed to check it? There was no videotape."

In the 1950s and 1960s, officiating in the NBA was a part-time
job for men such as the late Earl Strom and Norm Drucker. Strom
was recently inducted into the Hall of Fame, but for much of his
career he worked during the day at General Electric and then called
games at night on the East Coast. That's because the pay in the
NBA was terrible and the security was worse.

Officials were invited to try out for the league, and that meant
no training, no seminars—here's a whistle and you make the call.
The rookie would be paired with a veteran official. He usually
worked three games. If the veteran liked him, then he might be
back for the rest of the year. If not, he was gone in a week.

One of the greatest officials ever was Sid Borgia. He went directly from the Madison Square Boys Club to the Basketball Association of America—the forerunner of the NBA back in 1946.

In 1959, Borgia was also the supervisor of NBA officials and he
hired John Vanak, who was a policeman in Lansford, Pennsylvania,
who had called a few local high school and college games. He
received a call from Borgia on a Monday night and was told to
report on Wednesday to Philadelphia, where he worked a game
with Borgia. The NBA was paying refs $40 a game.

After fourteen years in the NBA, Norm Drucker was making
only $140 a game—and he was one of the higher paid officials.

In the infancy of the league, officials were supposed to be a part
of the show. Pat Kennedy was so flamboyant that he often was
mentioned in advertisements for that night's game. "People go to
The Garden first to see Mr. Kennedy officiate and second to watch

the basketballers play," wrote New York columnist Joe Williams.
"Mr. Kennedy does everything but throw himself through the
hoop."

Borgia was colorful, prone to dramatic gestures and saying
things like, "You, Jerry West, you traveled. But you traveled because Sam Jones pushed you. We won't call a foul on Jones, we'll
just give the ball to West out-of-bounds and take it from there."

Borgia preached the spirit over the letter of the law. He believed
that you "let the players decide the game," so you simply don't
blow the whistle in the final few seconds. He trained longtime
officials such as Joe Gushue, Earl Strom, and John Vanak—and
they brought a certain personality to the game.

These were men of enormous ego.

"I remember having a conversation with Earl Strom about
three officials," said Wally Rooney, a retired official. "Earl told
me, 'Well, three officials are okay working a game. And two officials are all right. But you know, one guy can do it.' Of course,
Earl was talking about himself. I loved Earl as a person, but he
would embarrass the guy he was working with. His idea of a
partner was a guy who made out-of-bounds calls, then rubbed
up the ball and handed it to the players to pass it back into play.
If you did anything else, Earl thought you were stepping into his
territory."

Of course, there are those who insist that Strom was the Magic
Johnson of officiating. He could see the entire court, make all the
right decisions, and handle any situation.

"Earl was unique," said Rod Thorn. "When we had debates
with Earl, I'd tell him that you can't train someone to be an official
like Earl Strom. Those guys just don't come along that often."

Until the 1980s, officiating in the NBA was a closed club.
Most of the officials were from the New York or the Philadelphia
area. Virtually all of them were white. They served an appren-
ticeship with a veteran official, and either learned on the job or
were fired.

"Even in the 1970s, the way we'd prepare for the season was to
have a three-hour meeting before training camp and then they'd
send us home with a new rulebook," said Madden.

In the 1970s, an official might view only a few game films a year
to see how he was doing his job.

"So much of that stuff in the early days was just vaudeville," Darell Garretson has often said. "You could blow the whistle with reckless abandon. If they didn't like it, you could go out and get a job that paid as much or more money. If my guys tried some of that stuff today, it would cost them a lot of money."

Garretson has been the NBA's supervisor of officials since 1981, and no one has had a greater impact on the profession.

Talk to former officials such as the late Strom and John Vanak, and you come away with the impression that Garretson is the Devil Himself. You can't talk to today's officials about Garretson—the NBA won't allow it—but most veteran officials will tell you off the record that the guy is a dictator and they hate his guts. The young guys won't talk to a reporter, period; they are afraid of what might happen if Garretson should learn that they even had a casual conversation with a member of the media.

"Darell has a lot of officials just scared to death," said Billy Saar, another longtime official, who retired in 1994.

"No matter what you may think of him, Darell has really improved how officials are trained and just brought more professionalism to the job," said Madden. "A lot of things he has implemented over the years have really made things better."

Today's officials have a starting pay of $67,000, and the top scale for the most experienced referees is $177,000. They work between 75 and 77 regular season games. An official appearing in the first round of the playoffs will earn another $13,000. If you work the playoffs into the Finals, that's an extra $30,000. Officials also receive a healthy $210 per day to cover their hotel, meal, and rental car expenses.

"It's safe to say that these guys don't spend $210 every day," said Thorn. "They also make a very respectable salary with excellent benefits. Yes, we ask them to do more than in the old days, but we are paying them a lot more."

Officials must show up in shape and stay in shape. For a 6-foot-1 former New York policeman turned official by the name of Billy Saar, this wasn't easy.

"I could run well, but they had a weight clause in everyone's contract," he said. "You were given a target weight at the start of the season, and then you were weighed again at midseason. You'd be told two weeks ahead of time that you were going to be weighed and how much you were supposed to weigh. For two weeks in the middle of the year, most of the officials are in a rotten mood because they are starving themselves to make the weight clause."

You can bet NBA coaches are thrilled to hear that.

"I never was fined for being overweight," said Saar. "They wanted me at 218 pounds and I usually got there, although I hardly ate for a few weeks to do it. You don't want a lot of fat slobs out there, but some of us veteran officials thought that the league made too big of an issue out of it—because they knew it would be tough on us."

Thorn became the NBA's director of operations in the summer of 1986. He is commissioner David Stern's "basketball man." He also is Garretson's boss, meaning he is the ultimate authority over officials.

"I never remember fining any official for being overweight," said Thorn. "But I didn't work a guy for the last month of a season. He got too heavy and couldn't lose it, so I didn't assign him any games."

Losing those games cost the gentleman perhaps $20,000—and it sent a message to the other officials that the league was serious about weight. But in his final few years as an official, Garretson seemed rather pudgy and some veteran officials wondered why his weight wasn't an issue—implying Garretson did not have to abide by his own rules. That issue became moot when Garretson retired as an official in the summer of 1994, but he remains the supervisor and the heavy hand that makes key decisions that affect the lives of the NBA's officials. He wants his guys to look neat and trim. Officials run about five miles a night when working a game. The average NBA official is forty-five years old, and several are approaching sixty, so physical conditioning is critical.

"That is part of the reason we went to three officials [in the 1988–89 season]," said Thorn. "We thought it would be less wear and tear on our older guys, and it would prolong their careers. Before we hired the twenty-six new officials [in 1988–89], the average age of our officials was near forty-nine. We needed some young blood."

Wally Rooney found himself caught in this age trap.

"When I was hired by the old ABA in 1969, one official told me that if I planned to make it a career, come up with a basketball age," he said. "So I shaved off five years. I worked in the ABA until the merger in 1976, then I went over to the NBA. I'd go for my physical and the doctor would ask my age. I'd say, 'See what I was last year and then add one more.' The league found out about it a few years ago and they were very upset. I told them that in our preseason one-and-a-half-mile run, I had a better time than half the officials in the league. I was over twenty years older than some of those guys. But Rod Thorn said, 'Wally, you lied.' I said, 'Rod, I said I was over sixty.' "

Well, that was true as far as it went.

"They thought I was sixty-one," said Rooney. "But I was really sixty-six. Someone told the league to check my age. I didn't know who or why. But I also know that I wasn't the only official with a basketball age. The league really doesn't want anyone older than sixty-two working games, so I retired. But from what I understand, I was the oldest official ever to work an NBA game."

Thorn declined to comment on Rooney's situation.

Officials fight injuries—just like players.

"In my last ten years in the NBA, I had three knee surgeries and a major back surgery," said Madden. "Because of my knees, I couldn't run in the off-season. To stay in shape, I took long walks outside or on the treadmill. Look, I'm not crying about our life-style. I loved officiating and you are treated well, but the travel and loneliness can beat you down. It isn't uncommon for an official to have a sixteen-day trip working nearly every night and in a different city every day. Then I hear the coaches and players complaining about a ten-day road trip where they played five games and they say they are totally exhausted. These are mostly young guys in their twenties. Today they have private planes. They don't have to buy an airplane ticket. They don't even have to carry their own bags. They have forty-one home games. I'm not even talking about the money they make, but the way they travel and are cared for—they are treated like kings. They don't have any excuses as far as I'm concerned."

Or as Wally Rooney said, "There is a reason that six of the top twelve officials are divorced. This lifestyle is great if you like travel and being in the center of the action, but it can really kill a marriage and a family because you never have any home games."

What do officials and players say to each other?

According to Wally Rooney, there was a game when Charles Barkley approached him by the scorer's table, going on and on about something.

ROONEY: "Charles, if you don't cool it, I'm going to call a T."

BARKLEY: "Wally, I haven't said anything yet to get a T."

ROONEY: "So far, you're right."

BARKLEY: "Besides, I make too much money for you to call a T. on me."

ROONEY: "Charles, I don't know about that."

BARKLEY: "Wally, can I get a T. for thinking something?"

ROONEY: "No."

BARKLEY: "So I have to say it. You can't just call it."

ROONEY: "You do."

BARKLEY: "Okay, Wally, I think that was one lousy fucking call."

Rooney nailed Barkley with a technical foul, and Barkley laughed.

"That is one of the things I miss about the game, the guys," said Rooney, who retired in the summer of 1993 after twenty-three years as an NBA and ABA official. "There is a lot of discussion about trash talk these days. Well, the guys did talk. Larry Bird would say, 'Wally, they don't have anyone who can guard me.' Or when Barkley was doubled-teamed and scored, he'd run down the other end of the court and yell back at the opposing bench, 'Next time, you better put four guys on me.' But it was usually good-natured. Guys would say it with a smile and we laughed about it."

Officials also talked between themselves about the players, especially before a game.

"There is a checklist that we'd go over, and that included the matchups," said Jack Madden. "If two guys had a fight the last time they played, we were aware of that and we wanted to make sure that we'd jump in quick if things got a little heated again. We'd talk about the individual players' tendencies. Rick Barry liked to drive into the lane, stop, and jump into the defender to draw the foul. He got a lot of foul calls on that move, but often it was a charge and the officials would remind each other to watch him closely on the move. Reggie Miller kicks his legs out after taking a jumper to draw contact and make it look like he was fouled. Laimbeer would flop all the time, acting as if he had been run over even though he was barely bumped."

"The player's style does have something to do with how we call the game," said Billy Saar. "There was one game where Charles Oakley was telling me that the guy guarding him was 'beating the hell out of me.' I can't remember who the guy was, but if you ever saw Oakley play you know that no one ever beat the hell out of Charles. He beat the hell out of everyone in the league."

Players have similar discussions about officials.

If you are playing on the road, you wanted Earl Strom and now you want Dick Bavetta with a whistle in his mouth. Both are known as road refs. The home team was winning two of three games in the 1980s, but when Strom or Bavetta came to town, the home team usually won only 50 percent of the time.

But Bavetta calls a close game with a lot of fouls. Strom was from the Let the Boys Play school, and he was interested in felonies only. When the players go on the court for a loose ball, Bavetta is likely to blow the whistle quickly for a jump ball. Strom would let the players roll around, saying, "I wanted to award the most aggressive guy for coming up with the ball." So he held his whistle.

Coaches tell the players these kinds of things before a game, once they learn the identity of the officials. The officials are different for every game—unlike baseball, where the same umpiring crew will work an entire series. Nor are the officials announced in advance. But the moment they walk into an arena about ninety minutes before a game, word filters into both dressing rooms about who will be blowing the whistles that night.

While the league wants all the officials to be the same, Strom said he never favored the road team: "I just didn't bend to the home crowd. Some other officials would go with the flow because it's easier. You need guts to make the tough call against a home team and bring the house down on you."

The facts are that in the 1990s, the home team was called for an average of 6 percent fewer fouls than the road team.

"I remember a game where Stan Albeck told me that his team was 2-13 in games where I worked," said Bill Saar. "He said that he had no chance with me. I told him with his team, he didn't have a lot of chances to beat anyone, anywhere—because Stan had a lousy team that year. But coaches will say things like that to try and get inside your head."

Early in his career, George Karl was convinced that his team would never win a game when the official was Ronnie Nunn. But then Karl's team did win a few games with Nunn, and his name was replaced by someone else on the hit list.

Another favorite move of coaches is to tell a veteran official who is working with a couple of young refs, "I feel sorry for you being stuck with those guys. You've got to carry the whole load, and that's a shame."

"You have to ignore stuff like that, and instead be steady and consistent," said Rooney. "We know that the coaches are going to work us over, and we'll listen to some of it. But you can't let them run down a fellow official. You tell them to cut it out. Most of the time, the things said are pretty harmless."

Of course, there was the game back in the 1970s when Cleveland coach Bill Fitch picked up a folding chair and threw it at official Bob Rakel. Luckily for Fitch—and Rakel—it missed.

"That stuff is scary," said Rooney.

Has there ever been a time when an official went after a coach?

"I can only speak for myself, and it happened once," said Rooney. "I had known Hubie Brown for years. We even went to Niagara at the same time. He lost a close game and he was screaming at me that I didn't have guts enough to call John Havlicek for stepping out-of-bounds. He kept saying I 'didn't have the guts' to blow the whistle on Havlicek. He was calling me dishonest, and I took off after him. I was always known for being very calm under fire, but I would have fought Hubie that day if a couple of players hadn't stepped between us and restrained us. I wasn't proud of how I acted, but Hubie also was out of line. The league office looked at it and decided that we both were wrong. They called it a wash and didn't fine either one of us."

In the NBA, traveling isn't always a violation. Palming seldom is, and you can be camped in the lane and not be called for three seconds.

"I call it the pro call," said Earl Strom. "You can watch a guy shuffle his feet before he dribbles. Did he walk in the strictest sense? Yes. But in the NBA, we ask if that little move gave the player an extra advantage. If it did, then it's traveling. If it didn't, we let it go."

This will come as news to most NBA fans, who simply thought NBA players are permitted to walk with and/or carry the ball because they are stars. But what Strom terms the Pro Call is a part of the NBA's officiating doctrine. It is even something that Strom and Garretson agreed upon.

"When we see a guy maybe turn the ball over with his hand [which would be considered a palming violation in high school and college], we don't automatically blow the whistle," said Bill Saar. "We ask ourselves if that move gave the player an advantage over the defender. If he stands out there dribbling and palming the ball over and over but not going anywhere—well, that's not a violation."

Sound crazy and arbitrary?

Well, it comes straight from the top. In one of his rare interviews, Garretson told *Sports Illustrated*'s Leigh Montville, "We're always looking at the advantage/disadvantage situation. Did the person do something to create an advantage for himself or put the opponent at a disadvantage? If he did, it's a foul [or violation]. If not, we don't make the call. . . . You get familiar with a player who spends 38, 39 minutes a night on the court. This isn't college, where you only might see a player three–four times a year. You get to know how players play. Suppose Julius Erving, every time he went to his left, took a little baby step. Maybe he walked, but he never got any advantage from it. That was the way he always played."

And the officials let him play that way.

When Patrick Ewing catches the ball at the low post and makes his move into the middle of the key, he often takes one of those famed baby steps. He has been doing it ever since he came into the NBA. He might have been called for traveling a few times as a rookie, but never since then. Why? Because it's his move and the officials don't think that move gives him an advantage—although those guarding Ewing might disagree.

Some NBA coaches insist that no player was ever allowed more latitude when it comes to traveling than Michael Jordan.

"Trying to deal with Michael and traveling was tough," said Jack Madden. "He had this spin move and made it so quick . . . if you were right on top of him like we were, it was hard to know what he did. From fifty feet away in the stands or on videotape, you might see it. But when you are that close and he moved that fast . . . I often let it go because I just wasn't sure that he did anything to give himself an advantage."

Madden was hardly alone.

"Suppose the game was a blowout and Jordan was in the open court, going for a dunk," said Strom. "And I saw him take an extra step before he dunked. I wouldn't call it. It was not a close game. The crowd wanted to see Michael dunk. Heck, I wanted to see Michael dunk. I let it go."

So did a lot of officials.

In 1991–92, Jordan was whistled for only five traveling violations. That's right, *five*. In 1992–93, it went up to nine. No wonder Michael decided to play baseball. He probably thought the officials were picking on him.

But seriously, consider how many times Jordan handled the ball in the final two years of his "first" career—and he walked only fourteen times? As a rookie, Shaquille O'Neal was called for walking seventy-four times. Christian Laettner was second with forty travels in 1992–93. And Ewing was third with thirty-six, so maybe the officials didn't let him get away with as many baby steps as it seems.

"It's easy from the stands to see what you think is walking from a player like Jordan," said Saar. "The guy isn't human. His hands are so big that it was no trouble for him to carry the ball. He didn't move, he exploded to the basket. His moves were quicker than the human eye."

NBA officials tell you that players not only have outgrown the court, they've become bigger than the rules—or at least the rules of basketball with which most of us grew up. Because of the size of these men, there is a foul on every play; you aren't supposed to bump or lean on anyone. But in the NBA, it is almost impossible for someone not to be pushing or leaning on someone else.

"Some of the stuff is really hard to call," said Wally Rooney. "Suppose you have a game where Shaq and Ewing are banging against each other. Ewing is trying to establish position in the low post to catch a pass. Shaq is trying to bump and use his body to push Ewing as far away from the basket as possible. You ask yourself, 'Who had the position first? Who is pushing whom off their spot?' It's not easy."

One thing most officials would like to see is the no-foul-out rule, whereby a player can pick up more than six fouls and stay in the game—although his team would be penalized with two free throws and loss of possession of the ball every time that player commits a foul after number six.

"Officials like to say that they aren't aware of how many fouls certain players have, but you know," said Bill Saar. "Guys are yelling it from the bench. You know when a star is in foul trouble, and the no-foul-out rule would mean that when a couple of guys foul the same player, you don't have the temptation of calling a foul on the lesser player to protect the star."

Officials are human. They know that fans pay to see the stars, and they don't want the stars to foul out. Neither does the market-crazed NBA, so you often see a strange call on a rookie who is just watching a play where a star seemingly commits a foul.

"When you officiate in the NBA, the idea is to keep the game moving," said Strom. "An official shouldn't nitpick. If he sees some little violation away from the ball that has absolutely no bearing on the play [such as a man standing in the corner of the key for what should be a three-second violation], I'd let it go. Why interrupt the game for something that has nothing to do with the play itself?"

But there is something troubling about all this talk of the Pro

Call. Why shouldn't the pros be held to the same standards as high school and college players, both men and women? It would seem that the last thing a player such as Jordan, Erving, or Ewing needs is an extra step—or the right to carry the ball.

Yes, there is going to be more contact because the players are too big for the court, and the arena design—with all those lucrative courtside seats—means that we won't see the court being enlarged in the near future. The NBA considers such a change too radical, even though it would actually increase the number of courtside seats. Fouls are and should be called differently in the NBA than anywhere else. But why can't we ask the pros to keep both feet behind the line when in-bounding the ball after a made basket?

Or why can't we ask them to follow the standard traveling and palming rules? Several officials have said that they allowed palming because so much handchecking was taking place on defense. Therefore, the man dribbling the ball needed an extra advantage to neutralize the advantage that the defender was given from hand-checking. Sounds like that is one Pro Call on top of another until both the letter and the spirit of the rules are gone.

But in 1994–95, the NBA began strictly enforcing the hand-checking rule, and the players adjusted. Certainly they can adjust to the same dribbling and palming rules that they played under in high school and college. All the league has to do is have the guts to make the calls.

"No one can clean up the game or set the tone of how it will be played better than the officials," said Gary Fitzsimmons. "All they have to do is call it by the rules. I loved the [1994] World Games where the Asian officials called Dominique Wilkins for charging on that spin move of his, where he turns right into the defender and runs the guy over. It has always been a charge, but the NBA officials let it go because it was 'Nique's Move.' Well, the Asian officials didn't know Nique or his moves, and they just called it like a normal basketball game. Our guys could learn something from that."

Amen.

No game is officiated quite like the pro game.

Take the end of a game.

"It's not written anywhere, but an official knows that he's not supposed to decide a close game with a call," said Wally Rooney. "I learned that the hard way."

Rooney's nightmare came in 1991, the opening game of the first-round playoffs between Houston and the L.A. Lakers. The Lakers were in front, 94–92, with three seconds left. But Houston had the ball under the Lakers' basket, trying to pass it in-bounds for a shot at tying the game.

"Otis Thorpe was passing the ball in," said Rooney. "You have five seconds to pass the ball in-bounds. I checked and Houston had a timeout that they could use if they didn't get the ball in-bounds within the five seconds. I handed the ball to Otis Thorpe, and I started counting 'One-thousand-one, One-thousand-two . . .' As I said, 'One-thousand-five,' Thorpe called for a timeout. I said, 'Too late,' and gave the ball to the Lakers. L.A. hung on to win that game. As I walked off, I was with [officials] Jess Kersey and Tommy Nunez. I asked them what they thought, and they said, 'Wally, it was very close.' I felt bad when I made the call, and that made me feel worse. Then we went into our dressing room and put in the tape. We put a stopwatch on it, and it turned out that Thorpe called timeout at 4.9 seconds. I was just sick when I saw that. Rod Thorn later put a watch on it, and he came out at 4.7 seconds. All I knew was that night I couldn't sleep. I'd cost Houston a chance to win that playoff game—or at least get it into an overtime. [Houston coach] Don Chaney is a good man and he deserved better than that."

As it turned out, the Lakers swept the Rockets in three games and ended up losing to Chicago and Michael Jordan in the 1991 Finals, so in the grand scheme of things Rooney certainly didn't prevent the Rockets from winning a title.

"I know that," he said. "But I made the wrong call. In some of our meetings, we talk about situations like that. At the end of the game when it's close to a five-count, give them the timeout. Don't take the game away from them by making that kind of call."

But you might make that call in the second quarter?

"Perhaps," said Rooney. "It certainly would not have been as big a deal."

This is a kind of justice that drives many purists to the edge of madness.

Why is something a good call in the second quarter, but not in the final seconds of the game?

Consider Game 3 of the 1994 Finals between Houston and New York. With twenty-nine seconds left, the Knicks had the ball. Houston was leading 89–88. Patrick Ewing set a pick to free John Starks for a shot, but official Jake O'Donnell called Ewing for an offensive foul. The ball went back to Houston, and the Rockets hung on for a 93–89 victory.

After the game, reporters demanded that O'Donnell explain why he called an offensive foul on Ewing. Even if it was a foul, aren't the officials supposed to let it go in the final minute and "let the players decide the game"?

"It was a judgment call," said O'Donnell. "The play was a pick-and-roll. He moved his hip out. Then he did it again. I wasn't going to let it go twice."

This brings up all sort of questions:

1. If it was a foul the first time, why didn't O'Donnell call it right away?
2. Since he didn't call it the first time, can anyone blame Ewing for thinking that it is okay to do—which explains why he did it twice?
3. Should he have called it in the first place?

"One of the things they tell officials is that they don't remember the call you don't make," said Rooney. "Where you get in trouble at the end of the game is for the call you did make. That is why you see the officials just let things go in the final seconds while the players clobber each other. It is not written anywhere that this is what you are supposed to do, but it is understood. Look at what happened to poor Hue Hollins in that Chicago–New York game."

In Game 5 of the 1994 Eastern Conference Semifinals, the Bulls had an 86–85 lead. The Knicks' Hubert Davis took a jumper from the top of the key as time was about to expire. The Bulls' Scottie Pippen appeared to graze Davis's arm, and Hollins called a foul on Pippen.

Davis went to the foul line, made the shots and the Knicks won, 87–86. That gave them a 3–2 lead in the series, which they eventually won in seven games. On October 12, 1994, Darell Garretson told Melissa Isaacson of the *Chicago Tribune* that Hollins made a mistake with that call in such a critical part of the game. He was subscribing to the theory that you let the players decide a close game.

"When your boss says you blew a call like that, you never live it down," said Rooney. "It also sends a message to the other officials."

There were ramifications to the Hollins-Garretson fiasco.

Garretson makes himself very scarce when it comes to interviews, letting his boss, Rod Thorn, handle that department. The Bulls were convinced that Hollins had something against them, and coach Phil Jackson was fined during the 1994–95 season for saying that Hollins had "an attitude" and "antagonism" toward his team. When Hollins made some calls that went against the Bulls in a loss to Dallas, Jackson said that Hollins was "brutish" and "irresponsible," and that he was picking on Scottie Pippen.

In his next five games where he was assigned to the Bulls, Hollins called Pippen for four technical fouls. Then Pippen jumped in by saying, "We don't get the calls anymore because we don't have the established players like Michael [Jordan] and Horace [Grant]. You won't ever see Will Perdue get a call. Bill Wennington draws a charge every game, but they never give it to him. If there is any kind of judgment call, it is going against us."

"That kind of stuff bothers me," said Bill Saar. "Bad teams think they don't get as many calls because the officials have something against them. But the real problem is that they are bad teams. You hear that all the time, that officials favor good teams or stars. It's just not true."

"The star call is a complete fallacy," Jack Madden said. "The coaches ingrain it in these kids' heads. They tell rookies that they won't get any calls in their first year, so don't expect any. Then when they are called for a foul, they think it's because they're a rookie—but the fact is that they made a rookie mistake. It is just like the makeup call—that's another fallacy. If an official kicks a call, he is not going to make it up right away at the other end of the court. Sometimes, it seems like that happens because people are looking for it, but that's just coincidence."

*   *   *

As if dealing with hostile players, coaches, and fans on top of a brutal traveling schedule wasn't enough, officials must also keep in mind that the league itself is watching their every move, a fact it makes clear in none-too-subtle ways. The late Earl Strom viewed Darell Garretson and the NBA front office as the Kremlin and he was Aleksandr Solzhenitsyn. Strom believed that Garretson wasn't training officials, he was building an empire of disciples.

Listen to the debate:

EARL STROM: We teach our officials where to stand, how to hold their arms up, how to run—but we don't teach them how to deal with people. Handling people is as much a part of officiating as knowing the rules. A good official is like a cop on the beat—he ignores the jaywalkers and watches out for the muggers. You reward aggressive play, but nail the hatchet men and the bullies. You use some judgment, but the NBA wants to take the human element out of officiating. How can you call a game when you are always worried about where you are supposed to stand and how you should hold your shoulders?

(Strom said that this passage should be purged from the NBA rulebook: "Refrain from talking to players, coaches and trainers during a game unless absolutely necessary. At no time should officials speak to fans seated about the court. Do not initiate conversation with players, coaches, fans or other club personnel. Remember, legitimate questions may require a brief response, but statements need not be answered.")

That is exactly what an official should *not* do. Officials are people, too, and a dialogue is an important part of officiating.

WALLY ROONEY: Earl called the new school of officiating the Stepford Wives. Darell Garretson believes in teaching the officials to see and call the game the same way. Earl believed that there is a need for individuality. Earl is from the old school, where you watched the players play and then blew the whistle when they got out of hand. You adjusted to the players. Darell believes that you control the game by blowing the whistle and having the players adjust to you.

EARL STROM: They tell you to treat all people the same. What sense does that make? For example, if I worked a game where Lenny Wilkens was one coach and Chuck Daly was the other, you better believe that I treated them differently. If Lenny ran down the sidelines to challenge a call, I'd listen for a while to what he had to say. Lenny didn't do that to show you up. If he won't shut up after a while, then you bang him [with a technical]. But with a coach like Lenny, he gets a longer leash. Chuck Daly, he was a showman. He'd prance up and down the sidelines wanting to get the crowd into it and maybe even get tossed. I had a much shorter fuse with him.

WALLY ROONEY: I liked to try and control a game with the use of my voice. Rather than blow the whistle all the time, why not just tell two guys to "knock it off and cut it out." But they now tell officials not to do that. They say it is like coaching the players. We shouldn't coach them, we should just make the calls. But I believe in preventative medicine rather than rehabilitation. If you can warn guys, even if you have to get in their face and tell them in their own language to "cut that shit out," and it keeps a problem from developing, what is wrong with that?

ROD THORN: We don't tell our officials never to talk to players or coaches. But we also don't think an official needs to spend a lot of time explaining what he did or didn't call. Some of these coaches will debate you all night if you give them the time. We want our officials to conform to the same standards. What we hear from players and coaches all the time is that they want some consistency in how the game is called. Well, we are trying to give them that by training everyone the same way.

EARL STROM: When I worked a game, I was never afraid to call a timeout and then tell each team to cool it or I'm going to start throwing guys out. I'd stick my head in a huddle during a timeout to get my point across. I'd rather do that than just throw a bunch of technical fouls around.

JACK MADDEN: Some officials are afraid to call technicals because they don't want to upset people. They are afraid that the NBA office will see all the technicals and think you can't control the game, or maybe they are afraid that someone will call the NBA office and complain. They want to be friends with the players and coaches so they go out of their way to be nice to them and explain things all the time. Part of the reason is that the players and coaches help evaluate the officials, and these guys want good ratings, so they buddy up to these people. But you can't let people run all over you. Some of these coaches will try anything to gain an edge. No matter what anyone says, they are not your friends. Some people said I had rabbit ears. I think I still hold the record for the most technicals called in a season, it was eighty-seven in 1971–72. Part of the reason was that I was working with a lot of young guys who needed to be protected. But if I had to call a technical, I never hesitated. Every official is different, but I think some of Earl's criticism of Darell [Garretson] is that he just didn't like Darell personally. He had an axe to grind.

JOHN VANAK: Darell did some good things when he became supervisor, but my problem is that he runs a czarship. He divides officials into his guys—the guys who are his friends and the guys he hired—and everyone else. And he made his son [Ron] a lead official, and that was ridiculous.

BILL SAAR: Darell's personality just overpowers a lot of guys. He rules through intimidation, and some of the officials today would do better if they could relax instead of looking over their shoulders all the time. I mean, you'll call a game and maybe something happened. At 2 A.M., your phone will ring. Darell or someone from the league office saw it on tape, and they are grilling you about the play. They can't even wait until the next morning. Or you'll travel the next day, and when you check in, there is a fax waiting for you, a memo about something they want you to do. Officials now travel with their own VCRs. After a game, you'll sit down and watch a tape of the game you just worked. They want you to critique it that night, or the next day. It's a stressful job already, and I think a lot of this stuff just adds more stress.

WALLY ROONEY: When Darell took over, one of the first things he said was that players and coaches watch videotapes of the games and use them as teaching tools, so why can't we? That never bothered me much. You can overdo it like anything else, but in the past, we hardly watched any tape at all—and that wasn't good.

BILL SAAR: Tape can be used very effectively, but veteran officials also have a lot of knowledge from all their experience that they can impart to the young guys. But more than once I heard Darell say, "Don't listen to the veterans," and I think that's wrong.

EARL STROM: That's because Darell doesn't want anyone to question him or his tactics. Among officials, we have what I call the Whispering Society. You have guys calling Darell, maybe telling him something about another official. Too many guys are playing politics, worrying more about getting on the good side of Darell than in doing their jobs right. A guy like Ed Middleton is a good official, but Darell always puts him down because Ed would talk to girls in the stands and liked to go out and have a few beers. He doesn't genuflect to Darell. He's just a good official with a lot of guts. Some veteran officials have been run down and second-guessed so much that they've had their confidence shaken. Darell can really ridicule and berate you, just so you know your place in his universe.

ROD THORN: You have to take most of what Earl said about Darell with a grain of salt. Earl wanted to be the supervisor of officials. He and Darell just didn't like each other. At the end of his life, I think part of what kept Earl going in his retirement was attacking Darell. Sure, Darell is a hands-on guy. But we want that. We want our officials critiqued and we want them to know they are accountable. If their confidence is such that they are going to be shaken because they are being evaluated, then they have a problem. Players have shootarounds during the day of a game, so why can't our officials look at tape? I like our officials to be a little on edge. But it's not like we are firing these guys. In 1988 and 1989, we hired twenty-six new officials and twenty-two are still with us. We probably lose only one or two guys a year [who are fired]. I just don't buy a lot of Earl's criticisms.

Officials are evaluated from several sources. NBA coaches and general managers comprise 40 percent of the voting. The other 60 percent comes from Thorn, Garretson, and NBA Observers, who are men hired by Thorn and Garretson to sit supposedly unnoticed in the stands and watch the officials, then give a full report to the league office. The officials are rated on areas such as knowledge of the rules, comportment on the court, and handling game situations.

"I always thought it should be at least 50–50 with the coaches and general managers having as much say as the league office," said Strom. "That's because it is the coaches and general managers whose jobs are on the line, based upon how the games are called. I usually rated number one with the coaches and general managers, but my rating with the league office would vary depending upon how I got along with Garretson that year. One season, I was really having trouble with Darell, and he rated me below Tommy Nunez. Tommy is a nice guy and everything, but he is an average official at best. The whole thing is very political and arbitrary. In fact, the officials themselves aren't supposed to know where they rate, but you are told where you personally were rated. So the Whispering Society goes to work. The ratings are passed around and it isn't long before the list is known to all the officials."

Why are the ratings important?

"Because it determines how many playoff games you get," said Strom. "The higher the rating, the better official you are supposed to be. The best officials [at least the highest rated] work the Finals, and that can be worth a lot of money. My point is that the ratings often mean that you really don't get the best officials in the most important games."

A number of NBA coaches and general managers will agree with Strom, but they aren't about to speak out. They worry about incurring the wrath of Garretson and the league office. Others have simply resigned themselves to view officiating like the weather —it's never really what you want and you can complain all day about it, but what can you really do?

Other coaches and general managers try to tell themselves that the calls will even out, despite the fact that they don't believe it. Part of it is human nature. You always remember the call that may have cost you the game, but you immediately forget the critical decision that went your way. That's because coaches and players believe they are owed a break when they get one. When they don't, they just figure that everyone from the heavens on down to Darell Garretson is conspiring against them.

Meanwhile, Thorn and Garretson deserve some credit for trying to make the situation a little better—namely, adding a third official. Thorn originally sold it as "another cop on the beat" when the rule was put into place for the 1988–89 season.

"It helps to have another pair of eyes out there," said Thorn. "But we also needed to get younger. By bringing in twenty-six officials [over two years], we are breaking in the younger guys to take over when the older guys retire. We also are prolonging the older guys' careers because they don't have to run as much in a three-official system."

All of that sounds reasonable, but some veteran officials have objections.

"My problem with the three officials is that everyone was supposed to have their own area," said former official John Vanak. "The court is divided up into primary and secondary zones. There is a crew chief, who is supposed to be a veteran guy in charge of questions about the rules. But they tell you to pretty much watch what goes on in your area, and not blow [the whistle] over another official if you see something in his area. I never liked that, because a foul is a foul no matter where it happens on the court. If you see it, you should call it. But if you do that too often and step on another guy's toes—even if the guy you are working with doesn't have a clue—you get a memo from the league office about it."

"I broke in using the two-man system and I liked it because it was more like an art form," said Bill Saar. "You and your partner just watched the game. You didn't get hung up on who is supposed to stand where. I guess there was just more individuality with two officials."

According to Saar, "With three officials, anything that happens in the paint is fair game for any official to call. But the rest of the court is divided up and it's best not to make a call in another guy's zone unless it's something blatant."

While many of the veteran officials who worked with only one partner weren't thrilled when the change was made, most have come to terms with the three-man system.

"No matter what anyone says, it made for a better-officiated game," said Jack Madden. "With an extra guy, you can cover the court better. That just makes sense."

"Here is the real inconsistency with the three officials," said John Vanak. "The league is using the CBA as its primary training ground of officials. And how many officials do they use in the CBA? Two. If you are going to train these guys right, have three officials in the CBA. Don't tell me that's an extra expense. It's pennies when you consider the budget of the league office."

Well said, and three officials should be the rule in the CBA, just as it is in the NBA.

Those who object to the three-man system probably are the same officials who don't like the idea of having to watch a lot of videotape of their games. They broke into the league when there were only two officials, and when a referee was a law unto himself in the tradition of Sid Borgia, Mendy Rudolph, and Strom.

However, Garretson at his worst swings things to the opposite extreme. Strom and others are right that officials can be tied in knots by the rules on how they are supposed to handle action on the court. They should be encouraged to communicate with players and coaches, not act as if they are above the game. They rightly feel harassed by the late-night phone calls and the constant barrage of letters, faxes, and sometimes petty fines.

Officials can be fined anywhere from $50 to $1,000.

"If you mess up a rule, it will cost you at least $50," said Madden. "If you do it again, it will cost more. If you don't notice that a team has tried to slip the wrong free throw shooter to the line after a foul, that will cost you at least $100. Most of the time, when a guy is fined, it is justified."

Wally Rooney said the largest fine he'd heard of was $1,000— and he and two other officials received it when they were snowed in and showed up twenty minutes after the scheduled start of a game in Sacramento. The league thought they should have taken an earlier flight, or simply figured out how to get there. Officials are supposed to be at a game at least an hour before the start, and if they are a few minutes late that will cost them $50.

"We expect our officials to know the rules of the game and to follow the rules we set down for them," said Thorn. "If they don't, they will be fined. But we don't fine a guy for what would be considered an error in judgment [such as Madden and Kersey failing to see Parish clobbering Laimbeer]. We talk to them about it and show them the tape of the play and try to figure out why they missed it, but we don't fine them."

"That method can be good or bad, depending upon how it is handled," said Saar. "Ninety percent of the time, when an official kicks a call, he knows it. He doesn't have to have his nose rubbed in it."

Saar's objection to the heavy-handedness of the NBA office is a common one heard from NBA officials. In fact, so many officials will tell you about it in an off-the-record setting that it is pretty clear that the league has a problem—not so much in its policies, but in how those rules are enforced. Over and over, you are told that the league will "humiliate" and "embarass" officials behind closed doors. Thorn replies that a lot of these guys are just too sensitive and can't take a little criticism.

"I think you have to look at the overall picture," said Madden. "If you honestly ask yourself if the games are being called better today than they were twenty years ago, you have to answer that they are."

You also have to say that there will no longer be the great officials such as Strom and others, who were raised in the Wild West days of the NBA. Garretson's approach doesn't allow room for much personality on the court—although Garretson himself was never afraid to talk to players or coaches and seemed immune to some of his own rules. The NBA office replies that veteran officials such as Jake O'Donnell, Joey Crawford, and Mike Mathis are allowed more latitude when calling the games, and when some of the younger officials trained under Garretson mature, they also will be given more freedom.

But will they know what to do with that freedom when they get it? Will the right older officials—men such as O'Donnell, Mathis, and other veterans who may not be favorites of Garretson—be permitted to become mentors to young officials? Some have insisted that Strom will be the last official ever named to the Hall of Fame, because from now on all officials will be robots, which may be the result of Garretson's system. And if that's the case, will the game be worse off? The NBA thinks not. Veteran officials have another opinion. The answer may only come after Garretson steps down and the on-court officials feel they have some room to breathe.

12 Selling the Game

For seven years, Mark Heffernan was "game day director" for the Cleveland Cavaliers.

That meant he was the guy who picked the music the fans heard, decided when that music would be played, and hired cheerleaders and halftime acts.

Larry Brown recently said, "We've ruined the game. It has turned into a burlesque show with all the music and dancing at the games. The way it is now, we may as well put on dresses and let the players sing and dance." Brown was talking about guys like Heffernan, and as the years passed and the NBA continued to push its franchises to hype the game, Heffernan found himself agreeing with Brown.

"I knew that something was wrong during Lenny Wilkens's last season with the Cavs [1992–93]," said Heffernan. "Lenny had asked me to play softer music if he called a timeout at the end of a close game so the players could hear him. There was a game where the score was tied with seventeen seconds left. Lenny called a timeout. Usually, the marketing people want you to blare the music and really get the fans wound up, but I remembered what Lenny said. I went with softer music. The Cavs came out of that timeout and made the shot to win that game. I felt really good, but the next day I got a memo from my boss criticizing me for not cranking up the music. It didn't matter what Lenny wanted, all they cared about was getting the crowd excited."

Heffernan worked in this capacity for the Cavs from 1987 to 1993.

"When I was hired, teams were just starting to go in for the cheerleaders, the halftime shows, and all that we have today," he said. "Those were exciting times, because we were putting together programs. I played small-college basketball. I love the game and I understand it. I tried to pick things that wouldn't get in the way of the game. But I was amazed that some of my superiors were so concerned about what music I played, why I didn't play it louder—things like that."

Doug Collins sympathizes.

"When I coached the Bulls, in some places they played the music so loud that I couldn't communicate with my players," said Collins. "I'm in arenas now where they are playing music while the game is going on. I mean, the guys are playing and the music is blaring. You've got horns blowing, wolves howling, and rubber screeching. When Gary Payton makes a good play in Seattle, they use a sound effect of screeching tires. There is a time and a place for music, but damn it, people are there for a basketball game. Let's let them play!"

Collins may think so. Even a marketing person such as Heffernan can understand that concept. But it escapes many people running NBA franchises. That's because there is a split in the administrative offices of most franchises. It used to be that the president or general manager was in charge of both the basketball end and the business side, which includes ticket sales, promotions, and public relations. But now most teams divide the responsibilities. For example, the Cavaliers' basketball operations are run by general manager Wayne Embry. But the business side comes under the control of whoever happens to be the president of the Business Division. The Cavaliers have had a number of men in that position during Embry's tenure. Some of these guys would love to make trades, sign free agents, and leave their fingerprints on the team on the floor. But like most good general managers, Embry guards his turf like a pit bull. So that leaves the selling of the game to the business types.

To some of these men in seemingly big positions, no detail is too small. Heffernan said that one of the Cavaliers' vice presidents didn't like the team song, so he made himself a lyricist for the weekend and rewrote the words.

"The song was by [veteran rocker] Michael Stanley, a Cleveland native who had cut eight albums," said Heffernan. "I think he knew a little bit about what he was doing, but they rewrote him anyway."

He also said that one of the team's executives didn't like some of the music Heffernan picked, and the man came up with his own playlist.

"I kept wondering why this guy didn't have more important things to worry about than the music and when the cheerleaders were on the floor," said Heffernan.

Ah yes, cheerleaders.

It started with the Laker girls and the bikini-clad girls at the Miami Floridian games in the ABA.

"The Cavs had cheerleaders during the early 1970s, but they disbanded them when they found out that a couple of the girls were—how shall we say this delicately?—professional entertainers at certain nightclubs," said veteran Cavs broadcaster Joe Tait.

But the NBA kept pushing for cheerleaders—excuse us, dance teams. Anyway, the Cavs came back with some in the early 1980s. That was when Ted Stepien was the owner, and these women were "models" who often worked the lingerie shows at one of Stepien's clubs. They didn't last long, either. Nor did the polka—yes, Stepien had a polka for the team song. When Heffernan was hired in 1987, one of his first jobs was to assemble a dance team for the Cavs. During the 1993–94 season, the dozen women were paid $35 a game and told not to date the players, although that rule was not always followed. Some women didn't survive the season, and others were hired. Even though it's only $35 a game, there are no shortage of volunteers. Heffernan said that the Cavs spent about $25,000 annually on their cheerleaders, a choreographer, and three sets of uniforms. Others estimate that it is now at least $50,000. No doubt, some franchises in bigger markets than Cleveland are spending over $100,000 on their dance teams.

If you think you hear the same music in every NBA arena, you do. The league doesn't mandate the music, but teams check each other's playlist and talk about what songs are best received by the fans. So you end up with a steady stream of "We Will Rock You," "Devil in a Blue Dress," "Old Time Rock & Roll," "Wooly Bully," and "Everybody Dance."

Then there is the matter of the volume.

"The NBA has joined the 'Let's Deafen America' club," said

Tait. "They believe in jacking up the volume until your ears are ready to bleed. Even if the song is good, they'll play it so loud that it sounds like three guys banging on garbage can lids and belching."

Heffernan said that some of the Cavaliers' deep thinkers have spent hours with him, wanting to go over what music would be played when—as if they were a group of football coaches putting together a game plan. This situation is not unique to Cleveland. Virtually every NBA franchise has marketing fever.

"That's because these knuckleheads think this stuff really matters," said Tait, an NBA broadcaster since 1970. "To me, the typical NBA marketing mentality was the 1994–95 opener in San Antonio. The Spurs put on this indoor fireworks show, but the smoke set off the smoke alarms and the sprinklers turned on, drenching the fans for fifteen minutes. I watched that and said, 'That's exactly what you idiots deserve.' I remember going to a league meeting where [Spurs marketing director] Russ Bookbinder spoke, and he talked about how it was just as important what kind of bells and whistles you put around the game itself. He said that the marketing department could put people in the seats regardless of how well the team was playing. I wanted to barf. The most important thing always was and always will be the team. Winning is the best promotion. When the Celtics won all those titles, no one cared that their idea of a halftime promotion was the ball rack sitting at midcourt."

No one is saying to just can the music, dump the cheerleaders, and play the game as if it were in the middle of Grant's Tomb.

But it seems that the league won't allow the fans a moment of silence when they can speak to the person next to them without screaming. Nor does the league think that the fans will know when to cheer on their own, so they keep flashing NOISE on the scoreboard. Some franchises don't believe their fans can read so they show a pair of hands clapping. Some fans will tell you that the music gets in the way of the cheering. When the home team has made a run and a timeout is called, the fans stand and clap for their heroes. Then the music cranks up, and their cheers are quickly drowned out. So they just sit down.

But it is nice when the home team comes up with something clever.

During the 1992 playoffs, the Cavs were being called "marsh-mallows" in the Chicago newspapers. When the Bulls came to the Richfield Coliseum, Heffernan pulled out a film clip from *Ghostbusters* of Bill Murray battling a huge marshmallow man on the scoreboard telescreen. It fit and it had never been done before and Cavs fans went wild. Commissioner David Stern saw it and sent out word that this was a good idea. Now, most teams use film clips to ignite the fans, usually a scene from *Animal House* where John Belushi tells his bozo buddies that "this thing isn't over until we say it is over." And another good idea became an instant, homogenized cliché.

The remarkable result of the marketing frenzy is the development of a cottage industry of halftime acts going from arena to arena.

"I once hired a group of Chinese acrobats," said Heffernan. "Their manager drove up in this small truck. He opened it and about thirty acrobats piled out. They were stuffed in there for hours and they were hungry. None of them spoke English. We led them to the floor a couple of hours before the game, and they ate all the food that was put out for the fans who sit at courtside. We needed them to sign a release for insurance purposes, but they didn't write in English. They all used the Chinese symbols that said Lord knows what. Then they began walking all over the arena. I told their manager to round them up. About forty-five minutes before the game, I was upstairs and I saw these two Oriental people. I screamed, 'Get your ass down on the floor! You don't belong up here!' The guy looked at me and said in perfect English, 'I bought a ticket, buddy, what's your problem?' "

Heffernan said that once he brought in a bear and his trainer from the Moscow circus. "I knew that bear was smart, but I was a little shocked when I walked out of the arena after the game and saw the bear in his van," he said. "The bear was wearing Larry Nance's jersey and sitting with his paws on the steering wheel."

If you are a regular at NBA games, you probably have seen these halftime acts. There are the Bud Lite Daredevils, who dunk basketballs while leaping off trampolines.

They make $3,500 plus expenses.

There is Christopher, a guy who has five dummies and does a

Michael Jackson routine. He's also a $3,500 act, although rumors about Jackson's sex life have not helped the guy's business.

There are the Quidlers, three guys who stuff themselves into huge sacks. They walk on their hands and drag their legs behind them. All of these are in sacks. They have a yodeling routine, where you just see a big farmer's head at the front, while the legs are behind them inside a bag decorated like a cow, so you have a big head dragging around a big cow.

"That was the weirdest act ever," said Heffernan. "Fans were walking out at halftime and just stopped and stared. They had the same response I did when I saw them on tape. You can't have a regular diet of the Quidlers, but once in a while, they are so bizarre that it works."

Heffernan said that his budget was about $50,000 for halftime entertainment. The top acts receive $3,500, but you can get a good Frisbee-catching dog or a trick dribbler for $1,500. There are also free acts such as wheelchair basketball, pee wee basketball, and fan free throw contests.

Anthem singers in Cleveland receive $25 plus two free tickets to the game.

"We had everything but a mascot," said Heffernan, though the Cavs once imported the Phoenix Gorilla.

"He wore a Ron Harper jersey," said Heffernan. "The problem was that the Cleveland fans didn't know the Gorilla, and some people saw him in Harper's jersey and called the next day to complain it was racist."

The Cavs did try one more mascot, but the guy wore a suit that made him look like a spark plug, and the plug was mercifully pulled on him after one game. Top mascots such as the Gorilla can earn $50,000 a year—not just from the team, but from making appearances at parties thanks to the exposure they receive from the NBA.

Boston experimented with mascots.

"One poor woman dressed up as a leprechaun and lasted one night's worth of being pelted by debris," wrote the *Boston Herald*'s Michael Gee. "That fat moron who spelled out 'Celtics' with his body a couple of seasons ago was cordially hated by the fans and has not returned. . . . To attend a Celtic game was to be transported back to 1954, which is when the gum was left under your seat at the Garden. Celtic promotions tend to consist of club dignitaries handing out checks to various charities, or halftime enter-tainment like the endearingly freakish Balloon Man, the guy who enveloped himself inside one."

"The Balloon Man is a very good act," said Heffernan. "He gets top scale, the $3,500."

The Celtics hired their first marketing director as they prepared to move into their new arena in the fall of 1995. It will have 3,000 more seats than the old Boston Garden, but no Big Three of Bird, McHale, and Parish.

"God help the poor dancing girls who take the court during a 30-point loss to the Timberwolves," wrote Gee.

"The best acts are kids and animals," said Tait. "I hate halftime shows, but I'll watch a baby race, a turtle race, or a dog doing tricks. But if I owned a team, I wouldn't have a halftime show."

Why not?

"Because I'd want my fans to head out to the lobby and buy concessions so I'd make more money," said Tait. "I said that to some marketing people once and they looked at me as if I'd lost my mind."

In many arenas, there is never a moment's peace as the various marketing departments try to outpromote each other. When a timeout is called, cheerleaders are on the floor . . . or some guy is trying to throw in a half-court shot to win a trip to Aruba . . . or a mascot is showing an eye chart to an official.

"During my last year, I didn't know if they wanted to have a basketball game or if it was supposed to be the World Wrestling Federation," said Heffernan. "I would talk about how we needed a happy medium and we had to respect the game. They just talked about the music, the acts, and what else we could do to entertain the fans. They didn't believe that basketball was why fans came. They thought that ticket prices are so high that they can't just give them a basketball game. It has gotten worse since Magic and Larry retired. It's like they don't trust the game and these players to entertain the fans. That really bothered me, and that's part of the reason I left the Cavs."

After the 1993–94 season, Heffernan resigned from the Cava-liers to work as a director at a Cleveland television station. He probably wanted to work for a place where the audience has the right to turn down the volume.

*   *   *

Music and halftime acts aren't the only things that drive NBA front offices into a complete state of distraction.

So do team colors and logos.

It cost the expansion Toronto Raptors over $750,000 in research and design before they decided upon their new logo.

Think about that—$750,000 just to figure out what should be *on* the uniforms. No wonder the guys in the uniforms making an average of $1.5 million believe they are underpaid.

Anyway, the Raptors' marketing gurus knew that black and teal were the hot colors. Research told them that. The Chicago White Sox and L.A. Kings saw sales of their shirts and other team clothing nearly double after switching to a scheme where black is the dominant color. The NBA's leading merchandiser in the early 1990s was the Chicago Bulls, their main colors being red and black. The fact that Michael Jordan wore those colors just may have had something to do with the sales. The Bulls would have been a terrific seller if Jordan had come out in a pink and paisley jumpsuit. Just remember how he revolutionized the tennis shoe market with the introduction of Air Jordans, which looked to many fans like nothing more than black and red army boots. But kids loved them—primarily because Jordan wore them. Then other shoe companies copied the design and now the shoes don't look clunky at all; marketers will tell you that they are high-tech.

But during Jordan's hiatus, the Chicago Bulls fell from first place in the sale of caps, shirts, shorts, socks, bed sheets, towels, and anything else with the Bulls logo.

The new leader was . . . the Charlotte Hornets?

You got it. For the year 1994, the Hornets were number one.

"We're proud of the fact that our merchandise has been successful without being black," Hornets president Spencer Stolpen told reporters. "We're the first to really click without black."

Actually, the Celtic green and the Laker purple did just fine in the 1980s, but that's ancient history to today's NBA marketers. The Celtics? The Lakers? Green? Purple? UG-LEE. Our research shows that no one likes those colors, they'll tell you.

Well, no one may like green or purple since Larry Bird and Magic Johnson retired.

Anyway, number one is the Charlotte Hornets, a team that has never gone beyond the second round of the playoffs.

But the Hornets were . . . well . . . teal.

Teal is hot and teal is cool. Kids like teal. Adults like teal. Everyone seems to like the Hornet logo. As for the team, little kids do love 5-foot-3 Muggsy Bogues, because he is their size. Adults like him, too, because he plays so hard and doesn't seem threatening—unlike Larry Johnson and Alonzo Mourning, two other Hornet players. But some fans, especially teenagers, like the twin scowlers of Johnson and Mourning. Others are enamored with Johnson's Grandmama commercial where he wears a dress, though it's hard to figure out why.

Anyway, the Hornets were laughed at when they hired designer Alexander Julian (and reportedly paid him over $100,000) to design their new uniforms, and Julian came back with teal, "because it goes with any complexion." He also put thin, purple pinstripes in the uniform, to give it the look of an Italian suit.

Incredibly, he knew what he was talking about.

For 1994, the Hornets were first in sales, followed in order by the Bulls, Orlando Magic, Phoenix Suns, and Seattle Supersonics.

Now other teams are looking at a form of teal—while the Hornets went to a darker blue, hoping the new look would sell even more shirts.

For the 1994–95 season, the Cleveland Cavaliers changed their uniforms to a wimpy pale blue—although it was sold to ownership as "Cavalier blue," as if the team was about to pioneer a new color. Right. The North Carolina Tar Heels have been using it for years. Anyway, the Cavs' new uniforms were named the ugliest in the NBA by ESPN, and sales have not exactly soared. On the road, the Cavs put black in their uniforms, to go with the wimpy blue. Given all the injuries the team has sustained in the middle 1990s, black and blue may be the perfect colors for the Cavs.

As for the $750,000 spent by the Toronto marketing wizards, the Raptors settled on a red dinosaur dribbling a gray basketball, with purple and black as the background. Within the first six months it was on the market—before the team even picked a roster or hired a coach—the franchise claimed it sold $30 million in merchandise and ranked seventh in sales.

Obviously, there are huge dollars in all this. During the 1984–85 season—Jordan's first year in the NBA—the entire league sold $115 million of merchandise. For 1995–96, the projections are over $3 billion. To the NBA's credit, all the teams share equally in the royalties from the sales of NBA products. Therefore, spending $750,000 to decide on a logo is nice, but it won't help your bank account.

That is why teams are now in love with luxury suites and court-side seats—that's where the real money is.

In 1974, what is known as club seating (courtside) and loges made up about 5 percent of the average income of an NBA team. Now, it's close to 35 percent and growing every year. Lakers owner Jerry Buss started the frenzy when he noticed that stars such as Jack Nicholson and Dyan Cannon liked to sit at courtside—where they could be seen, but also where ushers could keep most of the fans away. He also knew that those folks were filthy rich and would pay outrageous prices for a prime seat, so he charged outrageous prices.

As Nicholson, Cannon, and other Hollywood stars attracted TV time, Jack and Dyan wannabes anted up for courtside seats. Some were other stars, such as Billy Crystal and Lou Gossett, who sit courtside at L.A. Clippers games. But in most cases and in most cities, those courtside seats are purchased by rich guys (and their wives) who consider it chic to be as close to the action as a guy wearing a uniform and sitting on the bench. The Knicks charge $1,000 for courtside seats—that's $1,000 per seat, per game!

Most experts will tell you that having prime seat and luxury suite locations is one of the major considerations when building a new arena.

The Miami Arena was opened in 1987, but it has only eighteen luxury suites, and they are up near the roof. The Miami Heat's lease expires at the end of 1998 and there is serious discussion that the Heat will leave the building (which cost the taxpayers $52 million) for another city—unless renovations are made to supply more luxury suites.

Teams love luxury suites for more than just their price—even though many of them are sold for $10,000 or more a year, and the six or eight people in the suite must also purchase separate game-day tickets for another $50 to $100 each. What's so attractive is the commitment a team can extract for the suite. The leases on many of these luxury suites are for three to ten years. Teams can pocket that income and be shielded from the year-to-year or even month-to-month ups and downs that are a part of an NBA franchise.

If the average fan who goes to maybe five games a year thinks that his NBA team has forgotten about him, he basically is right. The priority is on the loges, the courtside seats, and the prime-location season ticket holders.

Consider the new Gund Arena in Cleveland. The luxury suites went for $85,000 to $150,000 annually, the leases being for ten years. There are ninety-two of these suites, so the Cavs' yearly luxury suite revenue has to be close to $10 million. Because the leases are for ten years, the Cavs can count upon $100 million over the next ten years from those loges.

"I'll tell you how amazing it was," said Cavs broadcaster Joe Tait. "I helped host a lottery for the first twenty-eight loges—the prime locations, the ones that cost $150,000 a year. There were about fifty people representing corporations there, and over twenty of them were really upset after the lottery because they couldn't pay $1.5 million over the next ten years for those prime suite locations. I was astounded."

At Gund Arena, courtside seats sell for $200.

Near the courtside seats and luxury suites, waiters and waitresses hover about to sell $4 beers, $5 burgers, or a dozen chocolate chip cookies for $18.

For a good seat in the center of the arena that isn't near the ceiling, the prices are $75 and $48 each. The Cavs had the fourth-highest ticket prices in 1994–95—an average of $36. Only the Knicks, Larkers, and Suns were higher.

Remember, this is Cleveland—not New York or L.A.

In Toronto, over 4,000 seat locations were sold at $10,000 each for the team's first season. No, not the actual seats themselves. For $10,000, a fan had the right to say where he wanted to buy a seat—and then to pay for the tickets later. Top price was $85, so it cost about $3,500 for the tickets—or a total of $13,500 for a prime season ticket in that first year, and it was just a seat, not a luxury box.

Some marketing experts insist that by the year 2000, the income earned from all the facets of these luxury suites and prime seats will equal the local radio and television revenues in many cities.

It is astounding that there are so many people (or, more to the point, so many corporations) willing to shell out these kinds of dollars. But the corporations use them for entertainment purposes, especially to impress out-of-town clients.

All of that is very nice . . . and very lucrative.

But it has changed the kind of fans at the game. Some aren't even fans at all; this is just a place to go for an evening. Maybe that is why there are so many cheerleaders, so much music, so many pleas from the scoreboard (and sometimes, the public address announcer) for the crowd to "get up and make some noise!"

Some of the suits in the corporate boxes have no idea when they are supposed to cheer—or even why.

Marketing people are often oblivious to the players and their needs. During the last week of January in 1995, Orlando's Horace Grant hyperextended his knee when he slipped on the Orlando floor, which was wet. What promotion did the Magic front office plan for the next game? They had fans grease up and slide across the floor. Think about that for a moment. The floor is already slippery, and you lose one of your star players because of it. So what do you do? You have a halftime promotion where you grease the floor. The Magic were playing host to the Chicago Bulls that night, and the second half was held up for forty minutes as the players and coaches from both teams demanded that the entire floor be wiped up. Furthermore, this game was broadcast nationally on WTBS, with Chuck Daly serving as the analyst. He wasn't thrilled with this stunt, and said so.

In essence, Daly's point was: Guys, try to remember what matters the most happens on the court, not in some marketing meeting.

Yes, the NBA is a bottom-line business, and right now, business in the NBA is very good. But never forget that the product is being diluted by Stupid Marketing Tricks and petulant young stars.

"Even with some of the crazy salaries and other problems, I still consider the NBA to be a good business," said Red McCombs, the former owner of the San Antonio Spurs.

Why not? McCombs bought the Spurs in 1988 for $47 million. He sold them in 1993 for $82 million. Part of the reason was that the Spurs had David Robinson. Part of the reason was that the Spurs moved into the new Alamodome with their own luxury suites. And part of the reason is that there always seems to be someone out there willing to pay an outrageous price for an NBA team.

"But I do think the new arena was critical to enhancing the value of the franchise," said McCombs. "We wanted to build a dome that also could be used for football in case we could attract an NFL franchise. We also wanted it paid for. We took it to the voters, fought a hard campaign and won an election [53 percent to 47 percent] whereby the voters approved a half-cent sales tax for five years. We paid off the $180 million we owed to build it and have another $20 million in reserve. The whole thing is paid for, and not many cities can say that about their facilities."

But talk about gall! After two years in the Alamodome, the new Spurs owners have threatened to move the team unless a new "basketball only" arena is built. They want fewer seats but more luxury boxes to sell.

By comparison, Cleveland's Gund Arena was budgeted at $120 million and cost close to $150 million. The financing came partly from a sin tax on cigarettes and alcohol in Cuyahoga County, partly from loge revenues, and partly from county bonds. But they were still about $22 million short early in 1995.

There may not be any more NBA owners such as McCombs, who is a San Antonio car dealer. He purchased the Dallas franchise of the American Basketball Association in 1972 for $2 million—and he moved it to San Antonio, where it became the Spurs. In 1982, he sold his share in the Spurs and purchased a controlling interest in the Denver Nuggets. In 1986, he sold the Nuggets (for an estimated $20 million profit), and in 1988, he bought the Spurs again.

"As time went on, I learned that there was a lot of money to be made in owning franchises," said McCombs. "There still is. I got out because I was sixty-six years old and it takes a lot of time and energy to own one of these things if you're going to do it right. But I also see wealthy individuals such as Paul Allen in Portland, who can buy teams—although most will probably be owned by corporations."

But McCombs has one other vision, the perfect marriage of the NBA and marketing.

"Eventually, a company such as Nike is going to buy its own

NBA team, and then you'll have all the players wearing Nike's equipment and under both playing contracts and merchandising contracts with Nike," he said. "Why not? It makes sense."

Actually, owning a team probably doesn't make sense for Nike. How would they sell shoes to rival fans? And how could the NBA allow a shoe company to sign players on opposing teams—in effect, to have your opposition under contract to you? More likely would be ownership by a named sponsor in an unrelated business, like Great Western in L.A. or Fleet Bank in Boston. Corporate names for teams are standard operating procedure around the world; are the USAir Bullets or the Neiman-Marcus Mavericks a part of David Stern's global vision for the future?

Television is just as guilty as the teams themselves when it comes to hyperventilating about the game.

"It used to be that we presented games as competitions," said Bob Costas. "Now, we sometimes show these things as confrontations. We have lost the distinction between intensity and mean-spiritedness. Intensity is something you want to sell. It shows that there is a passion involved in an important game. But too often, we presented some of these things as a mean-spirited turf war, and that bothers me."

Costas is one of the most thoughtful men in network sports television. He is known as an avid baseball fan, but he broke into broadcasting doing play-by-play with the old Spirits of St. Louis of the ABA. He currently is the host of the NBA pregame and half-time studio shows.

As the game became more violent in the late 1980s and early 1990s, television celebrated the fights—while denouncing them at the same time. The broadcasters would say how this was terrible, how the league had to step in and stop the brawls before someone got hurt. But the newscasts would show the fights over and over. Then the cable and national networks would hype their games with video clips of what Costas accurately called a "mean-spirited turf war."

"There have been times when I've softened the teasers for certain games and times when I have changed the script that they wanted me to read," Costas said. "I was really unhappy with how the [1994] Knicks-Bulls playoff series was marketed. Every clip seemed to be a basket, then chest-bumping, finger-pointing, or guys in each other's faces. No one is naive enough to think that these things are tea parties. All high-level athletic competitions where a lot of pride is at stake have the possibility of spontaneous eruptions of emotion, even violence. But there is a difference between that happening occasionally and it being the whole undercurrent of the game."

Or as TNT analyst Hubie Brown stated: "Some of the teasers for the NBA looked like they were promoting the World Wrestling Federation."

Chuck Daly is believed to be the first to say that the NBA was really marketing itself as MTV basketball.

"It came to me when I was being interviewed by Cindy Crawford on MTV," said Daly. "What I mean by MTV basketball is that a kid who is eight to twelve today and watching TV, what does he really see about the game? He gets the commercials, where two of the greatest players ever—Michael Jordan and Larry Bird—are playing H-O-R-S-E like it was a video game, shooting balls over skyscrapers and from outer space. Then they see Shaquille O'Neal tearing down the rim and destroying a playground. There are other commercials, and many are cleverly done. But all we are talking about is running, jumping, dunking, and tearing down the backboard. You don't see anything about how to execute a pass, how to pivot or make a normal jump shot. You never see anything like the great pick-and-roll plays our great guards in Detroit ran. Kids today are growing up with a different mentality about the game. They are being taught to go to games to see dunks, ripping down the rim, and maybe long three-point shots."

"The players have caught on to what the cameras want," said Costas. "They know what postures and noises will get them on the air. They know that cameras are under the basket. So a guy dunks the ball, looks right at the camera and screams. That stuff is terrible. There is too much emphasis on the power and the assertion of power for its own sake. I'm just tired of this 'In Your Face' thing."

Wayne Embry goes further.

"Sometimes, I wonder if they think they're selling basketball or a gang war," said the Cavaliers general manager. "We are selling some of our players as nothing but street kids, and some of them aren't from the inner city. But that's become the image that is cool. You can see what television is doing. They are targeting the younger audience and accenting the negative. As an African-American, I know that my race is about more than the street, but you watch TV and it makes you wonder why they keep accenting the negative. Why do we make such a big deal about Dennis Rodman?"

Wayne, the answer to that one is easy: TV ratings.

Ever since Rodman started dying his hair every color of the rainbow, dating Madonna, and turning himself into the Illustrated Man with over a dozen tattoos, his presence on most NBA games meant an extra 25 percent in terms of viewers.

"Unbelievable," said Embry, shaking his head when he heard that fact from Nielsen Land.

Rodman runs around telling everyone, "The NBA is scared to death of me. The league doesn't know what I'm going to do next." He has adopted the same outrageous public persona as Madonna: Rodman believes he has to keep topping himself, and that just makes everything worse for his coaches and teammates. But to many young people—and to TV executives—Rodman sells and he was promoted by TV shamelessly in the 1995 playoffs.

Consider that one of the 1994 playoffs' bigger draws came in Game 6 and Game 7 of the Indiana–New York series. That's because the Pacers' Reggie Miller got into a trash-talking episode with film director Spike Lee, who was sitting courtside at Madison Square Garden as Miller shot the Knicks out of the game—and shut Lee up in the process.

For old-line basketball fans, the appeal of this is impossible to comprehend. But this was also pure MTV—talking big and loud, with a movie celebrity in the middle of it. Like it or not, this is marketing, NBA-style.

13 The Toughest Basketball League in the World

Here is how it is to coach in the Continental Basketball Association:

The place was Rapid City. The Coach was Eric Musselman, whose Rapid City Thrillers had just lost to Yakima. This was December 1994. Musselman is the son of legendary CBA coach Bill Musselman, but Eric has carved out a reputation of his own in pro basketball's underworld.

Heading into the 1994–95 season, Eric Musselman had a 160-64 record in four seasons coaching the Thrillers—all before his thirtieth birthday. But as Musselman stood in the dressing room of the Mt. Rushmore Center on that blustery December night, his team was 9-9.

"I'd never been 9-9 before," he said later, as if it were 9–90.

Yakima was ahead of Rapid City in the CBA Western Division standings, but they were a team that Musselman believed didn't have near the talent of his own.

"I'm not going to yell and scream at you guys," said Musselman. "But I just have a simple question: Do any of you guys know what is at stake here?"

Musselman walked over to Rumeal Robinson, who had spent the previous four seasons with three different NBA teams.

"Rumeal, can you name one team in our division?" asked Musselman in a soft voice.

Robinson looked up for a moment and shook his head.

Musselman walked over to Bo Kimble, a three-year NBA veteran.

"How about it, Bo?" he asked. "Who else is in our division?"

Kimble said he didn't know.

Musselman's next stop was LaBradford Smith, a three-year NBA veteran.

"LaBradford, can you help me out here?" he asked. "Name another team in our division?"

Smith didn't know.

Forward Mark Randall was drinking water from a paper cup. When Smith couldn't answer, he threw the cup at the wall. This was Randall's second tour of duty in Rapid City. In between, he'd had stops in Chicago, Minnesota, Detroit, and Denver.

"You guys are hopeless," Randall said as he walked out of the room.

Then Keith Smart stood up and addressed the three Thrillers who had just earned dunce caps: "Guys, Yakima is in first place in our division. We just played them. I mean, at least fifteen times today Eric has talked about how we had to beat Yakima because they are in our division."

A star at Indiana whose jumper gave Bob Knight his last national title, Smart is a lot like Randall: he has played in the NBA, CBA, and Europe, and has been a true professional everywhere he wore a uniform.

Musselman didn't say a word. He left the locker room, went to his office, and within a day he had traded Smith, Kimble, and Robinson for future CBA draft picks.

"Mostly, it was a dump job," he said. "Those guys had talent, but I had to get them out of here. I mean, if they can't take the time to look at the newspaper to see the standings . . . if they don't hear a thing I say to them about who we're playing . . . how am I supposed to win with these guys? Well, within twenty-four hours all three of them were gone and I'm glad I did it."

Robinson, Smith, and Kimble all had million-dollar contracts in the NBA. They were used to $60 a day meal money. Even though they were in Rapid City making $12,000 and $15 a day for meals, they still thought they were in the NBA.

"At the start of the season, I had five NBA first-round picks in training camp," said Musselman. "I know it was the most talent I've ever had in my time here, and we've had some great teams. No CBA team ever went to camp with five first-round picks."

The five were Randy Breuer, George McCloud, Robinson,

Smith, and Kimble. Breuer was thirty-four years old and hampered by injuries; he was cut. But that still left four.

"Some of those guys were bad guys," Musselman said. "Others just didn't care. Bo Kimble is a nice kid, but all he worried about was his points. He didn't guard anyone. It didn't matter to him if we won or lost. In the last four years, we have sent more players to the NBA than any CBA team, partly because we have good players and because our teams win. We don't keep selfish guys. I had been hearing about the new breed of player; with this group, I saw it."

Musselman also held the CBA rights to Lloyd Daniels. When Daniels was cut by Philadelphia in late November of 1994, Musselman contacted his agent to see if he wanted to play in Rapid City and perhaps earn a ticket back to the NBA.

"His agent told me that if Lloyd was going to the CBA, he had to be guaranteed playing forty minutes a night," said Musselman. "I told him that I don't guarantee any player any time—the player earns it. He said that Lloyd either was guaranteed forty minutes a night or he wasn't reporting."

Musselman was not about to let any player hold him hostage, so he traded Daniels's rights to Fort Wayne. No one is sure if Fort Wayne promised Daniels that he'd play forty minutes, but Daniels reported to the Fury, averaged 28 points and played over forty minutes most nights.

"The great thing about this league is that the coach has total control," said Musselman.

"You better believe that," said Jerome Lane, who has bounced back and forth between the NBA and the CBA. "In the CBA, the coaches actually make more money than the players. If they want your ass out, they trade your ass the next day."

The average CBA coach earns $50,000. The players make between $12,000 and $20,000.

"We have a salary cap, but it's pretty much an honor system," said Musselman. "Besides, everyone is making about the same and none of the contracts are guaranteed. So it's real easy to trade people, or just get rid of them like I did with [Smith, Kimble, and Robinson]. A couple of years ago, I picked up Melvin Newbern in a trade. He had been in the NBA with a couple of teams. His agent told me that Newbern wanted to play the point, although his best position was shooting guard. Anyway, I played him at the point for one game. He was on the court for twenty-two minutes and all he wanted to do was shoot. He'd get his numbers, but you'd never win big with him. So the next day, I traded him. I had him for one day and twenty-two minutes."

"This league is the complete opposition of the NBA," said Mo McHone, a veteran NBA assistant who coached Yakima to the 1995 CBA title. "In the NBA, the salary cap and the huge contracts make it hard to work out almost any trade. In this league, it's so easy that teams trade every day. It's like bubble gum cards. I swear, if Michael Jordan were in the CBA, he'd have been traded at least three times."

The CBA is supposed to be the farm system for the NBA, but it's unlike any farm system you've ever seen. None of the CBA's sixteen franchises are affiliated with any NBA team. In 1994–95, they were scattered across the continent from Yakima to Pittsburgh to Mexico City to Hartford, and yes, Rapid City, a town of 80,000 in the Black Hills of South Dakota.

The NBA sends the CBA only $100,000 a month, which the CBA uses to pay the salaries and expenses of its league office. The NBA also pays the salaries of the officials.

But everything else—coaches, players, and front office salaries along with all expenses—is paid by each franchise.

"Last season [1993–94], only two teams made money," said Musselman. "We [Rapid City] led the league in attendance with a 6,200 average and cleared $72,500. I understand that Oklahoma City made about $5,000. A lot of teams lost $100,000, even $200,000."

In 1994–95, only Souix Falls, South Dakota, showed a profit.

Any CBA player can be called up by any NBA team. The CBA team loses the player, most likely its star, and receives only $2,000 from the NBA in return.

Imagine an entire league on a ten-day contract. So it's conceivable that three Rapid City players could be with the Thrillers for a month and not know who else is in their division. No, it's inconceivable; no one should be that selfish and/or oblivious. But it is a reflection of the state of mind of many players.

So if a player wants to quit at halftime—as Duke's Thomas Hill did one night in Fort Wayne—he just walks out. And gets traded to Fargo, North Dakota, the next day.

"Guys come and go at any time," said Musselman. "One year, I had three guys leave the same day. They all got better deals in Europe and Turkey, so they were gone. You only have ten guys on your roster, so if you lose three, you're down to seven. And if a couple of guys are hurt, you may not have enough players to put on the floor."

If a player is injured, he can be cut. In the NBA, the Players Association ensures that an injured player remains on the inactive list (and the payroll) at least until his injury is healed. Not so in the CBA.

"With about a month left to go [in the 1993–94 season], Jerome Lane hurt his ankle," said Musselman. "He could have stayed in town for a few weeks and maybe played again, but he decided to go home—and we didn't encourage him to stay. So he didn't get paid for that last month, and we replaced him on our roster. We do have an injured list, but most CBA owners don't like you to use it because they don't want to pay that extra salary."

Players can—and do—leave at any time.

"Right in the middle of the [1994] Western Conference Finals, Billy Thompson called me at 4:30 in the afternoon," said Musselman. "We had a game that night. Billy had been in the NBA for five years. He was an ordained minister and was the best person I've ever worked with. He was our team captain. We are talking about a great guy. But right in the middle of the playoffs, Billy said he had this offer to play in Turkey, and he was going to take it. I asked him to at least play that night. He said that he had to get his stuff together and go—and that was the last I saw of him. We got $15,000 from his team in Turkey, and Billy was paid $25,000 for two months. It was nice to get the money, but we really didn't want to let Billy go. But he was leaving, and we didn't want to start suing a team in Turkey, so we just let him go."

The typical CBA team goes through thirty to thirty-five players per year.

"It's the most existential of all basketball leagues," said veteran CBA coach Charley Rosen. "There is no carryover from one season to the next. Sometimes, not even from one month to the next. You scout a team, and three days later they have three new players.

That happens a lot. It's constant turmoil and turnover. People say, 'Why don't you bring in some young players, develop them and you'll be strong by playoff time?' [Veteran NBA coach] Tom Nissalke tried it in Rapid City [in 1987–88] and he just got his ass kicked [a 16-38 record]. I tried it one year in Rockford. It lasted about half the season, and I knew I had to get some veterans in there and win some games. Your owner and your fans aren't interested in development, they want to win now. As a coach, you had better win, or your ass will be gone, too. When Henry Bibby coached at Oklahoma City [1991–94], he was famous for bringing in all these talented guys who had some kind of drug rap. The idea was that he'd get as much mileage out of them as he could. When the guys started to turn sour, he'd dump them and bring in someone else. The point of the whole league is win, win, win. No one has any patience. No one has any loyalty. Rarely does a guy even make the whole season with the same team."

"If you have the same guys from day one until the end of the season, you'll never win," said Musselman. "Day one players are mediocre guys. They are players who were cut early in NBA training camps—or weren't even good enough to get an invitation to an NBA camp. As the NBA season goes on, players are cut. You want those players. Or guys who signed to play for $250,000 in Europe are sent home. You want those players, too. Those are the players who help you win. You have to keep shuffling the deck."

Here is the CBA mind-set: Late in the 1993–94 season, Rapid City lost Jay Guidinger and Ben Coleman to the NBA—Guidinger to Cleveland and Coleman to Detroit. Those were Musselman's two big men in a league where players over 6-foot-8 are few. Musselman picked up the rights to a guy by the name of Darren Morningstar, who had been a second-round pick by Boston in 1992. He had played briefly with Utah and Dallas. Fargo had his CBA rights.

"I played one game for Fargo," said Morningstar. "Actually, it was only six minutes. I got into it with the coach, just quit. I left the arena, bought a case of beer, drove off, and never looked back."

Musselman traded a few low-round draft picks for Morningstar and another player by the name of Clinton Smith. Morningstar showed up in Rapid City wearing Elvis Presley sideburns and looking like he had spent a lot of time with the King dining at the Cheeseburger in Paradise. He was 6-foot-10, 250 pounds, with most of it around his gut.

"I kept telling myself that somehow he had started 16 games for Dallas early that season, so he must have done something right," said Musselman. But in the 1993–94 season, Musselman probably had better players than the Mavericks, who won a total of 13 NBA games. Morningstar lasted 12 games and was cut.

But that was longer than Clinton Smith. He played one game, and was traded the next day for Jerome Lane.

If you are confused by all this player movement, don't worry about it. No one can keep track—which is exactly the point.

"It just gets insane," said Rosen. "One night, I got into it with Eric Musselman after a game. I got him against the wall and I thought I was going to strangle him."

Musselman is about 5-foot-8 and 150 pounds. Rosen is a foot taller and 100 pounds heavier. Musselman was swearing and spitting in Rosen's face as he tried to get Rosen's hands off his neck.

"Despite that, we always have been good friends," said Musselman.

"That's true," said Rosen. "Of course, I'm out of the league now. I started to lose control. In another game, I threw a punch at [Grand Rapids coach] George Whitaker and I wound up spending a night in jail. That's when I knew it was time for me to get out. It is that kind of league. After a while, it can turn anyone into a lunatic. You spend about 25 percent of your energy on coaching and the rest on insanity. This player is screwing that guy's wife, and the woman's husband wants to kill your player. I had a player who was selling drugs. I had guys fighting in the dressing room. When someone gets called up to the NBA, half of the league goes into a depression because those guys thought they should have been called up instead, and you have to deal with that for three days. Guys are quitting, guys are being cut. You are constantly looking for more players. Nothing is guaranteed. Everyone is volatile. It is life on the edge because anyone can be gone tomorrow."

The NBA has a very orderly process of procuring talent. You can do it through the college draft, trades with another team, or by signing free agents. Each NBA roster consists of twelve players. You can put three more players on the injured list.

That's it—a maximum of fifteen guys.

In the CBA, the key is a rights list.

The CBA has a seven-round draft. Even if the player doesn't sign with you, the team that drafts him keeps his rights for two years. Until 1994, it used to be forever. Anyway, if that player wants to play in the CBA—he must play for the team that owns his rights.

"In this league, when you make a trade you try to get as many draft picks or rights to players as you can as part of the deal," said Musselman. "You want the rights to good players, guys sitting on the bench in the NBA, or guys playing in the best league in Europe. You never know when they'll be cut. Then you can maybe talk the guy into playing for you—or trade his rights to another team for more draft picks or the right to other players."

When Musselman took over the Rapid City Thrillers in 1988, the team had the rights to about thirty players—about average for the league.

"Now we are close to a hundred," Musselman said in 1995. "We also have a list of another fifty guys whose rights we want. I can't tell you how Karl Malone and John Stockton are playing in Utah, but I know who the eleventh and twelfth men are on the Jazz, how they are playing, and who has their rights. I know all the eleventh and twelfth men in the NBA and my goal is to get the first crack at those guys if they're cut."

The rich get richer. The more players' rights you have, the more power you have to make trades that will bring you more players and more access to acquiring other players.

"Eric learned that from his father," said Rosen. "Bill Musselman won three titles in the CBA because he got the best players. His black book was legendary. He had the players' names, their agents' names, their wives' names, and their girlfriends' names. He knew the mothers and their old coaches. He could trace down anyone. And because he got good players, those guys went up to the NBA. So part of his sales job to a guy from Europe or who was just cut was, 'I'll get you into the NBA.' He could talk about Mike Sanders, Tony Campbell, Scott Roth, Sam Mitchell—a lot of guys who made the jump. He also had absolute discipline because he had so many players on a string, he could cut or trade a good player and bring in a guy who was just as good the next day."

"Eric is unbelievable," said Bill Musselman. "I came back to coach [in Rochester, Minnesota, in 1993–94], and Eric held me up. I wanted one of his players, and he kept squeezing me for another draft pick plus the rights to two more guys."

Or as Eric Musselman said, "Every night, we seem to play a team that has at least three of my former players."

All of this instant access to talent gives CBA pep talks a certain flavor you'll never find in the NBA.

One night, Musselman was mad at his guards. He stormed into the dressing room at halftime and berated them for their selfishness.

Then he wrote the name of John Bagley on the blackboard.

"If you guys saw the paper this morning, you know I just got Bagley's rights," said Musselman. "With one phone call, he's here and one of you guys is gone. So get out there and pass the ball."

This kind of motivation does work, because there have been names on the blackboard one day who ended up in uniform the next. In the NBA of guaranteed multimillion-dollar contracts, a coach who tried that would be ignored or laughed out of the room.

This concept of hoarding players' rights usually confounds the former NBA players who want to try coaching in the CBA. The best CBA coaches are also the general managers; they put the team together, coach it, and make all the moves during the season.

"[Former NBA backup center] Mark McNamara wanted to try coaching, so we hired him as an assistant in the fall of 1994," said Musselman. "He lasted about six weeks. He thought all he had to do was work with the players on the floor. Well, we spend ten to twelve hours in the office, talking to players, agents, scouts, and NBA people to keep building up our rights list. We also want to know who might get cut or come back from Europe, so we can trade for their rights. To us, this is the natural way of doing business. To guys from the NBA, it's a shock, and most of them are not about to put in the work."

McNamara quit Rapid City a few days after the opening of hunting season.

"Someone accidentally shot Mark's dog," said Musselman.

"Mark was really close to his dog, and he got very depressed. He didn't come to practice the next day, because he was upset about his dog. The following day, he came in and said he was moving back to the West Coast. He had been in the NBA for seven years, and made a lot of money. He told us that he was going home. He had just built a million-dollar house or something like that. To him, it wasn't worth it."

The CBA's top coaches have been Mauro and Dan Panaggio (a father-son combination), Flip Saunders, Mike Thibault, Bruce Stewart, and Calvin Duncan. None played in the NBA. Only Duncan even played in the CBA.

All of this may sound fun, at least in a rotisserie-league sort of way, but it does not make for a good farm system for coaches or players.

"All the emphasis on winning works against that," said Musselman. "But the NBA doesn't help, either. They tell us to develop players. Sure, they sometimes sign young guys like John Starks, Anthony Mason, Marty Conlon, and Michael Williams—but most of the time, they take our older guys. Charles Jones was signed out of this league at the age of thirty-eight. John Long was signed at thirty-five, Earl Cureton was thirty-four. Do they take some of our younger players and really work with them? Not often. They want to win now, so they go for the veterans."

Another problem is the lack of size.

If you watch the NBA, you know that most teams don't have decent backup centers. Some simply use a 6-foot-10 power forward in the middle when the big man rests.

"In our league, it's even worse," said Musselman. "Most centers are about 6-foot-8. Pat Durham was a center in the CBA, and he went to Minnesota as a small forward. In the CBA, you end up with a lot of guys playing out of position. Power forwards become centers. Small forwards are power forwards. Shooting guards are small forwards, and you can play a 6-foot-2 shooting guard in this league if he can score. The league is based far more on speed than size."

And that doesn't help you develop NBA players, either.

"Even the game itself works against the development idea," said Rosen. "The guy who owns your team doesn't care how many players you send up to the NBA, all he cares about is winning or losing. Most of the coaches don't even have fully guaranteed contracts, so they can't worry about development. One year, I got fired with 11 games to go in the season. I had a $50,000 contract, but only $30,000 was guaranteed. Do you think that I was real worried about developing young players for next year or the NBA?"

But there is an even bigger problem.

"In the CBA, they have this quarter-points system," said Rosen. "You get a point for each quarter of the game you win. Then you get three more points for winning the game. So there are seven points on the line in each game. The idea is to eliminate garbage time and make each quarter into a separate game, with a standings point at stake. But that's dumb. I've lost games by 40 points, but still won two quarters. You don't deserve anything if you lose by 40 points. This is like giving a point for each inning that you win in a baseball game. Why?"

But rewarding the winners and losers isn't Rosen's biggest objection.

"If you want to develop players, then you can use that garbage time to play the young guys on the end of the bench," he said. "But the quarter-points rule encourages you to play your starters more, and forget the guys on the end of the bench. It just seems that everything about the CBA is designed to work against development."

Musselman agrees entirely.

"Over the years, I've picked up rookies who had just been cut by the NBA," he said. "One year, I signed Gary Voce. He had been cut by the Cavaliers at midseason. He was horrible. I had him for 10 games and let him go. Another year, it was Demetrius Calip, who was with the Lakers for a few weeks. He was awful, too. Both of those guys lasted only a few weeks with me. Maybe they would have worked out in the long run if I'd had time to bring them off the bench, but the veterans in our league were chewing these kids up. There was no reason for me to keep them, so I cut them in favor of older guys who had been in our league before."

It doesn't have to be this way.

The CBA could be a great place to develop players.

It could be the perfect place to train and develop coaches.

It could be an excellent way for an injured NBA veteran to play himself back into shape for a few weeks, then rejoin his NBA team.

"But the league doesn't do any of those things—or at least not as well as it can," said Phil Jackson. "The NBA needs a real farm system, like baseball. The CBA is right there. Everything is in place to make it work. You have [NBA] teams being sold for $125 million. You have players signing contracts for $50 million. Then they say that it would cost too much money to use the CBA as a farm system? That argument doesn't make it with me. I hear that the Players Association doesn't want it. Well, why not?"

One reason is that the Powers That Be in the NBA don't see the potential of the CBA.

"I think the CBA setup is fine the way it is," said commissioner David Stern. "We support the league. The CBA has given us players like John Starks and Anthony Mason. Phil Jackson and George Karl coached there. I don't see a need for big changes."

Maybe that's because Stern doesn't see any tremendous marketing advantages to be gained by turning the CBA into a full-fledged farm system.

"That's not it," he said.

Stern's objections are these:

1. He says that NBA teams like the idea that they can sign any CBA player. If it were a farm system like baseball, then certain CBA players would only be available to the NBA team paying their salaries.

    "What is wrong with that?" asked Phil Jackson, who coached in the CBA for five years. "What do you think NBA teams do now with the three spots on their injured list? They hide young guys all the time. They concoct a phony injury and let the guy sit there all year. The league knows this. Hey, let every NBA team have a three-man taxi squad, and allow those guys to play in the CBA and get experience. That will help them a lot more than sitting on the injured list."

2. The Players Association doesn't want NBA teams stockpiling players in the CBA.

    "The union is worried about these guys going up and down from the CBA," said Phoenix Suns owner Jerry Colangelo.

"But wait a minute. If each NBA team has a three-man taxi squad, make a rule that requires those three guys to make at least the NBA minimum [$125,000] instead of the $10,000 or whatever they'd make in the CBA. What the taxi squad does is create more members and high-paying jobs for the union. I just wonder if anyone ever really took the time to explain that to the Players Association."

3. Stern said that he fought for the idea of allowing NBA players to rehabilitate from injuries while playing in the CBA for a couple of weeks, "but I lost that one to the Players Association, too. They were worried that NBA teams might use this rule as a way to punish players by sending them to the minors."

"Well, he should bring it up again," said Jackson. "You can make a rule like in baseball that a player with a certain number of years experience in the NBA would have to approve a rehabilitation assignment to the CBA. We really need this. Once the season gets going, there just isn't that much practice time between games, and the CBA would be a perfect way for players to work themselves back into shape quickly."

4. Most NBA teams would rather have the guys on the end of their bench.

"That's crazy," said Doug Collins. "You can say all you want about practicing every day against a Patrick Ewing or a Hakeem Olajuwon, but once the season starts, a young player doesn't often get that chance. Either there are too many games that cut down the practice time, or because of the heavy schedule your stars don't scrimmage that much during the season. There comes a point in the career of every young player when he has to *play*, and I mean competitive game experience. Sitting on the end of the bench does nothing for you."

In fact, it has hurt many young players.

"I don't know how many guys come into our league who had been number one draft picks and then have spent a couple of years on an NBA bench," said Musselman. "You see these guys play and they look terrible. They've lost their games. They don't even look as good as they did in college, because all they did was sit for two years. The whole thing is backwards."

How so?

"Suppose you draft a guy in the first round, but you see that he's not going to play for you right away," said Musselman. "The best thing to do would be to send him to our league right away after training camp. Let him play. Let him learn the pro game that way. Maybe Danny Ferry would have come along faster if the Cavaliers could have done that with him. I don't know for sure. I remember how Dave Jamerson was on Houston's bench for three years. He came into our league and he was awful. He was supposed to be able to shoot, but I didn't see that. Like a lot of number one picks who spend too much time on the bench, they forget their strengths and what got them to the NBA in the first place."

Players such as Mario Elie, John Starks, Anthony Mason, and Michael Williams were successful because they had a lot of CBA experience early in their pro careers, *then* they went up to the NBA. It's common sense. You play in the minors before the majors.

Jackson is joined by Wayne Embry, Doug Collins, Hubie Brown, and Jerry Colangelo in saying that if the league really wants to improve the game on the court, it should turn the CBA into a real farm system.

Heres how to do it:

1. Make the NBA's injured list a real injured list. Make it two spots, and make sure that the guy is really hurt, no vague injuries like "tendinitis of the knee." As Embry said, "That is something teams use because it's true—every player has some kind of tendinitis in his knees."

2. Allow each team to have a three-man taxi squad. You don't have to have three players, but you are not allowed to have more than three players. Each of these players must be paid the NBA minimum salary and the salary must be guaranteed for the year as they work on their skills in the CBA.

3. A player with three or more years of NBA experience must give approval if he is to be sent to the CBA to rehabilitate an injury or simply to receive some playing time.

4. Two NBA teams can share a CBA franchise. This setup is often used in the summer leagues. The CBA team can be supplied with up to six members of the NBA's taxi squad—and it can sign six of its own players to fill out a twelve-man roster.

5. If an NBA team doesn't want to take part in the CBA plan, fine.

That NBA team can still sign any CBA players not being paid by another NBA team.

6. If an NBA team can reach an exclusive agreement with a CBA team whereby that CBA team works only with that one NBA team, that's okay, too.

7. The CBA players not on an NBA taxi squad are still eligible to sign with any NBA team.

8. Hiring coaches is the tricky part, because coaches decide playing time and the style of play. The best situation would be for an NBA team (or two NBA teams) to pick and pay the coach. That way, they can make sure that their players receive the amount of court time and coaching the NBA team deems best. If a CBA team wants to hire its own coach, then the NBA teams would have to work that out. But given the financial state of most CBA franchises—the average franchise lost over $150,000 in 1994–95 and only one team showed a profit—having someone else pay the coach's salary will appeal to most CBA owners.

"I coached in the CBA for five years and it is a great training ground," said Phil Jackson. "But it will be even better if you make the game more like the NBA. It would be a great way for a former player to see if he likes coaching, or if he has the aptitude to do it. You often hear that this player or that player would make a good coach. Well, send him to the CBA and let's find out. The CBA can also be a good place for college coaches who want to see if they like the pro game."

Well, maybe not the top college coaches, but assistants who'd like to try the pros.

But the NBA needs to make the investment—probably $500,000 per franchise—to take the emphasis away from winning and put it on development of players and coaches. Money talks, and the NBA has plenty of money to spend. The only question is, how do they want to spend it?

Here is what will probably happen: Some teams will pass on a chance to have a farm team. They probably will be teams that have been constant losers, teams that take shortcuts in scouting and other areas.

Other teams—highly successful franchises such as Chicago,

Phoenix, and Cleveland—will either combine into one CBA franchise, or they will decide to get their own deal with a CBA team. The teams that aggressively pursue the CBA will develop players and coaches. Other teams will see it and follow. Soon, the CBA will have to expand, as every NBA team may want their own CBA farm team. Minor-league baseball has been a major fan attraction and a profitable business, despite the teams being stocked from the big-league team on top. Why can't the same thing happen in the CBA?

14 Improving the Game

WHY NOT: ALLOW ZONE DEFENSES

Actually, some zone defenses are already permitted in the NBA. What is a full- or half-court trapping defense? It's certainly not a man-to-man defense, but teams play it all the time and it's legal.

Or what is it when Shaquille O'Neal catches a pass at the low post, about eight feet from the basket, and three defenders swarm all over him? Is that not a zone?

As former center Kareem Abdul-Jabbar recalled being double-teamed, "If that's not a zone, then those guys should at least have been given some parking tickets."

Actually, you can double-, even triple-team a man if he has the ball. Those certainly are zone principles, and they are legal in the NBA.

But old-fashioned 2-1-2 or 1-3-1 half-court zones are not. Nor are some other strange hybrids, the likes of which former Kentucky coach Adolph Rupp once called, "The old stratified, transitional, hyperbolic paraboloid."

So what is an illegal defense in the NBA? Don't even ask.

"I know it when I see it" is how the late, great official Earl Strom explained it. "Just don't make me explain it."

"That's because Earl knew that the illegal defense rule was stupid," said Pete Newell. "If you watched his games, he seldom called it."

Basically, you are supposed to play pure one-on-one defense—and you also are supposed to drive fifty-five miles per hour on most interstates. But there are times when you are allowed to double-team the ball. There are other stipulations that have made the league's illegal defense rules nearly as complicated as the salary cap. In March of 1979, official Richie Powers grew weary of trying to decipher and enforce the illegal defense rules, so he announced to both teams that he would ignore it in a game where New Jersey beat Atlanta, 97–95.

The league fined Powers $2,500 for his benign neglect.

"That rule is like a beard I've been tripping over for 20 years," Powers told *Sports Illustrated* in 1979. "I'd like to see zones allowed in exhibition games just to see if it will be the 'piranha eating up the game' that the owners think it is. I don't believe it."

This is a subject of real debate. Listen in:

HUBIE BROWN: If you can play a zone, no one would ever get to the middle and score inside. The college game is played at rim level. The high school games and the women's games are played below the rim. The NBA is played above the rim, maybe a foot over the rim. You put a zone in there with all the great athletes and you'll never get shots in the lane. It will force a perimeter game. Everything will be jump shots.

DOUG COLLINS: But what is it today? [NBA supervisor of officials] Darell Garretson keeps saying that allowing zones will take away individual play. Well, I beg anyone to go to an NBA game and tell me how many dunks happen in a half-court situation. The dunks come on fast breaks and in transition. Now, the defenses usually take away the drives to the basket—even with all the illegal-defense rules. Coaches just find ways to get around it. I just don't think big men can see any more double- and triple-teams than they do already with the illegal-defense rules.

ROD THORN: Everyone is worried about the dropping scores and the lack of offense. If you give coaches a chance to use zones, the scores will go down even more. There will be even more defense and a slower game.

DOUG COLLINS: The NBA game now is a zone anyway. Everything on the weak side [away from the ball] is zone. There is all this rotation on defense. It's really not much different than a zone, you have players just scrambling around trying to cover an open guy. No matter what the league says, every team is zoning away from the ball to some extent.

PETE NEWELL: We let high school kids play zone. We let girls' and women's teams do it. You mean to tell me that a women's team can figure out how to play against a zone, but an NBA team can't? Then what do we have all these coaches and assistants for?

Every time a big man is double-teamed at a low post, that means the three remaining defenders are trying to cover four guys—and that's a zone. We say that we have the best players, the best coaches, and the best basketball minds, let's see what they do if they are allowed to play any kind of zone defense.

LARRY BROWN: The illegal-defense rules have taken away movement on offense. They encourage isolation basketball. You have two guys using the pick-and-roll play on one side of the court, and three guys standing on the other side, pointing and screaming, "Illegal," trying to get the illegal-defense call. You also have the coaches yelling, "Illegal." The game comes to a stop as everyone tries to figure out if the defense is illegal or not. It's ridiculous.

BILL FITCH: I'm not sure if we want to legalize the zone, but anything that can take the officials' hands out of the game is inherently good. These guys spend a lot of time watching for illegal defenses when they should be looking out for more major violations.

PETE NEWELL: Why should we force officials to worry about what kind of defenses are being played? Isn't there enough contact out there to keep them busy? We've turned them into the kind of police who are writing jaywalking tickets when guys are getting murdered across the street. The illegal-defense call is just so arbitrary, I hate it.

LARRY BROWN: We should be playing the best basketball in the world and teaching kids how the game is played. I'd like to see us play more like the international game [where the zone defense is permitted]. I hate isolation basketball. I hate telling two or three of my guys that I don't want them to move on offense, that I want them thirty-five feet from the basket. But the way the rules are now, the best way to play is isolation for your best player, letting him beat his man off the dribble. As he drives to the basket, another defender picks him up, so he passes off to someone else for an open shot. I don't think this is good basketball. Playing against a zone would force you to use a motion offense with all the players involved. Zones would also force teams to try and run more, to beat the zone down the court for a shot before they set up.

HUBIE BROWN: To me, the beauties of basketball are the backdoor plays, the cutting through the lane—not a bunch of jump shots. I know that we have a lot of three-pointers being taken now, but I just think you'll see even more with zones. The great size and shot-blocking ability of today's players would turn the NBA into a jump-shooting fiasco with zone defenses.

PETE NEWELL: I've heard all the arguments about how zone defenses would hamper scoring, hamper star players, and dampen fan interest. Well, look at the college game and the international game. I don't see zone defenses bringing them to a stop. The hardest ticket in basketball to get is to the NCAA Final Four, and they allow zones. Part of the reason the NBA first eliminated the zone was to stop slowdowns, but that was before the advent of the 24-second clock. A big part of basketball is moves and countermoves. I do this to stop you, you try this to get around me. As the rules are now, coaches have decided that they don't have to run.

LARRY BROWN: A by-product of having three offensive guys standing thirty-five feet from the basket and not being part of the play is that they stop fast breaks. By being so far away from the heart of the offense, they are in great position to get back on defense and guard against the fast break.

PETE NEWELL: What is the best way to beat a zone defense? It's to run and get the ball down the court before the zone sets up. If coaches are smart, zone defenses should lead to more fast breaks.

DOUG COLLINS: Coaches tend to copy each other. If nothing else, maybe a zone defense would give a coach an excuse to allow his players to run.

In the words of Doug Collins, "Let 'em play zone." Or at least let 'em try it. The illegal-defense rules change every few years. They are like the tax code: every time the government tries to simplify it, they make it more complicated. Under the current setup, offenses have become stagnant.

Basketball man after basketball man will tell you these three things:

1. Three guys watch the other two offensive players execute a pick-and-roll play.
2. The ball is passed to the big man at the low post. He draws a double- or triple-team. He passes the ball out of the defense, usually to a teammate who is open for a three-point shot.
3. Even though today's great athletes grow up playing the running game and seem more physically suited to run than to play half-court basketball, coaches have put on the brakes and few teams make an effort to run.

Pete Newell, Collins, and others are right when they insist that the best and most logical way to attack a zone defense is with the fast break. Teams who dare to run should be rewarded under the new rules.

There is nothing sacred about the illegal-defense rules. They are changed every few years, so why not just throw them out? Let's see what happens for a couple of seasons. If it makes the game worse, you can be sure that someone, somewhere still has a copy of the old rulebook and we can bring it back.

WHY NOT: ELIMINATE FOUL-OUTS

On the surface, it sounds like a terrible idea: what do you mean, make it so no one can foul out of the game? You want a guy like Rick Mahorn to have unlimited fouls?

Actually, a basketball thug like Mahorn would—but there would be a penalty.

But first, let's talk about why the NBA should forget about its rule in which a player is sent to the bench for the rest of the game after his sixth personal foul.

"I remember the seventh game of the 1994 Eastern Conference Finals between New York and Indiana," said Doug Collins. "The Pacers' Dale Davis went up for a dunk. Patrick Ewing fouled him. He grabbed Davis's arm. You could see the official standing there, waiting to see if the ball went in before making the call. That's because he knew that Ewing had five fouls on him, and the sixth would have sent him to the bench for the rest of the game. Well, the ball went in, so the official let it go. In fact, he might even have let it go even if Davis had missed—you never know."

But Collins's point is that the officials don't just call the game—they also are aware of how many fouls are on star players.

"The other trick officials use is if there are two defenders close to a guy driving to the basket and a foul is committed, you give the foul to the inferior player—to protect the star from fouling out," said Collins. "It's ridiculous."

Pete Newell has been pushing for the no-foul rule for years. It was used in the American Basketball Association without any real problems.

"Here is how it should work," said Newell. "If a guy already has five fouls and commits a sixth, he stays in the game. But the player who is fouled automatically receives two free throws. Then the offense keeps the ball. So the penalty is severe—two free throws and possession."

So what's the argument against it?

"One year at a coach's meeting, Lenny Wilkens proposed it," said Newell. "One coach stood up and said, 'Hey, if you get two free throws plus the ball, why not just go right at a certain guy during the game to get fouls on him so you can get the penalty? It will screw up the whole game.' I won't tell you who the coach was, but he was a big name. I looked at him and said, 'What are you talking about? You can go at a specific guy now and foul him out of the entire game—so why would you do anything differently just to get a couple of extra free throws?' This whole thing is common sense."

Or lack of common sense.

The NBA doesn't want to change the six-foul rule, "because it's working okay as it is," said Rod Thorn.

But this would make it better. As Bill Fitch said, "Anything that takes the officials out of the game is good."

Certainly anything that keeps the officials from worrying about how many personal fouls a certain player has is a great idea.

Maybe some coach would leave Rick Mahorn on the floor to pick up a dozen fouls, but it's doubtful. Not when his team gives up two free throws and possession of the ball every time Mahorn commits a foul after number five.

Remember, the league's other reason for ejection—fighting, a severe flagrant foul, two lesser flagrant fouls, and two taunting fouls—all will remain in place.

The league gives the stars the benefit of the doubt on foul calls because they know the fans and TV networks pay to see these guys play. The no-foul-out rule would let them do just that—without any subterranean help from the officials.

WHY: HIGHER ISN'T BETTER

Every few years, you hear someone say, "Too many guys are dunking. It's too easy. They ought to raise the basket and bring the little guy back into the game."

Obviously, Dr. James Naismith never imagined players being seven feet tall, players dunking anything but doughnuts, or players who could jump and look down into the basket. It was back in 1891 when Naismith was a teacher at the Springfield YMCA that he had an idea for a game where you throw a big ball up into a basket.

He took a peach basket and nailed it to a railing in the Springfield College gym. The railing happened to be about ten feet above the floor. There was no backboard. The ball was about the size of a soccer ball.

Over the years, the size of the ball has changed. A backboard was developed and made of different materials, from wood to metal to glass. But the rim stayed ten feet above the floor.

The theory of raising the basket is that it would force big men to shoot the ball. At least, they couldn't just drop it down into the hoop.

There were a few 7-footers playing college ball before World War II, but it was the advent of 6-foot-10, 245-pound George Mikan that convinced basketball people to consider raising the basket. It wasn't that Mikan continually dunked. He almost never dunked. But he was so tall and strong compared to everyone else that he seemed to grab all the rebounds and own the area near the basket.

On March 7, 1954, Mikan's Minneapolis Lakers faced the Milwaukee Black Hawks—with a twelve-foot basket.

If you wanted to take Mikan out of the game, the twelve-foot basket sort of did the trick. He shot only 2-for-14 from the field. He finished with 12 points, thanks to 8-of-11 from the foul line. Rebounds were not kept, but it appeared that Mikan snared most of them.

"I played in that game," said Slater Martin, a 5-foot-10 Hall of Fame guard. "The basket was just too high. It took too much strength for us little guys to take long shots. The twelve-foot basket forced the game closer to the basket, because it cut down your shooting range. The closer the game is played to the basket, the more important big people become."

Martin scored 10 points and shot 3-of-11 in that game.

For the record, the Lakers beat Milwaukee, 65–63, and the two teams combined to shoot 30 percent from the field.

When former Chicago Bulls center Tom Boerwinkle played at the University of Tennessee in the middle 1960s, Coach Ray Mears held a scrimmage with a twelve-foot basket. The results were the same as the pro game in 1954.

At 6-foot-10, Boerwinkle shot a miserable 1-for-16. His only basket came on a jumper from the foul line. But the little guys didn't shoot much better. The Tennessee players combined to shoot 22 percent.

They also complained that a twelve-foot-basket made it nearly impossible to make a layup, "because you have to throw the ball straight up in the air," 6-foot Bill Justus told *Sports Illustrated*.

Boerwinkle said a big problem he faced was that he couldn't tip offensive rebounds back at the basket.

If you want to help the little guy, the last thing you want to do is raise the basket. If you bring it down to nine-feet, then little guys can make shots from further out because it takes less strength to get the ball up to the rim.

"At least that's my opinion," Hall of Fame coach John Wooden told *Sports Illustrated*. "If you want to help him, then lower the basket. But I'm against that, too. The basket has always been 10 feet and it should stay 10 feet. Why tamper with one of the basic concepts of the game?"

WHY NOT: A FOUR-POINT SHOT

"If you like the three-point play, why not put in a four-point play?" asked Dolph Schayes.

Why do that?

"It could be fun," said the former NBA coach. "Say you put the line thirty-two or thirty-five feet from the basket. When a team is down by four points near the end of the game, it isn't over. Kids can develop the shot. Maybe you only allow it in the final two minutes of the game. But it would be something else for fans to talk about and coaches to use."

Schayes is in the Hall of Fame. He was known for his long two-handed set shots, some of which may even have gone in from what he proposes to be four-point range.

"Guys take half-court shots all the time after practice," said Schayes. "Now, they would have a better reason to practice it."

But it also would give four points to a guy who threw in a heave from sixty feet right at the end of a quarter.

"So what?" asked Schayes. "They already get three points for that shot. If you make a shot from sixty feet, you probably deserve four points."

Why Not: Keep It Moving

Does it seem like the final minute of a close game takes an eternity?

That's because it does.

Too many coaches calling too many timeouts. Sometimes, they'll even call one timeout directly after another.

Fans don't like it. Players don't like it. Only coaches like it, but if some coaches had their way, they'd call a timeout after every possession.

But this is not a coach's game, remember?

Well, there is a way to fix it: Don't let them do it.

Pass a rule whereby each coach is allowed one timout in the final sixty seconds. One and only one. That's it. He can use it anytime he wants, but once it's gone, it's gone.

Why Not: A New Ball

Johnny Kerr was an All-Star center in the NBA, and he also coached the Chicago Bulls and Phoenix Suns before becoming the Bulls' television broadcaster.

"But one of my most memorable jobs was as GM of the Virginia Squires," said Kerr.

That was back in the American Basketball Association.

"The NBA took a lot of good things from the ABA like the three-point play, the Slam Dunk Contest, and keeping track of things like steals and blocked shots," said Kerr. "But they should have taken the red, white, and blue ball, too."

Why?

"Kids love it," said Kerr. "The brown ball we use now is boring. The red, white, and blue ball shows up better on TV. It fascinates kids. Even now, when you drive past a playground you often see kids with a different colored basketball."

The ABA sold nearly 30 million of its red, white, and blue balls, but the league forgot to patent the color scheme, so it missed a chance to earn royalties on those sales.

"Just imagine how much the NBA would make with its marketing of a tricolor ball," said Kerr. "It would be a great marketing tool, and a gold mine for the league. Every kid would want one for Christmas. Besides, it's just a better ball to play with—because you can see the rotation on your shot easier—and a better ball for the fans to watch."

Kerr had one more reason for a new basketball.

"It would be fun," he said.

WHY NOT: GROUND THE TIMEOUT CALL

When the NBA changed the "force-out" rule, it forced the officials to do the right thing. If a player has the ball near the out-of-bounds line and steps over the line, either he slipped or he was fouled. Nothing in between.

Now, the NBA has to keep with the spirit of that rule.

How many times a game do you see a player come up with a ball near the out-of-bounds line, and just before he steps over the line, he calls timeout so his team can keep possession?

It seems to happen every night—and that's not good.

Make this simple rule: A player cannot call timeout in order to keep possession of the ball. If he's in midair and calls timeout before he hits the ground, too bad. The official must wait until the player comes down.

From now on, all timeouts must be called by earthbound players.

Afterword

Is the NBA on the eve of destruction? Obviously, no, not yet. Most arenas are full. The television ratings for most of the 1994–95 season were slightly down over 1993–94 (when there was a whopping 17 percent drop from 1992–93). But then Michael Jordan returned and the ratings soared, sometimes to new record levels for Bulls playoff games on NBA, TNT, and TBS. In the end, it was a good year for the NBA on TV.

But the NBA cannot look at those numbers and be content. They must realize that the ratings were driven primarily by one man, and that Jordan is not going to play forever. Until Jordan's return, the league was floundering for its second straight season— despite major rule changes that dramatically cut down on the fighting and the bump-and-grind defense. The complaints about the NBA losing ground to hockey ceased, especially when hockey missed nearly two months because of a lockout. But there wasn't a real love of the game as it was being played. Most fans didn't think that they *had* to watch—until Jordan came back—even though the NBA had the weekly sports world all to itself.

That was evident not just in the pre-Jordan TV ratings, but in arenas around the NBA. There were numerous "blue seat sell-outs." The tickets were sold, but the seats were empty—or they were occupied by folks who received free tickets from corporations and came to the game with as much passion as a corpse. The ushers who hand out the free rosters, press releases, and programs in the luxury seat areas say that well over half the people sitting there don't even want the rosters and stat sheets. There are a lot of fans at NBA games who don't know who they're watching—and don't care. They're there for business reasons, or because it's a chic place to go where they might see a movie star or a local bigwig. Meanwhile, many real fans with children are relegated to watching the games on TV, especially with the average ticket price at $33 in 1994–95 and expected to be $50 by the end of the decade. The NBA must be careful. It can price itself out of the reach of the fans who love the game the most. It can also use all those corporate dollars as a narcotic, falling into the trap of saying, "Our guys don't fight that much anymore, the TV ratings are back up, and we still play to about 85 percent capacity—so everything is great."

During the 1994 Finals, the NBA was in trouble. By the 1995 Finals, things were better—but the NBA must continue the soul-searching that began in the summer of 1994. The problems remain. All you have to do is listen to men such as Wayne Embry, Hubie Brown, Doug Collins, and Phil Jackson—men who love this game and want to save it from the excesses that can drag it down as we head into the next century. Veteran basketball men know that the league's hold on the fans is precarious. Pro basketball does not yet have the luxury of the loyalty that carries baseball from one generation to the next—and through one stupid strike to the next. The NBA as we know it wasn't organized into one league until 1950—and it really didn't take center stage in the nation's sports psyche until the 1980s.

Then the league exploded because the game and the players had grace and style. Yes, they are huge men physically, but players such as Julius Erving, Magic Johnson, Michael Jordan, and Larry Bird seemed to be enjoying themselves so much that they brought children and their parents into the NBA mainstream. As Charles Barkley matured in Phoenix, he joined this circle. These guys really did respect the league and the game, and gave something back by being civil with the fans and media. Fans, broadcasters, and writers are thrilled when they deal with an athlete who comes across as a normal guy—he doesn't have to be Winston Churchill or Martin Luther King, Jr.

For most of their careers, Magic, Michael, Larry, and Charles gave us the impression that they really would play the game for free—that they'd love to get together on some playground for a two-on-two game.

While Shaquille O'Neal has worked very hard at improving his game and nearly led his team to a title in his third season, he has to make sure that he lets everyone know that he really loves basketball. He has to be careful to not get caught up in life away from the court. Kareem Abdul-Jabbar recently warned that players are becoming too consumed with their contracts and their celebrity status, often to the detriment of their own games and the NBA in general. This caution came to mind when O'Neal complained last season, "Rappers don't respect me." Well, he may be right. Professional rappers didn't like the idea that O'Neal was getting what they considered a free pass from record companies because he is a basketball star. But young players have so many agendas. They want to be respected for their athletic ability, for their singing and their acting—Shaq recently signed a contract to star in two movies for a major Hollywood studio.

Promoting Chris Webber sure isn't the answer. During the 1995 playoffs, it seemed that Webber was on more commercials, both for private companies and the league itself, than legitimate stars such as David Robinson, Hakeem Olajuwon, and Karl Malone. Webber came off as a lame Jordan wannabe when he took batting practice with the Chicago White Sox. That was in May, when a team with a talent such as Webber should have been in the playoffs. Webber's Washington Bullets won only twenty games, but they did rack up $15,000 worth of damage on a charter flight thanks to a very ugly food fight. Chris Webber has a lot to prove in this league. He may have won his battle with Don Nelson, but he lost a lot of respect in the NBA.

The Bulls' Phil Jackson sees how players want more than just the game—and how they do things to draw attention to themselves.

"They say basketball is entertainment, and they are entertainers," he said. "They say, 'What I really want is a commercial that establishes me as a unique person.' The Bad Boys like Dennis Rodman are in the commercials. The marketplace likes them. Before, the marketplace celebrated the warriors like Mickey Mantle or Stan Musial, who might come out and tip his hat."

David Robinson falls into the warrior category, but Robinson's main commercial exposure in 1995 came when he was in the same spot with—you remember, now—Dennis Rodman. Please! Rodman was insubordinate during the playoffs, refusing to take part in coach Bob Hill's huddles and being benched—but he was the biggest celebrity in the conference finals. There is more wrong with this TV picture than Rodman's Technicolor hair.

The money—especially the money given to players who have accomplished nothing in the NBA—means that guys who are in their early twenties are already looking for something besides the cash that can come from basketball. As Robert Parish said, "When you make a lot of money, especially at a young age, it has a tendency to give you an overinflated opinion of yourself."

But some people in the NBA shrug it all off as signs of the times.

"The whole idea of getting respect is at the crux of it," said Charles Grantham, the former head of the NBA Players Association. "When these players are recruited, it is for their athletic ability, not intellectual ability. As a result, what has developed is a plantation mentality. I'm not talking race, because it includes both black and white players. But the pervading feeling is, 'We own this team, so we own you.' It's not the money [that is the problem] that people think. That kind of attitude is the problem."

No, that kind of excuse is the problem.

A team pays a guy $30 million, and then it expects him to be on time, play hard, and listen to the coach. This is a plantation mentality? Come off it. If the NBA allows its players a free pass with cop-outs such as that, the league will be in danger within the next ten years. The NBA always has been a player's league, and its future rests with these players—and what the teams and league allow them to get away with.

Now the players are running wild. In the summer, the players union and the owners sat down and hammered out a deal to ensure labor peace into the next century. Finally, it seemed that someone had learned something from the sins of baseball, hockey, and other striking sports. The deal included a rookie cap, which is crucial to the financial future of the sport. It also addresses the issue of fairness—most rookies make too much money and most veterans are paid below market value.

But many of the players—inspired by their agents who worried about losing their 4 percent commissions on those mega-rookie contracts—rebelled against their own union and rejected the settlement. This was a first in the history of modern sports labor: management and the union skaking hands on a deal, then the union membership rising up to overthrow the union. You had players such as Michael Jordan—who should know better—insisting that he was never paid "what I was worth." Maybe that's true because Jordan in uniform is worth more than most franchises. But the average fan hears that Jordan earns over $50 million a year in endorsement revenues and he asks, "What else does Michael want?" Or the fans hear Seattle's Gary Payton whine, "People would have to cut their lifestyles. They'd have to live like penny-pinchers," if the new labor agreement went into effect. That was just as dumb as Cleveland Indians pitcher Dennis Martinez comparing the striking baseball players to the Cuban boat people. For the record, Gary Payton earns $3 million and he was the starting point guard for the team that was the biggest flop in both the 1994 and the 1995 playoffs. And for the record, even under the proposed "hard cap," the average salary in the NBA would be $3 million by the year 2000.

The mere mention of a strike or a lockout in a sport where the average salary is $1.3 million and the average ticket price is $32 is ludicrious, but that was the talk in the summer of 1995. It killed the good publicity the league received from the playoffs, and continued the NBA's fall from grace as the one sports league with its heart in the right place. It just brought back more memories of that *Sports Illustrated* cover featuring Derrick Coleman whining like a big baby.

The NBA is trying to clean up its image. It keeps telling us that for every bad apple, there are dozens of good ones.

Well, they should promote the best of the bunch.

Why doesn't the league make public service commercials that feature Juwan Howard earning his diploma? Howard signed a $37 million contract with the Washington Bullets, but spent the free time during his rookie year picking up the final thirty-two hours so he could graduate from Michigan with his class. Now there is a real Stay in School message, because Howard certainly didn't need to do it. He chased his degree just as he did his basketball dreams, and he did it to fulfill a promise to his deceased grandmother.

Or how about several spots with Kevin Johnson, the founder and financial backer of St. Hope Academy, a school for deprived children in Sacramento? Or use one of the league's classiest players, Jimmy Jackson, who donated $100,000 to his alma mater, Ohio

State. And the best way to sell piano lessons to some kids is simply to let them see 7-foot-2 David Robinson playing it—and playing it well.

The league is at a crisis point, not at the bank but of the heart. Does it want to reflect what is best about pro sports—as it did in the 1980s—or will it allow some of its young players to drag it down to the level of the 1970s, when the NBA was an afterthought in most cities? Do they want a league where spoiled players perform in front of yawning corporate crowds? These are the real questions as the league heads into the next century.

Index

Abdul-Jabbar, Kareem, 59, 69, 73, 87, 96, 182, 183, 194, 198, 292, 305
Adubato, Richie, 65–66, 87–88, 120–21, 142–43, 145, 153, 174, 184, 186, 188–94, 209–10
agents, 41–44
    certification of, 68
    contract negotiations and, 67–69
    fees of, 73, 75
    Players Association decertification and, 74–75, 306
    players' immaturity and, 119
    players instructed not to play by, 44
    at predraft camps, 68
    salary cap and, 42
    street, 51, 119
Aguirre, Mark, 111, 218–19, 228, 232
Alamodome, 272–73
Albeck, Stan, 129, 186, 188, 194, 244
Albom, Mitch, 35, 224, 229
Alcindor, Lew, see Abdul-Jabbar, Kareem
American Basketball Association (ABA), 15, 72–73, 85–87, 127, 241, 273, 297, 301
Anderson, Elijah, 107–11
Anderson, Kenny, 131, 133, 134, 135, 137
Anderson, Nick, 29, 98
Atlanta Hawks, 27, 51, 67–68, 117, 130, 155, 168, 181, 183, 185, 188, 191, 192, 195, 197–99, 293
Auerbach, Red, 39, 138, 148, 172–73, 223

Bad Boys:
    culture of disrespect and, 37, 220–37
    defense and, 111, 113, 161, 165, 166, 215–33
    fighting and, 220–37
    officials and, 225–26, 227
    taunting by, 225
Bagley, John, 211, 285
Bailey, Damon, 46–47
Barkley, Charles, 17, 27, 51, 52, 55–56, 57, 58, 60, 106–7, 114, 134, 162, 242–43, 304
Barry, Rick, 82, 91–94, 97, 98, 243
basket, height of, 24, 298–300
basketball, professional:
    above the rim, 157, 177, 195, 293
    blue seat sell-outs of, 303
    as boring, 19, 22–23, 164, 169, 197
    college game vs., 174–80, 184–186, 195, 199–200
    drop in scoring in, 18, 24, 160–168, 200–201, 226, 232, 293
    evolution of shooting in, 78–89
    as MTV basketball, 88, 121, 160–61, 275–76
    physical contact in, 20–22, 161–168, 177, 247–48, 294; see also fighting
    recommendations for, 292–302
    schedule in, 151, 176, 289

basketball, professional (*cont.*)
  timeouts in, 300–302
  as ugly, 18, 161, 162, 163, 166,
    167, 197
Beard, Butch, 27, 135–37
Benjamin, Benoit, 63–64, 133
Bianchi, Al, 182, 184
Bickerstaff, Bernie, 205–6, 212
Bird, Larry, 15, 17, 22, 23, 31, 34,
    52, 53, 55, 84, 88, 96, 114,
    160, 220, 222, 229, 234–36,
    242, 267, 275, 304
Blair, Bill, 30, 122, 135
Blaylock, Mookie, 130–31, 133
Borgia, Sid, 237–38, 258
Boston Celtics, 38, 53, 123, 148,
    160, 161, 163, 167, 168, 172–
    173, 175, 184, 185, 211, 217,
    220, 223, 229, 234–37, 264,
    266–67, 268, 282
Bowie, Sam, 17, 130, 133
Breuer, Randy, 278–79
Bristow, Allan, 71, 203
Brown, Hubie, 23, 84, 117, 118,
    124, 138, 145, 149, 150, 151,
    168, 177, 181, 186–201, 212,
    218, 244–45, 275, 290, 293–
    295, 304
Brown, Larry, 19, 41, 129, 169–
    170, 178, 185, 261, 294–95
Buckner, Quinn, 150–51

Carlesimo, P. J., 52, 175, 185
Carolina Cougars, 86, 210
Carter, Donald, 150, 155
Cartwright, Bill, 227, 230
Chamberlain, Wilt, 20, 72, 83, 94–
    95, 114, 117
Chaney, Don, 145, 181, 186, 209, 249
Charlotte Hornets, 71, 202–3, 211,
    268–69
cheerleaders, 262, 263, 267
Chicago Bulls, 45, 111–13, 123,
    144–45, 161, 163, 181–82,
    184, 185, 208, 211, 220–21,
    224–25, 249–51, 265, 268,
    269, 272, 275, 291, 301, 303
Christie, Doug, 63–64

Cleveland Cavaliers, 60, 62, 67, 70,
    87, 117, 123, 127, 133, 145,
    152, 164, 191, 211, 217, 220,
    224, 231, 261–67, 269, 271,
    282, 287, 290, 292
coaches, coaching, 139–212
  assistants to, 172, 182, 184, 186,
    194–97
  authority of, 146, 148–51, 194–95
  basketball as love affair for,
    154–56
  CBA as training ground for, 288,
    291
  clipboards and, 172
  college vs. pro, 174–80, 184–86,
    195, 199–200
  as control freaks, 18, 22, 160,
    171–72, 173
  decline in foul shooting and, 97–98
  and desire to be macho, 22, 113,
    158–59, 221, 228
  effects of firing on, 144–45
  endorsements by, 185, 223
  failure feared by, 142, 144
  family lives of, 143–44
  general managers' conflicts with,
    151–54, 169, 176, 178–80
  hiring of, 150, 152, 180–86,
    191–94, 196
  Hubie Brown's influence on,
    186–201
  interim, 202–12
  losing and, 144–46, 178, 204
  marriages and, 143
  and need to enforce discipline,
    19, 23, 37–38, 121–25, 131–
    132, 147–51
  of 1960s, 181–82
  offense strangled by, 18, 20, 22,
    157–73, 200
  officials and, 243–45, 253, 256–
    257, 258
  penalties for fighting levied
    against, 118–19
  as physically and mentally drain-
    ing, 141–42, 203–7
  players' defiance of, 24, 31, 44,
    131–32, 136–37, 148

players' egos juggled by, 146–50
as replaceable commodities, 142–
    143, 151–54
salaries of, 141, 146–47, 148, 151–
    153, 176, 185, 186, 210, 295
summer league, 48
superstars and, 218
trends in hiring of, 150, 152
as workaholics, 141–42, 143
"Code of the Streets, The" (Ander-
    son), 107–11
Colangelo, Jerry, 21–22, 43, 74,
    89, 99–100, 104–5, 171, 181–
    184, 288–89, 290
Coleman, Derrick, 17, 18, 27, 31,
    50, 53, 62, 124, 131–32, 134–
    137, 148–49, 165, 307
college basketball:
professional game vs., 174–80,
    184–86, 195, 199–200
recruiting and, 34–36, 49, 175–76
Collins, Doug, 23, 29, 57–58, 77–
    78, 84, 113, 119–20, 141–45,
    151–54, 162–63, 165, 169–
    170, 173, 185, 187, 211,
    220–21, 222, 225, 262, 289,
    290, 293–96, 297, 304
Continental Basketball Association
    (CBA), 106, 277–302
draft, 284
as farm system for NBA, 280,
    286, 287–92
injuries in, 281
lack of size in, 286
officiating in, 258, 280
pep talks in, 286
player development in, 286–87, 291
quarter-points system in, 287
rights lists in, 284–86
salaries in, 278, 279, 280, 285
salary cap in, 279–80
Stern on, 288–89
trades in, 278–80, 281
as training ground for coaches,
    288, 291
volatility of, 280–83
winning as priority in, 282–83,
    286, 291

contracts:
agents and, 67–69
holdouts and, 42–44, 58–60,
    63–66, 131
of officials, weight clause in,
    239–40
Costas, Bob, 112, 118, 274–75
Costello, Larry, 177, 189, 191,
    194
courtside seats, 270–72
Cousy, Bob, 58, 80–83, 85, 91, 138,
    157–58, 160, 166, 172–73

Dallas Mavericks, 60–61, 65–66,
    72, 111, 143, 145, 150–51,
    155–56, 160, 181, 182, 192,
    218, 232, 251, 282, 283
Daly, Chuck, 21–23, 28, 33, 52,
    100 –102, 113, 117–18, 121–
    122, 129, 133–35, 138, 141–
    156, 158–59, 166–68, 175,
    190, 191, 200–201, 215–33,
    253, 272, 275
Daniels, Lloyd, 48–49, 106, 279
Dantley, Adrian, 149–50, 216–17,
    218
Daugherty, Brad, 51, 60, 62, 223–
    224, 227
Davis, Dale, 83, 159, 297
Dawkins, Darryl, 86–87, 126
defense, 173
Bad Boys and, 111, 113, 161,
    165, 166, 215–33
as hand-to-hand combat, 18–22,
    111, 158–69, 303
as macho, 22, 113, 158–59, 221,
    228
of New York Knicks, 20, 22,
    159–63, 165, 168
zone, 292–96
Denver Nuggets, 33, 45, 83–84,
    152, 202–9, 211–12, 273
Detroit Pistons, 20, 37, 61, 100–
    101, 111–13, 121, 123, 133,
    147, 152, 156, 160, 161,
    165–68, 170, 174–75, 182,
    191, 192, 193, 200–201, 215–
    233, 234–37, 282

disrespect, culture of, 21, 99–125
  Bad Boys and, 37, 220–37
  code of the streets and, 107–13
  Fab Five and, 34–38, 42, 232
  marketing of, 18, 21, 161,
    274–76
  players' background and, 102–6
  race and, 125
  taunting and, *see* taunting
  team discipline and, 121–25
  violence and, *see* fighting
Dobek, Matt, 222, 226–27, 229
draft, 57–75
  ABA-NBA wars and, 72–74
  CBA, 284
  expansion and, 74
  lottery for, 69–72
  1960, 61–62
  1969, 69
  1973, 58
  1977, 59
  1983, 69–70
  1984, 70
  1985, 64, 67, 71
  1986, 62, 100
  1988, 67
  1990, 62–63
  1991, 65, 71
  1992, 63, 65–66, 71
  1993, 38, 62–63, 71–72
  1994, 41, 46, 57–61, 103
  1995, 51
Dream Team I, 52, 54
Dream Team II, 52–55
Drexler, Clyde, 16, 52, 164
drug abuse, 15, 24, 49, 102–6,
    116, 119
Dudley, Chris, 93–94, 98, 133
Dumars, Joe, 52, 53, 54, 55, 217,
    229–30, 232
Dumas, Richard, 104–5
dunking:
  and decline in fundamentals, 77–
    78, 84–89, 92
  marketing of, 84, 88, 161, 275

Edwards, James, 231–32
Elliott, Sean, 102, 177, 178

Ellis, Dale, 177, 207
Ellis, LaPhonso, 205
Embry, Wayne, 15, 21, 24, 31, 32,
    38, 51, 60, 67, 74, 99–100,
    101, 106, 107, 114, 115, 119,
    122, 123–25, 152, 180, 185,
    195, 220, 224, 225, 262,
    275–76, 290, 304
endorsements, 29
  by coaches, 185, 223
  Jordan and, 16, 54, 307
  by rookies, 31–32, 33, 41, 57–58
  as status, 31, 55, 121
  team obligations vs., 23, 31–32,
    149, 305
English, Jo-Jo, 18, 111–12
Erving, Julius, 73, 85–87, 127,
    223, 245–46, 248, 304
Evans, Mike, 204, 205–6
Ewing, Patrick, 52, 75, 116, 159,
    163, 190, 246, 247, 248, 250,
    289, 297

Fab Five, 34–38, 42, 232
Falk, David, 41–44
Ferrell, Duane, 108–10, 117
Ferry, Danny, 60, 65, 123, 147,
    290
fighting, 15, 18, 19, 107–19, 243,
    303
  Bad Boys and, 220–37
  code of the streets and, 107–13
  missed by officials, 234–37, 259
  penalties for, 118–19, 298
  in previous eras, 108, 109, 110,
    117, 223
  TV ratings and, 117–18, 274–76
Finals, 256
  1975, 172
  1976, 184
  1980, 44
  1982, 209
  1986, 160
  1988, 221–22
  1989, 219, 226–27
  1990, 227, 232
  1991, 249
  1993, 105, 162

1994, 22, 71, 160, 162–63, 250, 304
1995, 22, 29, 98, 163–64, 304
Fisher, Steve, 36–38
Fitch, Bill, 29, 70, 95, 117–19, 129, 130–33, 134, 148–50, 151, 154, 155, 156, 181, 199, 209, 244, 294, 298
Fitzsimmons, Cotton, 19, 22–23, 107, 121, 150, 165, 167, 171, 182–83, 184, 194, 200, 224–25
Fitzsimmons, Gary, 63, 64, 89, 165–66, 248
Five-Star Camps, 49, 145, 187, 189–94, 200–201
force-out rule, 301–2
foul shooting, 90–98
four-point shot, 300
Fratello, Mike, 130, 135, 145, 164, 186, 188–97
free agency, 40–41, 43, 176
fundamentals, decline in, 15, 23, 24, 76–98
    ball handling, 90, 157–58
    dunking and, 77–78, 84–89, 92
    foul shooting, 90–98
    pick-and-roll, 76
    shooting, 78–91, 166
    shooting percentages and, 82–83, 89
    33 and, 76–77

Garfinkel, Howard, 49, 189
Garretson, Darell, 239, 240, 245, 251–60, 293
Gee, Michael, 266–67
Golden State Warriors, 38–41, 61, 74, 83–84, 172
Goodwill Games (1994), 90
Grant, Horace, 83, 228, 251
Greer, Hal, 96, 97
Gund Arena, 271, 273

halftime acts, 19, 265–67, 272
handchecking rules, 19, 164, 169, 170, 248, 303
Hardaway, Anfernee, 29, 38, 40, 62–63, 71, 124

Harper, Derek, 18, 111–13, 150–151, 163
Harper, Ron, 62, 123, 266
Harris, Del, 69–70, 209
Harte, Dick, 161, 203
Havlicek, John, 81–82, 83, 84, 89, 110, 155, 244–45
Heard, Garfield, 150, 174–75, 210
Heathcote, Jud, 34, 36
Heffernan, Mark, 261–67
Hill, Bob, 101, 102, 186, 188, 193, 196, 209, 306
Hill, Brian, 29, 164, 191–94, 200
Hill, Thomas, 280–81
Hollins, Hue, 250–51
Home Shopping Network, 57
Horry, Robert, 115, 163
Houston Rockets, 16, 22, 69–70, 102, 123, 130, 160, 161, 163, 164, 179, 205, 209, 249, 250, 290
Howard, Jannie Mae, 35–36
Howard, Juwan, 35–38, 41–44, 45, 307

illegal defense rules, 19, 170, 292–96
Indiana Pacers, 46, 47, 67, 70, 87, 98, 117, 159–60, 181, 209, 276, 297
injuries:
    in CBA, 281
    of officials, 241
    of players, 281, 288, 290
interim coaches, 202–12
isolation offenses, 169–70, 294–95
Issel, Dan, 152, 202–7, 211–12

Jackson, Jimmy, 18, 65–66, 307–8
Jackson, Phil, 111–13, 123, 135, 146–48, 163, 166, 169, 170, 173, 229, 251, 288, 291, 304, 305
Johnson, Avery, 102, 178, 180
Johnson, Eddie, 171, 199, 211
Johnson, Kevin, 54, 170, 171, 307
Johnson, Larry, 53, 54–55, 71, 131, 203, 269

Johnson, Magic, 15, 17, 22, 23, 28–29, 31, 34, 44–45, 52, 53, 55, 58, 64, 70, 87–88, 96, 167, 171, 209, 229, 267, 268, 304
Johnson, Vinnie, 215, 230
Jordan, Michael, 16, 22, 23, 29, 31, 34, 51–55, 58, 75, 83–85, 96, 123, 162, 164, 169–70, 190, 208, 220–21, 224–25, 228–30, 246–48, 251, 275, 303, 304, 307
jump shot, 78–82, 87–88, 95, 96, 97

Karl, George, 33–34, 90, 211, 244, 288
Kasten, Stan, 67–68, 197
Kemp, Shawn, 33, 53, 90
Kennedy, Pat, 237–38
Kentucky Colonels, 188, 203, 210
Kerr, Johnny, 182, 184, 301
Kersey, Jess, 234–37, 249, 259
Kidd, Jason, 60–61
Kimble, Bo, 277–79
King, Stacey, 30, 147
Knight, Bobby, 46, 90, 183, 185, 278
Krause, Jerry, 152, 153–54, 169
Krzyzewski, Mike, 52, 65, 175, 185

Laettner, Christian, 18, 52, 65–66, 125, 149, 246
Laimbeer, Bill, 100, 117, 147, 215, 217–32, 234–37, 259
Lane, Jerome, 279, 281, 283
Layden, Frank, 141, 142, 144, 148–50, 151, 155, 186, 188, 189–95, 225, 233
Lee, Spike, 161–62, 276
Littles, Gene, 32, 188–89, 202–12
Long, Grant, 108–10, 117
Los Angeles Clippers, 61, 123, 154, 156, 181, 209, 270
Los Angeles Lakers, 20, 27–28, 33, 44–45, 63–64, 102, 146, 152, 163, 167, 171, 183, 209, 219–

220, 223, 229, 249, 263, 268, 270, 271
lottery, draft, 69–72
Loughery, Kevin, 129, 186
Lucas, John, 16–17, 28, 101, 106, 179–80
Luisetti, Hank, 78–80, 81
luxury suites, 270–73
Lynam, Jimmy, 43, 187

McCloskey, Jack, 152, 216, 218, 236
McCloud, George, 278–79
McCombs, Red, 24, 175, 178–80, 272–73
McHale, Kevin, 17, 114, 267
McKinney, Jack, 44, 187
McKinnon, Bob, 130, 210
MacLeod, John, 92, 183–84, 199
McNamara, Mark, 285–86
Madden, Jack, 234–37, 238, 239, 241, 243, 246, 253–54, 258, 259
Madonna, 101, 102, 276
Mahorn, Rick, 88, 100, 217–27, 231, 232, 296, 298
Majerle, Dan, 54, 171
makeup calls, 251
Malone, Brendan, 188, 190–94
Malone, Karl, 17, 52, 55, 57, 96–97, 123–24, 155, 165, 218, 284, 305
Malone, Moses, 55, 68, 134
Maravich, Pete, 73, 82
marketing, 261–76
  of Bad Boy image, 215, 216, 221–23, 233, 274–76
  cheerleaders and, 262, 263, 267
  clichés in, 263, 265
  courtside seats and, 270–73
  of culture of disrespect, 18, 21, 161, 275
  of dunking, 84, 88, 161, 275
  essence of game lost in, 19, 261–262, 264, 267, 272
  film clips used in, 265
  halftime acts and, 19, 265–67, 272

of Jordan, 88
of lottery, 71
luxury suites and, 270–73
mascots and, 266
music and, 261–65
sound effects and, 262
team colors and logos and, 268–70
television and, 274–76
Martin, Slater, 85, 299
Mason, Anthony, 113, 124, 159, 174, 286, 288, 290
Massimino, Rollie, 189, 192
Maxwell, Vernon, 16, 123, 163
Menendez, Al, 21, 37, 47–48, 90, 127, 128–29, 135, 161–62, 178, 232–33
Miami Arena, 270
Miami Floridians, 263
Miami Heat, 27, 185, 192, 227, 232, 270
Miami Tropics, 180
Miller, Reggie, 53, 159, 161–62, 243, 276
Mills, Terry, 131, 133
Milwaukee Black Hawks, 299
Milwaukee Bucks, 27, 38, 57–60, 69, 177, 191, 194, 195–98
Minneapolis Lakers, 299
Minnesota Timberwolves, 16, 30, 32, 61, 66, 72, 122, 125, 160, 209, 227, 286
Moe, Doug, 83–84, 170, 188, 197, 212
Morningstar, Darren, 282–83
Morris, Chris, 132, 135, 137, 149
motion offenses, 169–70, 295
Motta, Dick, 143, 150, 155–56, 181–82, 184, 194, 200
Mourning, Alonzo, 53, 71, 269
Mullin, Chris, 40, 52, 91
Musselman, Bill, 277, 284–85
Musselman, Eric, 277–87, 289–90
Mutombo, Dikembe, 83, 131, 206–8

Nance, Larry, 60, 87
Nash, John, 41–42

National Basketball Association (NBA), 215–302
ABA wars with, 73–74
average salary in, 307
Bad Boy image promoted by, 215, 216, 221–23, 233
beginnings of, 79
CBA and, see Continental Basketball Association
drug abuse in, 15, 24, 49, 102–6, 116, 119
expansion of, 74, 141
gross revenues of, 62
Observers, 256
Stay In School ads of, 51, 307
taxi squads for, 289, 290–91
three-official system adopted by, 236, 238, 240, 257–58
ticket prices for, 271, 304, 307
NBA Players Association, 68, 74–75, 105, 288–89, 306–7
Nelson, Don, 30, 34–35, 38–41, 43, 54, 152, 187, 194, 305
Newell, Pete, 24, 292–96, 297
New Jersey Nets, 16, 27, 47, 62, 64, 71, 100, 126–38, 146, 148, 149, 165, 293
New York Knicks, 20, 71, 111–13, 124, 128, 130, 134, 136, 146, 159–63, 165, 168, 171, 181, 188, 191, 192, 193, 197, 199, 209, 215, 221, 250, 270, 271, 275–76, 297
New York Nets, 223
New York Times, 80, 103
Nissalke, Tom, 211, 282
no-foul-out rule, 247–48, 292–96
Nunez, Tommy, 249, 256

Oakley, Charles, 115, 159, 165, 220, 243
O'Donnell, Jake, 250, 259
offense:
coaches' strangling of, 18, 20, 22, 157–73, 200
isolation, 169–70, 294–95
motion, 169–70, 295
Triangle, 169

officials, officiating, 234–60
  age of, 240–41, 257
  Bad Boys style and, 225–26, 227
  checklist of, 243
  as closed club, 238
  coaches and, 243–45, 253, 256–
    257, 258
  conversations between players
    and, 242–43, 252, 253
  divorces of, 241–42
  egos of, 238
  end of game and, 248–51
  evaluation of, 255–56
  fines of, 258–59
  as flamboyant, 237–39
  good teams favored by, 251
  home teams and, 243–44
  illegal defenses and, 292–94
  injuries of, 241
  makeup calls and, 251
  in 1950s and 1960s, 237–39
  Jordan and, 246–48
  palming violations and, 245–48
  Parish-Laimbeer fight missed by,
    234–37, 259
  pay of, 237, 239, 256
  perspective of, vs. fans, 236
  physical conditioning of, 239–41
  physical contact and, 247–48
  players' styles and, 243, 245–48
  Pro Call and, 245–48
  star players and, 247, 250–51,
    297–98
  supervision of, 239–41, 252–60
  training of, 237, 238, 239, 258
  traveling violations and, 245–48
  TV coverage and, 237
  videotape used by, 254–55, 258
  weight clause in contract of,
    239–40
  Whispering Society of, 255–56
Olajuwon, Hakeem, 18, 70, 160,
  163, 209, 289, 305
Olympics, 120
Olympics (1992), 52, 54
O'Neal, Shaquille, 29, 53, 54, 71–
  72, 83, 84, 91–92, 97, 124,
  246, 275, 292, 305

One Punch and You're Gone rule,
  118, 298
Orlando Magic, 16, 22, 62–63, 71–
  72, 98, 124, 163–64, 191,
  193, 200, 269
Owens, Billy, 27, 131
owners, 66, 121–22, 126–38, 131–
  132, 148, 149, 151

palming, 245–48
Parish, Robert, 217, 222, 234–37,
  259, 267, 306
Payton, Gary, 33, 262, 307
penalties:
  on coaches, 118–19
  for fighting, 118–19, 298
  for taunting, 116, 298
Perdue, Will, 228, 251
Perkins, Sam, 33, 63–64, 111
Pettit, Bob, 81, 109
Petrovic, Drazen, 131, 133
Pfund, Randy, 27–28, 29
Philadelphia 76ers, 28, 103, 127,
  223, 227, 279
Philadelphia Warriors, 72
Phoenix Suns, 30, 45, 69, 104–5,
  163–64, 170, 171, 174–75,
  181–84, 269, 271, 292, 301,
  304
Pippen, Scottie, 52, 75, 116, 169–
  170, 228, 250–51
Pitino, Rick, 47, 129, 186, 188,
  191–94, 196
Pittsburgh Condors, 86
players, modern, 25–138
  as "beyond fundamentals,"
    89–90
  as bigger than rules, 21, 247–48
  coaches defied by, 24, 31, 44,
    131–32, 136–37, 148
  coaches' salaries as viewed by,
    146–47, 148, 151, 152–53,
    176, 210, 295
  competitive fire lacking in, 28–
    29, 33, 88, 120–21, 134
  and desire for immediate gratifi-
    cation, 120
  education of, 51–52, 119–20

effect of bench sitting on, 289–90

endorsements as priority for, 23, 29, 31–32, 149, 305

fighting by, *see* fighting

holdouts of, 42–44, 58–60, 63–66, 131

immaturity of, 30, 119–20, 122, 138, 203–4

individualism of, 29, 31, 33, 77, 121, 305

individual statistics important to, 147, 279

injuries of, 281, 288, 290

loyalty lacking in, 33

as morally bankrupt, 100

odds against becoming, 50–52

officials and, *see* officials, officiating

playing time as priority for, 33, 40, 54, 137, 146–48, 204, 207, 208, 279

recruiting of, *see* recruiting

respect demanded by, 29, 30, 39–40, 108–11, 136, 305, 306

respect for game lacking in, 16–17, 29

selfishness of, 16–17, 28, 76, 100–102, 107, 279

sense of history lacking in, 17

skills of, *see* fundamentals, decline in

as spoiled, 28, 30–33, 42, 45, 119–20

stardom prematurely bestowed upon, 18, 31–33, 46–50, 55, 57–59, 63, 65, 306

veteran's advice ignored by, 54, 56

veterans' resentment of, 58, 60

winning no longer priority for, 16, 28, 31, 39

playoffs, 196, 200, 256

half-court game in, 160, 167–68, 170, 216

1981, 44

1984, 215

1987, 217, 234–37

1988, 146

1991, 114, 228–30, 249

1992, 265

1993, 133

1994, 18, 19, 33, 102, 108–10, 111–13, 134, 159, 160, 161–162, 203, 204, 250–51, 275, 297, 307

1995, 16, 33, 102, 159–60, 163–65, 276, 307

Pollin, Abe, 42–43

Portland Trailblazers, 94, 98, 175, 176–77, 232, 273

Pressey, Paul, 115–16

Price, Mark, 53, 54, 60, 78, 92, 224, 227

"Pro Call," 245–48

Rambis, Kurt, 28, 223

Ramsey, Jack, 149, 150, 186, 187, 199

Rapid City Thrillers, 277–87

ratings, television, 71, 103

fighting and, 117–18

for 1993 Finals, 162

for 1994 Finals, 162–63

1995 playoffs, 165–66

Rodman and, 276

recruiting:

college, 34–36, 49, 175–76

egomaniacs produced by, 34–36, 48–50

Five Star Camps and, 49, 189–90

at junior-high level, 46–47

summer leagues and, 48–49

Reed, Willis, 20, 113, 129–38, 146, 155, 165, 223

referees, *see* officials, officiating

restricted free agency, 40–41, 43

Rider, J. R., 18, 30–32, 122, 125

Riley, Pat, 20, 22, 34, 45, 111–13, 124, 149, 151, 152, 161, 163, 165, 171, 209, 219–20, 221

Robertson, Oscar, 82, 84, 85, 91, 96, 194, 198

Robinson, David, 18, 52, 102, 176, 177, 272, 305, 308

Robinson, Glenn, 57–60

Robinson, Rumeal, 133, 277–79
Rodman, Dennis, 16, 99–102,
    217–19, 227, 228, 231–32,
    305–6
rookies:
    endorsements by, 31–32, 33, 41,
        57–58
    salaries of, 23, 24, 32, 39–43,
        55, 57–75, 306
Rooney, Wally, 238, 240–41, 242–
    245, 249–51, 252–56, 258–59
Rose, Jalen, 34, 36, 111, 204, 207
Rosen, Charlie, 20, 281–87
Rothstein, Ron, 100, 186, 188,
    191–94
rules:
    force-out, 301–2
    handchecking, 19, 164, 169,
        170, 248, 303
    illegal-defense, 19, 170, 292–96
    no-foul-out, 247–48, 296–98
    One Punch and You're Gone,
        118, 298
    palming, 245–48
    taunting, 116, 162, 298
    traveling, 245–48
running game, lack of, 22–23, 44–
    45, 83, 157–60, 163–73, 197,
    200, 216–17, 295–96
Rupp, Adolph, 212, 292
Russell, Bill, 38, 85, 116
Ryan, Bob, 19–20, 22, 159, 163,
    230, 236

Saar, Billy, 239–40, 243, 244–48,
    254–55, 257–58, 259
Sacramento Kings, 209
St. Louis Hawks, 61–62, 109
salaries:
    ABA-NBA wars and, 72–73
    coaches, 141, 146–47, 148, 151–
        153, 176, 185, 186, 210, 285
    negotiation of, 66–69
    of officials, 237, 239, 256
    players' view of coaches and,
        146–47, 148, 151, 152–53,
        176, 210, 285
    playing time and, 146–48

of rookies, 23, 24, 32, 39–43,
    55, 57–75, 306
salary cap, 15, 40, 42, 62–66, 177,
    199, 306–7
    CBA, 279–80
    coaches' expendability and, 153
    draft picks and, 62–63
    rookie, 61, 74–75, 306
    veteran re-signings under, 62
Salley, John, 217–19, 227, 232
Sampson, Ralph, 69–70, 126–27,
    129, 160
San Antonio Spurs, 16, 44, 45,
    101–2, 106, 135, 174–80,
    181, 209, 264, 272–73
Sanders, Mike, 147, 284
San Diego Clippers, 70, 151, 156
Schayes, Dolph, 78, 80–81, 83, 95,
    96, 114, 172, 300
scoring, drop in, 18, 24, 160–68,
    200–201, 226, 232, 293
Scuttle (33), 76–77
seasons:
    1982–83, 69–70
    1983–84, 70
    1985–86, 161
    1987–88, 219
    1988–89, 83–84
    1990–91, 161
    1992–93, 160, 303
    1993–94, 160, 161, 164, 303
    1994–95, 19, 29, 83–84, 98,
        164, 248, 303
Seattle Supersonics, 33–34, 63–64,
    182, 206, 269
Sharman, Bill, 80, 114
Shelton, Lonnie, 115–16, 211
Smith, Clinton, 282–83
Smith, Dean, 175, 185
Smith, LaBradford, 278–79
Spirits of St. Louis, 127, 274
Sporting News, 50
Sports Illustrated, 18, 45, 54, 70,
    78, 106, 117, 188, 245, 293,
    299–300, 307
Stanley, Michael, 262–63
Starks, John, 112, 124, 161, 163,
    250, 286, 288, 290

Stern, David, 15, 18, 23–24, 70, 111, 112, 158, 265, 288–89
Stockton, John, 18, 52, 83, 97, 123–24, 155, 284
street agents, 51, 119
Strickland, Rod, 176–77
Strom, Earl, 115, 237, 239, 243, 244, 245, 247, 252–60, 292
Suhr, Brendan, 135, 190
summer leagues, 48–49, 51, 89, 91, 142

Tait, Joe, 263–64, 267, 271
Tarkanian, Jerry, 47, 48, 106, 135, 174–80
taunting, 15, 19, 23, 114–18, 232, 242–43
  Bad Boys as first in, 225
  code of the streets and, 107, 108–9, 112
  by Dream Team II, 53–54
  Fab Five and, 36
  penalties for, 116, 298
  promotion of, 18, 21, 161–62, 276
  rules, 116, 162, 298
  trash talk vs., 115–16
television:
  basketball influenced by, 274–76
  see also ratings, television
33 (Scuttle), 76–77
Thomas, Isiah, 52, 77, 89–90, 100, 165, 167, 193, 215–32, 235
Thorn, Rod, 22, 54, 116, 158, 221, 222, 235–60, 293, 298
Thorpe, Otis, 83, 249
three-official system, 236, 238, 240, 257–58
Tomjanovich, Rudy, 16, 119, 164, 209, 210
Toronto Raptors, 141, 193, 268, 269, 271
traveling, 245–48
Trent, Gary, 102–3

Triangle Offense, 169
Tripucka, Kelly, 215, 216
two-handed set shot, 78–80

USA Today, 18, 103
Utah Jazz, 45, 102, 123–24, 148–150, 155, 191, 211, 282, 284

Valvano, Jim, 51, 131–32, 133
Vanak, John, 237, 238, 239, 254, 257, 258
Virginia Squires, 85, 301
Vitale, Dick, 47, 174, 176, 189, 190, 192

Walk, Neal, 69, 182, 183
Wallace, Terry, 46, 47
Walsh, Donnie, 44, 161
Washington Bullets, 30–31, 41–44, 117, 172, 182, 217, 305, 307
Webber, Chris, 30–43, 71, 111, 305
Weltman, Harry, 65, 66–67, 126–130, 211
West, Jerry, 45, 82, 84, 96, 152, 155
Westhead, Paul, 44–45, 187, 203
Westphal, Paul, 55–56, 105, 163
Wilkens, Lenny, 52, 61–62, 77, 109, 143–44, 147, 148, 152, 186, 253, 261, 297
Williams, Buck, 115, 126
Williams, Jayson, 134, 137
Williams, Michael, 286, 290
Williams, Reggie, 207, 208
Willis, Kevin, 27, 67–68
Willis, Robert Keith, 67–68
Winter, Tex, 169, 183
Wooden, John, 97, 300
World Championships (1994), 52–55, 248
Wright, Sharone, 103–4

zone defenses, 292–96